W9-CUV-816

Praise for
Ya Gotta Believe!

"Tug is indeed a special person to me. We shared a unique camaraderie because we were both U.S. Marines and pitchers. Memories of our friendship are among my fondest in my forty years in this sport. His spirit and enthusiasm for life transcended the game of baseball." —Tom Seaver

"Two baseball autobiographies were released in recent months. One, Pete Rose's *My Prison Without Bars,* received all the publicity and spent weeks on the bestseller lists. The other, McGraw's book, came out with little fanfare, with plenty of copies still available at your bookstore. And that's a real shame. Where Rose offers halfhearted apologies for making mistakes in his life and begs to be put in the Hall of Fame, McGraw makes an honest appraisal of his life, owns up to the mistakes he has made, and comes away transformed. As you will too, if you read this book . . . the book turns very sad at the end, as McGraw is losing his battle with brain cancer. The details of his last few days are hard to get through, but the fact that his family, including Tim, is there by his side through the end is testament to how Tug McGraw turned his life around before it was too late. So put that Pete Rose book down. Donate it to your local library. Go out and get this book. You'll be glad you did." —*Los Angeles Times*

"[The] humorous and heart-wrenching autobiography of the beloved and kooky Mets and Phillies closer who finally succumbed to brain cancer. . . . You'll laugh through most of the first nineteen chapters as Tug, in his inimitable style, recounts the goofy exploits of his high-wire pitching career, and you'll feel his pain in detailing the estrangement and reconciliation with his famous son, Tim. The last couple of chapters, however, will make you cry as Tug and finally Yaeger describe his final days." —*New York Daily News*

continued . . .

"Poignant, confessional, witty at times, wistful, and optimistic, *Ya Gotta Believe!* is more than a rehashing of championship moments and locker room high jinks, and more than an extended mea culpa. It took McGraw many decades before he could do what Tim had done as a teenager—discover his past and thereby find himself. Whether that search was motivated by the onset of his fatal cancer or the approach of his sixties doesn't really matter. It was an important part of the journey."
—Rick Freeman, *The Trenton Times* (NJ)

"The book isn't a pity party. It's about how the human spirit endures through difficult times. . . . *Ya Gotta Believe!* isn't a baseball book. Parts of it will help Phillies and Mets fans relive the greatest moments in their teams' histories, but in the end, it's about being human and touching people's lives. Tug McGraw touched so many people's lives while he was alive. And before he died . . . he learned to treasure those close to him who touched his life. *Ya Gotta Believe!* will make you laugh. It will make you cry. And of course, it will make you believe, just as Tug was able to do when he was alive."
—Eric Fisher, Metro Philly

"I wanted to read this book the minute it came out and it's a terrific book. It talks about Tug and his brothers and parents, something I knew very little about. There are some sad moments and now I think it's amazing that McGraw was such a free spirit after all he had been through as a child and young man. The picture section is very cool! There are some amazing shots that I had never seen of the 1969 and 1973 Mets, as well as of the 1980 Phillies. Read about Tug outsmarting David Letterman after Letterman went back on his word. It's a hilarious story. Learn about who really coined the phrase that McGraw made famous! Learn how his son Tim, the famous country singer, fit into his life. Tug's life was fascinating. Find out which Phillies rode a bike to spring training in Florida from Philadelphia in 1978! This book has so many lessons you can learn and there are tons of ballplayers mentioned that are fun to hear about."
—Russ Cohen, Baseballology.com

ALSO BY TUG MCGRAW

Was It as Good for You? with William C. Kashatus
Lumpy: A Baseball Fable with Jim Ellis
Scroogie with Mike Witte
Scroogie #2 with Mike Witte
Screwball with Joseph Durso

Ya Gotta Believe!

My Roller-Coaster Life as a Screwball
Pitcher and Part-Time Father, and My
Hope-Filled Fight Against Brain Cancer

TUG McGRAW

WITH DON YAEGER

With an Introduction by
Tim McGraw

A SIGNET BOOK

SIGNET
Published by New American Library, a division of
Penguin Group (USA) Inc., 375 Hudson Street,
New York, New York 10014, USA
Penguin Group (Canada), 10 Alcorn Avenue, Toronto,
Ontario M4V 3B2, Canada (a division of Pearson Penguin Canada Inc.)
Penguin Books Ltd., 80 Strand, London WC2R 0RL, England
Penguin Ireland, 25 St. Stephen's Green, Dublin 2,
Ireland (a division of Penguin Books Ltd.)
Penguin Group (Australia), 250 Camberwell Road, Camberwell, Victoria 3124,
Australia (a division of Pearson Australia Group Pty. Ltd.)
Penguin Books India Pvt. Ltd., 11 Community Centre, Panchsheel Park,
New Delhi - 110 017, India
Penguin Group (NZ), cnr Airborne and Rosedale Roads, Albany,
Auckland 1310, New Zealand (a division of Pearson New Zealand Ltd.)
Penguin Books (South Africa) (Pty.) Ltd., 24 Sturdee Avenue,
Rosebank, Johannesburg 2196, South Africa

Penguin Books Ltd., Registered Offices:
80 Strand, London WC2R 0RL, England

Published by Signet, an imprint of New American Library, a division of Penguin Group
(USA) Inc. Previously published in a New American Library edition.

First Signet Printing, March 2005
10   9   8   7   6   5   4   3   2   1

Copyright © Frank E. McGraw, Jr., 2004
Introduction copyright © Tim McGraw, 2004
All rights reserved

 REGISTERED TRADEMARK—MARCA REGISTRADA

Printed in the United States of America

Without limiting the rights under copyright reserved above, no part of this publication may
be reproduced, stored in or introduced into a retrieval system, or transmitted, in any form,
or by any means (electronic, mechanical, photocopying, recording, or otherwise), without
the prior written permission of both the copyright owner and the above publisher of this
book.

If you purchased this book without a cover you should be aware that this book is stolen
property. It was reported as "unsold and destroyed" to the publisher and neither the author
nor the publisher has received any payment for this "stripped book."

The scanning, uploading, and distribution of this book via the Internet or via any other
means without the permission of the publisher is illegal and punishable by law. Please pur-
chase only authorized electronic editions, and do not participate in or encourage electronic
piracy of copyrighted materials. Your support of the author's rights is appreciated.

To my kids, Hank, and Betty; my fans; and all those fighting for their lives against cancer
—TM

To my nephew Josh: May the written word open up the world to you as it has to me. This is your year.
—DY

Acknowledgments

This book would not have been possible without the help and support of some very special people.

To my son Tim and his wife, Faith, who stepped up in a way I never thought possible. They were here with me from the first day I became ill, with their love and with the power of every resource they had.

To my children Mark and Cari for their love and support, and to my son Matthew, the youngest light in my family and in my heart.

To Jennifer Brusstar for caring so much and giving me hope with her own positive spirit, and for guiding me through my medical maze, and to Warren, her husband and my former Phillies teammate, for his patience. He is a lucky man.

To my "low-flying angels," Laurie Hawkins and Joan Czekaj, for getting me where I most wanted to go; Mike Mahoney for moving east to become part of my team; and Daine DeVillier, Tim's personal assistant, who found a way to make it all happen.

To the great fans of baseball, who inspired me on the field and off.

And most of all to my brother Hank, who added his own, special brand of McGraw wisdom to my life and to this book.

I thank Don Yaeger for helping me to take my crazy world and turn it into words.

Tug McGraw

A book like this one, filled with emotion, humor, pain, victories, and defeats, could only have been completed with the help of dozens of Tug's closest friends, family members, and teammates. To those who laughed while re-creating Tug's zany moments and cried while sharing details of his battle with cancer, I say thank you.

This book also would never have made it beyond the idea stage without the help of Jennifer Brusstar, Laurie Hawkins, Daine DeVillier, and the McGraw siblings—Tim, Mark, and Cari—who took time to tell me stories and open their hearts. The Tug story was not always pretty, and this group helped me gain an understanding of the man that made every interview more insightful. Tug's brother Hank was a godsend when it came to keeping oft-told stories straight.

There were also a number of journalists whose work was invaluable. Joe Durso and Dave Anderson of the *New York Times,* Ian O'Connor of *USA Today,* Bill Conlin and Paul Hagan of the *Philadelphia Daily News,* Bob Brookover of the *Philadelphia Inquirer,* Bruce Lowitt of the *St. Petersburg Times,* and Gary Smith of *Sports Illustrated* each crafted stories that shed new light on the McGraw story.

I also need to thank editors Terry McDonell, David Bauer, Rob Fleder, and Craig Neff at *Sports Illustrated,* who gave me time and support while working on this book. In

Tallahassee, Jill May and Sheri Cape also helped me keep this train on track.

Two fantastic writers, Sarah Bascom and Dan Wetzel, helped me craft and complete chapters so that they could be read to Tug while he was still lucid.

Every writer likes to think of his work as art, something that can't be improved. Doug Grad, New American Library's editor on this project, definitely proved me wrong. His efforts—and his love of the Mets—made this book immeasurably better than it was when I handed it in. Thanks for your patience and persistence.

Thanks must go to the team at NAL who helped make this book a reality faster than I thought anyone could, including Adrian Wood, Phil Wilentz, Ginger Legato, Jaye Zimet, and Doug's assistant Ron Martirano. And finally, thanks to the following for digging through their archives to come up with some great photos—George Kalinsky, Prem Kalliet at *Sports Illustrated,* Norman Currie at Corbis, Bill Fitzgerald at AP/Wide World Photos, Lorraine Hamilton and Mark Levine at the New York Mets, Larry Shenk at the Philadelphia Phillies, Angela Troisi at the DailyNewsPix, Paul Cunningham at Major League Baseball, and Michael Mercanti at the *Philadelphia Daily News*.

Don Yaeger

I want to thank Doug Grad for believing in and giving Tug's story the extra innings; and Jeff McMahon for helping me polish Tugger's final pages, but, most importantly, for discovering the missing "L" in his life story.

Jennifer Brusstar

Introduction

Everyone's life sets out on a path. There are quite a few things that happen along the way that change or, as I prefer, "form" that path. Hell, everything does. But I think it's the decisions that are made along the way in our lives, the way we choose to "deal" with these things, that make us who we are. You could say a lot of things about Tug McGraw, depending upon how well you knew him or when you knew him. I had an interesting perspective on both those views. I am his son, but I never called him Dad.

I think that it would be easy to assume that Tug was simply defined because of his reputation—he was a clown, a screwball; I mean, he was a lefty. But he wasn't simple. In my short time knowing him I came to realize that he was a very complicated character, struggling to find himself, searching for some way to define himself. I am not sure he ever did.

I don't know if he knew—I mean *really* knew—that he

gave me something, something that I can't define but I know it's there and it's very deep and personal.

I never called him Dad, but I think I will miss him as though I had him all along.

Strange how that works.

Go rest. Me and you—we're okay.

Tim
January 7, 2004
Nashville

• CHAPTER 1 •

The Day the Laughter Died

I love to laugh—almost as much as I love to make others laugh. I've often joked that I'm left-handed in every way, including my screwy sense of humor. But one of the downsides to living life as an unpredictable jokester is that when something's wrong, even those closest to you aren't sure when to take it seriously.

It was March of 2003, and I was in Clearwater, Florida. There is nothing quite like spring in Florida. The weather is beautiful, and a new baseball season right around the corner makes every day special.

In the past, I had always returned to Clearwater in the spring for the annual Old-Timers' Game. The Major League Baseball Players Alumni Association sponsors the game each year, which is a great opportunity to share a beer and some laughs with my old baseball buddies. There is also a party to help raise money for the Children's Hospital in Tampa, Florida... and I am always up for a party. Besides, all the folks down there, like me, love to celebrate St. Patrick's Day, which is March 17. I mean, I am a *McGraw*.

But this trip down was different. I still loved the parties and the celebration, but now it was about baseball. I had been recruited to work with the pitching staff for my boys, the Philadelphia Phillies. I was thrilled to be back in the game; it was like coming home.

This year I had rented a neat little condominium on the beach with my good friend John McManus. John is even shorter than I am, but with an athletic build. His hair and retro Fu Manchu mustache have gone practically white. John's green eyes are hidden by his thick-framed eyeglasses. He is a great sidekick, as he knows something about everything. He has a PhD in Psychology from Syracuse University, and John has written academic books on subjects like neurocognitive anthropology. He's led an interesting life, having managed bands and bars. John loves the hustle of city life. He can tell you about the most obscure music and talent acts that have performed in Philadelphia. John's gravelly voice almost sounds like a mumble when he speaks. He'll spin a stream-of-consciousness monologue, and if you listen in you'll often find he is really saying something thoughtful and interesting. He's one of the best and most loyal friends I've ever had. Despite our big egos, somehow we're a good match.

John and I were waiting for our friends Sam and Denise Miluzzo to come in for the weekend. Sam owned Golden Chrysler Plymouth in Roxborough, Pennsylvania. This is where I bought my cars. One year I bought three Plymouth Horizons from Sam—one beige, one burgundy, and one white. The cars were for me, my son Mark, and my daughter Cari. Although Mark was not pleased about my choice of a car for him—of course he wanted something sportier—they were on sale.

Sam and John had told me in recent days that I had been acting weird—but again, both of them just figured I was being just a little stranger than usual. During phone conversations, I would sometimes pause for long periods after a question. I would throw out comments that had nothing to do with the conversation.

For most folks, that would have set off warning signals. But as John, Sam, and Denise said later, they thought I was just distracted. I had been separated from my second wife for some time, and some of those closest to me worried that I was flirting with depression. I wasn't having as good a time with life as I had in earlier stretches, but it wasn't anything I thought anyone should worry about.

On the evening of March 11, I was grilling steaks with a buddy when Denise called to let me know their travel plans. After a few moments of silence on my end, she asked, "Tug, are you okay?"

All I could say was "I don't know."

"If you don't know, who does?" she asked.

I was confused by the question, so confused I didn't say anything. Frustrated, she joked that maybe I needed "the doctor," which is the nickname I gave Denise years ago because she was always taking care of people.

Little did we know.

I was less worried about Denise's assessment than I was about what John McManus thought. John had told me earlier in the evening that he was worried about me. While we were talking, he pointed out that I was short with every answer. He said I was playing with my food like a child, stuttering, and, as he said, "acting stranger than normal." He had only half jokingly told me that diagnosing a problem with me "would be tough, because you're so off the wall, the baseline is fluid. I can't tell if you are monkeying around or if you're really losing it."

He had noticed that my increased strangeness had begun a couple of weeks earlier, when I returned from a trip to

Philadelphia to visit my seven-year-old son, Matthew. John knew that the messy divorce I was going through was weighing heavily on my mind, and he told me he thought I was over-reacting to the situation. He also said he thought the stress of trying to serve as the life of the party at so many of the events scheduled over the next few days might be throwing me off.

The only clue that *I* caught suggesting something might be wrong was that I was awfully lethargic at the ballpark that spring. When the Phillies had invited me to work with them the year before I had made it a point to run from one place to another. I never walked because I was trying to set a good example for the players. I hustled my butt off. But this spring I could barely get myself to jog, let alone run, from field to field. In my mind I told myself to hustle. But my body wouldn't respond. Now that I look back on it, it all adds up. I figured I was just not in shape, as I hadn't done anything to get ready for spring training. And there again was a symptom that something was wrong, because doing well for the Phillies was really important to me.

On the morning of March 12, I got up and took a shower before heading to the ballpark. When I stepped out of the shower I reached over to the wall where the towels were hanging, and the next thing you know, I was pawing the towels like a cat would a pillow or something. I could not get myself to get off those towels. Oddly, I knew I was doing it. I knew it wasn't normal, but I couldn't stop myself. Somehow I shook that off, got dressed in my uniform, and headed over to Jack Russell Stadium.

In what should have been another sign that something was wrong, I didn't remember that Wednesday was a day off for the team. I was the only player or coach there. I went back to the condominium where John was just getting up. By the time he made his way into the living room, I was standing in the kitchen.

"John, we have a problem," I said.

And he said, "What you got, Frank?" He is one of the few people who calls me by my given name, Frank.

And I said, "I'm having trouble moving from task to task."

He said, "What do you mean?"

I said, "I just found myself in there kneading the towels like a cat, and I'm supposed to be going over and shaving and brushing my teeth, and it wasn't happening."

John just casually said, "Maybe we ought to call somebody." I went into the kitchen to make coffee, decided I had to go to the bathroom, and then just stood there and peed all over myself.

"John, something's *really* wrong here," I said. He walked into the kitchen to see me standing there in my shorts, pee running down my leg. "John, I'm having a stroke; I can't do anything." John later recalled that I was having a problem moving from room to room at this point.

"Call somebody, please," I said. "Get me to a hospital. I need help now." John sat me down on the couch and tried to reach Sonny and Mitzi Hepps, friends of mine from Philadelphia. When he couldn't reach them, he tried Debbie Schwab, who was my personal travel agent. Debbie was in Tampa, and she sent her husband Randy, who was working nearby, to come and rush me to the nearest hospital, Morton Plant. I blanked out and today can't remember anything from standing in the kitchen to arriving at the hospital.

When we arrived at Morton Plant's emergency room, they sat me in a wheelchair over in a waiting area. There was a nice lady sitting next to me with her sister, and I made a little conversation. I had some papers in my hand and rolled them up and held them to my eye like a telescope and stared at people. I thought I was being funny, but they were sure it was a sign I was really loopy. John hunted down the attending physician and offered his opinion that there was something wrong between my ears. Of course, he wasn't the first to make that suggestion over the years, but this time it was serious. The doctors said they'd get to my brain after my blood work came back.

While we waited there, John made a few calls to alert folks. His first call was to Daine DeVillier. Daine is the assistant to country music star Tim McGraw, who happens to be my oldest son. Tim was in Nashville with his family, and was heading to Florida on a concert tour the next day. John told Daine that I was in the hospital and, in his opinion, I had suffered a stroke. Daine decided to wait for test results from the doctors before he went over to tell Tim.

John, who suffers from emphysema, wasn't feeling well either at the moment. Though he knew I wasn't in the best condition, he didn't think anything I faced was life-threatening. The nurse he had talked to seemed to agree that I probably had suffered a stroke. So after a few hours of sitting around the emergency room, he left and went back to the condominium. Debbie Schwab, who had arrived during the wait, drove him back to the condo. While John was leaving, a few other friends got the word and started showing up. Ed Wade, general manager of the Phillies, and Dan Foster from the Major League Baseball Players Alumni Association met at the emergency room to sit with me.

About an hour later, the doctors finally took me in for an MRI to get a look inside my noggin. I was hoping for a result like the one Dizzy Dean received after he was beaned by a double-play throw while pinch running in Game Four of the 1934 World Series. He was rushed to the hospital, and the next morning's newspapers reported that "X Rays of Dean's Head Show Nothing." It was wishful thinking on my part. Almost immediately I was moved up to the intensive-care unit. I wasn't there long before a white-coated doctor walked in and laid it on me.

"I do not like to mess around with this kind of thing," the Middle Eastern–looking doctor said. "We got your scan back. I tell you straight out. You have three weeks to live. We see two masses in your head. Generally when you see multiple masses in the brain that means you have cancer in your brain and cancer elsewhere in your body. In my opinion, you won't live long."

I don't know where he went to medical school, but he must have played hooky on the day they covered bedside manner in class.

"What?" I said as I tried to understand the death sentence he'd just handed me.

"This is right. You have three weeks to live," he said when I asked him what he meant by "won't live long."

I was stunned. How do you react when, sitting there by yourself in one of those bare-butt hospital gowns, someone drops a line like that on you? You have three weeks to live. I tried to think of a joke, something funny to say, but all I could do was cry.

About then, Sam and Denise arrived from the airport. Sam, at five-foot-eight, looks like a Las Vegas pit boss, the guy who watches over the card dealers. His younger wife, Denise, is a perky, candy-faced blonde. She practically prances when she walks! I don't think Denise owns a pair of shoes with less than three-inch heels. They, along with Ed and Dan, came up to the ICU right after the doctor had left me. I was lying on the bed, hooked up to a couple of IVs and a heart monitor, when they walked in. I was hysterical, crying and pounding my head as I looked at them and said, "Sam, Denise . . . cancer." They didn't have a clue what was going on.

She went in search of the doctor. Denise said it was impossible that I had cancer. "This man just had a physical," she said. "If he had cancer in his body, it would have shown in his blood work."

The doctor was as blunt with her as he was with me. "The number and size of the masses in the brain tell me he has cancer elsewhere in the body," the doctor told her. Denise asked if he was a neurologist, and the doctor said that while his specialty was internal medicine, he was positive of his diagnosis. "How unprofessional," Denise said after he walked out of the room. "They take one MRI and they're giving you a death sentence."

I was hysterical, just going out of my mind. Where do you go from there?

Sam called Daine back in Nashville to give him the test results around 10 p.m., and Daine rushed straight over to Tim's home. Tim was in bed, but Daine told him he needed to hear this. Within the hour, Tim was arranging for my other kids and my brother Hank to fly into Tampa the next day.

Fortunately, Tim was already scheduled to head in my direction early that next morning to start a concert stretch in Florida. My middle son, Mark, was at work in Oregon, and my daughter, Cari, was working in her new business in Southern California. My brother Hank was home in the Napa Valley area.

Sam called Tim and Daine again to alert them to an appointment scheduled with the hospital's neurosurgeon the next morning at seven. Sam said he would keep everyone informed. Tim asked for calls on the hour so that he could do anything possible to help.

That night I began having small seizures, the result, I'm told, of the pressure the tumors were putting on my brain. I would grab things and hold on tight, put straws and wrappers in my mouth and chew on them. I floated in and out of being coherent. I kept trying to pull the IV tube out of my arm. My friend and former Phillies teammate Larry Christenson gave me a baseball to fidget with.

At one point Denise climbed up on the bed just to cry with me and offer a little comfort. I must have come back about that time, because I finally found something funny to say. "This is the first time I've ever been able to get you in bed," I said. It was the first time I'd laughed all day.

By the next morning, word had reached the Phillies camp that something was wrong with "Tugger." Several folks started calling the hospital, and the news media figured it all out.

Ed Wade and Dan Foster came back the next morning to join Sam, Denise, and me in the meeting with the Morton Plant neurosurgeon.

The neurosurgeon had the same opinion that the doc had given me night before. I definitely had tumors growing in my brain, and they wanted to see how far the cancer had spread in my body. The doctor told me he was ordering a body scan to see if the cancer had metastasized. Once the body scan was complete, they ordered a PET scan.

PET stands for positron-emission tomography. If I hadn't been sick I would have found this kind of cool. The fact that this machine even exists means that man predicted the existence of, discovered, and is now using antimatter. (A positron, I found out, is the antimatter equivalent of an electron.)

To get the PET scan, I was injected with a small dosage of a chemical called radionuclide combined with a sugar solution. The radionuclide emits positrons. The PET scanner rotated around my head to detect the positron emissions given off by the radionuclide. I was told that since the malignant tumors were growing at such a fast rate compared to healthy tissue, the tumor cells would use up more of the sugar, which had the radionuclide attached to it. A computer then translated the measurements of the amount of glucose consumed to produce a color-coded picture.

Denise kept asking why the doctor felt so comfortable in saying that this was cancer. She told the doctor about an auto accident I'd had a few weeks earlier and mentioned that I'd hit my head.

"I'm very sure about this," the doctor said, taking away her hope. "If the scans show there is cancer elsewhere in the body, we'll go there first. If the cancer is only in the brain, it gets tougher to do a biopsy."

Ed asked what my chances were, and though I was sedated and groggy, I heard the message loud and clear: "This isn't good. I will tell you this is probably a terminal situation." I started crying again.

It was the beginning of a day full of tears. One by one family and friends started making their way over to the hospital. As somebody came up, I would look at them and laugh, and then just burst out crying. Tim was the first to arrive. He had to give a concert in Orlando that night, so he flew into Tampa first. He wanted to talk to the doctor himself.

When he arrived, there was a frenzy around the hospital. Obviously, when one of America's most popular music stars shows up, people lose their minds. Sam and Denise had made sure the doctor stayed around to talk to Tim.

By the time Tim got to him, the neurosurgeon had all the scan information available. He stuck with his prediction that things were grim and that there weren't a whole lot of days in my future.

That was when Tim uttered the two words that set lifesaving decisions in motion: "That's unacceptable." Ironically, a well-wisher later sent me a book about a brain tumor patient entitled *Unacceptable*.

Tim asked the doctor what it would take to transfer me to another hospital. The question took the doctor by surprise.

Tim pressed again, and the doctor finally agreed I could be transferred, but said it would require a special ambulance to make it happen. Tim asked Denise to start looking for one. Seeing that Tim was serious, the doctor offered to help.

At that stage, everyone knew who was in control. Tim, busy with concerts, public appearances, and his own young family, stepped in to save my life. The most important thing he did was just take over. He probably was the only person in my family who had the life experience and personality to make everything happen.

The scene at Morton Plant quickly became bizarre. There were a number of ballplayers in town from my era for the Old Timers Game, and one by one some of the biggest names in baseball from the 1960s and 1970s started making their way to Morton Plant. Brooks Robinson, Fergie Jenkins, Mike Schmidt, Jerry Koosman, Harmon Killebrew, Larry Bowa, and Greg Luzinski all dropped by.

Then some of the current Phillies players, coaches, and management came over. Everyone was looking for a way to boost my spirits. Warren Brusstar—another old Phillies teammate—Larry Christenson, and Phillies broadcaster Harry Kalas gathered around my bed to sing "High Hopes." I hope all those guys never quit their day jobs! Harry piped in with his version of my final pitch in the 1980 World Series, the pitch that struck out Willie Wilson and earned us the world championship. It was pretty uplifting stuff.

Tim's presence added to the craziness. Rumors that his wife, Faith Hill—a country star in her own right—was with him increased the buzz even more. The media got wind that all this star power was gathered in one place, and it wasn't long before TV trucks and newspaper reporters converged outside. We had become the story of the day. That added to the stress everyone was feeling, because the question of what to say and who should say it isn't something any of us were ready to handle. When we didn't offer lots of information, rumors began to spread. That was even worse.

Everyone had agreed at that point in time that nothing would be said to the press about anything. There was an agreement between the kids and the doctors that everyone would say I was in for evaluation and testing, end of story, nothing more than that.

Unfortunately, nobody had bothered to mention this plan to my soon-to-be ex-wife, Diane. That first evening, when Diane was walking out of the hospital, she told reporters, "Tug's in here because he has a brain tumor." That was like calling in the circus. Suddenly every entrance to the hospital was staked out. The phones at the hospital PR department were ringing off the hook. Our brief effort to keep my condition private and quiet was blown.

Larry Shenk, the public relations director for the Phillies, did an incredible job fielding all the calls from reporters trying to sort things out, making sure all the information was accurate. It seemed like things were spinning faster and faster, and all the while I kept wondering if the doctor was right. Three weeks?

Late in the afternoon, Tim had to leave for Orlando and his concert. I was given a video later showing him in Orlando where, while onstage, he slapped his thigh with his right hand, just as I did all those years in the majors. Maybe no one in the audience knew he did that for me, but it really hit me hard. He arranged for all of his Florida concerts to be videotaped and had copies sent to me in the hospital. Several fans, there to see and listen to Tim, held up signs for me, encouraging all of us with "Ya Gotta Believe." During each of his concerts, he made some gesture that was to tell me to keep fighting. Almost every night while he was playing, Tim called from his cell phone to let me hear the crowd, but it was so loud I couldn't really hear anything. That week, with all that was happening, I really didn't grasp the tribute Tim was paying me. But later, when I watched the video of that Orlando concert and I saw what he had done, I lay in my bed and cried. He even had a giant king-size bedsheet that had been painted with me in Elvis hair, wearing a baseball uniform and an Elvis buckle. He brought it up onstage and held it up, and sent it to me the next day. All that stuff has to add up and get to you. It did me, anyway.

Throughout that week, he'd go perform at night, make twenty thousand people happy, then fly to Tampa the next morning to deal with my issues, my soon-to-be ex-wife, and the rest of my family. How he did it I have no idea.

Over the next twenty-four hours, my family and closest friends all made their way to Tampa. While it was great to see them, having them there all together really told me how serious this was. When that doctor laid the three-week line on me, I chose not to believe it. But when I kept looking up and seeing someone new walk through the door it hit me. *Man, this is serious!*

Everyone was trying to be on their best behavior. They didn't want to freak me out. They didn't want to say, "Hey, Dad, you're dying." They didn't want to be like that first doctor.

While my memory of this time period is a little weak, there evidently were a couple of times where, because I was in a tough spot when somebody came in, I guess I just lost it. I don't like to get emotional, and yet I do it all the time. Always have. To me it's a weakness; yet it's a weakness that I exhibit quite frequently. I'll get emotional in front of a TV set, or at a movie. Seeing other people upset affects me. But at a ball game, standing on the mound, you've got the bases loaded, you just toughen up and you don't allow yourself to get emotional until the inning or the game is over. You're trained not to. If you get emotional in the middle of a ball game, that means you're not doing your job . . . or you're getting ready to get shelled.

I was happy to see my son Mark when he arrived, but I was curious about why he was there. I didn't think I was sick enough to merit that. Then Cari came walking in, and she always gets me. I remember looking at her and saying, "You, too? What's everybody doing here?" I can't remember the order in which everyone came in.

But as I lay there in the hospital, the event that really took me over the edge was when Hank got there. I know he doesn't like to fly, yet he flew to Tampa to be there. When I opened my eyes and saw Hank, I had one of those "oh, shit" moments.

A lot of folks, handed a death sentence, go out looking for "closure." I don't believe in that stuff. I don't believe in running around trying to right nearly sixty years of issues with people. I'm not saying there aren't mistakes out there that I regret; I'm simply a big believer in going forward, doing my best not to look back. As the great pitcher Satchell Paige once said, "Don't look back; something might be gaining on you." Some call that wrongheaded; I call it life.

I know mine has been a flawed life—I'm even willing to name those flaws. I've made mistakes in relationships, made huge mistakes as a parent, made mistakes professionally, made unimaginable mistakes financially. But going back and rehashing those mistakes won't fix them. In some cases, bringing them back up only makes matters worse. Maybe I'm just not smart enough, but as I lay there in a hospital bed I wasn't going to burn my remaining brain cells thinking about the forks in life's road and what would have happened if I'd made other choices. I'm just not that deep, and I couldn't see myself starting to try to be now.

So I chose to move forward. That's been a lifelong philosophy I learned from my father, who didn't want to look back at what, for him, had been a pretty difficult life.

Still, when you hear that "forward" may last only three weeks, you know there are things you have to do. I nearly had a breakdown in the hospital trying to list all those things in my mind.

I knew my life was a mess. *Complicated* doesn't even begin to cover it. *Mess* is a much better word. And I needed more than three weeks to get my life right.

My first thoughts were of Matthew, my youngest son. He's seven years old. He is my pride and joy. With him, I finally understood the love a father could have for a child. I also saw him as my opportunity to get this father thing right. I had vowed to learn from the mistakes I had made with Tim, Mark, and Cari for his benefit. Matthew was going to get it all. But I thought I had decades to give it to him. And now . . . three weeks.

The biggest thing that hit me about Matthew was how he was going to be growing up with just his mom. It was going to be hard enough on him that his parents would be divorced. Now one of them might be out of the picture altogether. I hoped Diane could set the course for him as I wanted to. I would like to see him get good grades. Naturally, I'd like to see him become a good athlete. I'd like to see him be responsible and truthful as he grew up. I didn't know if his mother would be able to give that to him. I wanted more for Matthew.

All of my life's experiences were going to go into Matthew's upbringing. So this illness suddenly kind of changed all that. As I was there in the hospital, I kept thinking that I had to hurry up and get the cornerstone set in there with Matthew, and hopefully make it strong enough so he'd always be able to go back to that belief in himself. You don't know how much time you have to set that cornerstone. Right then he didn't act like he was absorbing anything. Obviously he was absorbing all the things that seven-year-olds absorb. But when it came to our relationship, it was a tough call as to whether I had done the one-on-one time I should have.

It was really rough when Matthew made his first visit to see me in the hospital. He knew that I was sick, but he didn't know how sick, or why I was sick. It was my request that he not know. He knew that they were going to operate on my coconut. And once it was over, he knew the doctors had left me with, as his five-year-old friend Jack, who is Warren Brusstar's son, called it, a "baseball head," because the stitches in my now-shaven head resembled the seams on a baseball. I guess I now resembled Mr. Met—the Mets' baseball-headed mascot—only without the costume.

I lay there looking at him, wondering what more I could give him. How could I make sure he got what he needed from me?

As my mind filled with thoughts and questions about Matthew, other things started flooding in. What about the other kids? Yeah, they're adults now. But I felt it had just been in the last few years that I had started to be a friend, if not really a father, to Tim, Mark, and Cari. In my mind, none of them needed me anymore, which was a hard thing for me to grasp. Just when I thought I was available, it seemed I wasn't needed.

Mark works as a full-time fireman and an emergency medical technician with the fire department in Eugene, Oregon. I like to say he has more saves than I ever did. Mark has turned out to be somewhat of an adventurer and thrill seeker—a bit of an adrenaline junkie. He has been known to live on boats in the South Pacific and wait to surf the "ultimate big wave." When not at sea or saving lives, Mark can be found climbing Machu Picchu in Peru. I am proud that he has the balls to give things a shot—and the skills to succeed at them. Cari and her husband had just opened their own business at the time, a neat drive-through coffee place in Hemet, California, near Palm Springs.

And what can I say about Tim? He had developed into a superstar as both an entertainer and family man. He was outperforming me in all aspects of life. But I felt those relationships had just gotten to where I was in a place to offer advice when asked. I still wasn't in touch as often as I should have been, but I felt I was getting better—a tough admission for a guy fifty-eight years old.

Then there were my brothers—one whose life has gone completely off the rails and the other a wanderer. I've tried to be helpful to them. What would happen now?

While I was not looking for the elusive "closure," I did reach out to my first wife, Phyllis. She was there when the good times were rolling and put up with a lot of my bad behavior. I told her I thought that had we been able to communicate better, things might have worked out differently, and I would take the blame for that.

Phyllis and I have been friends since we've been divorced, and we've had versions of this conversation in the past. But it was never with death staring us in the face.

Though I was basically broke and without a steady paycheck, I had all kinds of other things going on. I had paid speaking engagements, appearances, and commitments to the Phillies. I became fixated on Matthew and these life issues and just started telling myself there was no way these doctors were right.

Amazingly, the more I thought about all these commitments, the more I realized that while I always thought everything in my life was simple, figuring out how to clean up my life was really pretty complicated.

I had always said I would live life one day at a time. Now

someone told me I had only twenty-one of them left. It definitely changed my perspective on what everyone else saw as the happy-go-lucky life I was living.

Actually, that's probably one of the greatest misperceptions about me. People see the public Tug, who is always laughing, always there with a joke and a toast. But in the years since I retired, there have been long stretches where life was a roller coaster heading downhill and I seemed to be stuck in the valley. It didn't stop me from making those public appearances and putting on a show as the "laughing lefty," but inside I'd been struggling for quite a while.

It is tough, when you have an upbeat public persona, to maintain that façade when life is in the crapper. It's even tougher when, playing off the whole "Ya Gotta Believe" phrase I became famous for during the 1973 season with the Mets, I was being hired occasionally as a motivational speaker. Here I was telling people about the importance of positive thinking when I was mired in a series of personal crises that had me cursing and thinking any way *but* positively.

Now I had to put all that aside and get my life together. Fortunately, through my little one-man company, I had just hired a wonderful and energetic lawyer, Laurie Hawkins. I had met Laurie in early 2001 when she was the regional director of communications at the American Heart Association in suburban Philadelphia. I had been recruited to serve as the celebrity spokesperson for a national event the association was holding—CPR Weekend—and it was her job to promote my involvement with the media in the Philadelphia area. The event was to provide free CPR training to the public, and I was asked to become involved for three reasons.

First, I have atrial fibrillation, which makes my heart beat irregularly and puts me at a higher risk for heart attack or stroke. Second, my friend and former Mets teammate Tommie Agee had only recently died of cardiac arrest. I had served as a pallbearer at his funeral, and his death had affected me greatly. Finally, I had a personal connection, in that my son Mark is an EMT and paramedic and helps people who have suffered cardiac arrest and need CPR.

To her credit, during the time I worked with Laurie, I somehow didn't turn her blond hair gray! When I met her, I learned that she was an attorney with a law degree from Temple University, and that she had many years of experience in marketing and public relations, as well as in law and business organization, and that she'd run her own company for eight years. In the summer of 2002, I began to talk with her about helping me in the new company I'd formed on my own, the Tug McGraw Company.

I had many ideas for projects but with the goal of not traveling a lot for personal appearances. I had been going out on the road, making speeches and appearances for two to three weeks out of every month, and I wanted to spend more time with Matthew. I wanted her to find a way that I could accomplish this, so she put together a business plan for me that included the Ya Gotta Believe in Baseball campaign. The plan was to bring in revenue with corporate sponsorship and advertising, in addition to appearance payments.

I also told her that for many years I had wanted a restaurant of my own, and we discussed how this could happen. I loved to cook for people, so we began to look for places where I could do this. She handled all of my public relations and was developing some exciting new opportunities for me, and we were beginning to really get them going when I left for spring training.

When the brain tumors were discovered, the plans had to change. Fast. Laurie says now that the two-year plan we had for increasing my nonappearance revenue became a two-month plan, but luckily many of the things we'd started could still be used. We got my Web site going, and parts of the Ya Gotta Believe in Baseball campaign, like the fan involvement part, were still good.

When I returned from Tampa, Laurie put that law degree to work. She and Jennifer Brusstar, wife of Tug's Phillies teammate Warren Brusstar, helped me draft a living will along with all those kind of things that I had to have in order—for my kids, for the law, and for my tax situation to be straight before life's end. Those were things I should have had done a long time ago anyway. Most important, she took control of my floundering divorce case, making sure I ended that relationship while doing all I could to leave things behind for Matthew. If I had a lot of money in the bank or assets that needed to be divided up and distributed, the job would have been tougher for Laurie. But by the spring of 2003, I just didn't have much left to fight over—just a storage locker full of Sharpie pens, old fan mail, self-help books, golf tees, and hundreds of photographs from golf outings. Not much when you consider all I had been able to earn over the course of a lifetime.

CHAPTER 2

Picking Up the Pieces

It was important to my health that Tim took control. Diane was down in Florida to take Matthew to Disney World, and her presence caused confusion with my other kids. She had actually told doctors that she was my wife—conveniently leaving out the fact that we were getting a divorce—and that she was to be the decision maker on what procedures I would or wouldn't undergo. When my kids heard that, they asked me if, in fact, I was getting back together with Diane. I said no, which caused a full-blown family feud in the hallway—all of which was settled when Hank stepped in to calm everyone down. No one wanted to question his judgment or whether he had my best interest at heart.

Tim made all the right decisions, including getting me out of Morton Plant. He and Faith had worked their network of friends and contacts to quickly gather information on the best hospitals in the world for my kind of brain tumor. The centers where I had the best chance of survival were scattered from Houston to San Francisco to Baltimore. Amazingly, one of the top ten was just a few miles away in Tampa—the H. Lee Moffitt Cancer Center.

Maybe I've been too hard on the doctors at Morton Plant because of the way my time there started out. I know they've done good work with the Phillies as the team's spring training hospital for years. But brain cancer was not one of their specialties.

I needed a hospital that specialized in the field. Moffitt was the place. After three days, the folks at Morton helped arrange for a private ambulance to take me to Moffitt. But that wasn't made easy. There was so much media attention on this story that I had to sneak out at about eleven-thirty at night.

The meat wagon rushed me across the bay, and that was the night I met one of the great angels in this story, Dr. Steven Brem from the Moffitt Cancer Center. Dr. Brem is one of the most respected brain tumor specialists in the world and, as luck would have it, he had grown up a huge Phillies fan. When he got the call asking if he could help me, I'm told he said he never expected to work on someone who had once been a personal hero.

Dr. Brem doesn't usually meet patients at one in the morning, but he came to the hospital to talk to me that night. Gathered around were Hank, Cari, Jennifer, Warren, Diane, Denise, and Sam, as well as Marta, the family advocate from Moffitt. Dr. Brem took time to explain to all of us what I faced. He gave it to me in a really positive way. He didn't say, "You're going to die in three weeks." He said, "We're going to make you better. We're going to get rid of these tumors, and you're going to be fine."

Then Dr. Brem went through the procedure, explaining what we could expect. The most important package that was supposed to come with me in the ambulance was the MRI pictures, but somehow they had gotten lost. Dr. Brem had hoped to read those MRIs before the family talk, but without them, he just moved on with complete confidence. By the time he was finished talking, it didn't even occur to me that I was going to die.

Dr. Brem scheduled me for an MRI later that day. Anticipating that I would need surgery, he scheduled me for the following day, and planned to cut open my head and, as he said, "carve out" the two growths. It sounded to me like we had caught this early enough, that maybe a little carving would save my life. The good sign, he said, once he'd seen the MRI, was that the cancer had not spread beyond my brain. The bad part, obviously, was that I had cancer in one of the most difficult places on a person you could operate on.

There were many questions concerning the surgery. Brem said, "If you went in playing the piano you would come out playing the piano." He just "tickles" the brain.

Though we were all full of hope after listening to Dr. Brem, the family gathered around me in my hospital bed, and Father Victor Eschbach, who is as close to a family priest as I have, had also flown in, and led everyone in the Lord's Prayer. Father Victor is a large man with a boyish face who enjoys a good smoke and can tell impressive jokes for a man of the cloth. When Father Victor had read in the papers that I had taken ill, he jumped on a plane and flew down from Pennsylvania. After I went under the knife, Father Victor held a mass at the hospital that many of my friends and family attended.

Of course, I would be unconscious for the entire operation. But I knew a bit about what the doctors would be doing while the drugs I received through an IV knocked me out. I'd be given the Mr. Clean look, minus the earring—head shaved completely, while my dome was marked up for the correct spot to make the incision. I hoped they wouldn't be playing tic-tac-toe with the markers up there while I wasn't paying attention. There would be bleeding when they cut into the scalp, but there wouldn't be much in the way of bleeding from the brain in the actual tumor removal. They had really bright lights in the OR, microscopes, loupes—all the stuff the doctors would need to see what they were doing. And then a bunch of scary-looking instruments like power drills to cut through the bone and things that looked like big shoehorns to open up a flap in my skull—this was for the craniotomy that would allow the doctors access to my brain. Hey, if they had a clean room at Home Depot, Dr. Brem would feel right at home. After the tumor was cut out, the flap would be replaced, and I'd be sewn up, although probably not with the 108 double stitches in every regulation baseball. I hoped everything would go all right.

Six hours after they rolled me into the operating room, I came out, I was told, as a new man. I was in recovery when Dr. Brem and his entire staff gathered everyone in a room to give them an update. Dr. Brem explained that the cancer was a level IV glioblastoma multiform (GBM), the most aggressive and fatal of brain tumors. I'm told everyone sat there waiting for his next sentence. Tim, who had asked for some honey-roasted peanuts to snack on, sat there with them cupped in his hand, never putting one in his mouth. He was so tired from balancing concerts and my situation—mixing the two by bringing the hospital staff T-shirts and hats from the road—that he even curled up on the floor during my operation and took a nap.

Then Dr. Brem gave them the good news: He said they got everything visible. He felt his surgery team had hit a home run, and that the surgery had gotten 99.9 percent of the tumor, and that, with radiation and chemotherapy treatment, I had a strong shot at beating this thing.

Everyone got excited at the news. Everyone except Jennifer Brusstar. Jennifer is a longtime family friend. Then, fifteen years ago, she was drawn even closer to the McGraw mess when she married my former teammate Warren Brusstar, a man I always loved to call "the best-looking man in baseball," and moved to the Napa Valley area. Jennifer, Warren, and their sons, Jack and Dylan, have been there for our family through good times and bad.

Jennifer has worked as a flight attendant at American Airlines for nearly twenty years and is one of those people who knows how to work the phone and time zones to keep in touch with everyone. If she landed from a flight and it was too early to call her family on the West Coast, she'd call mine on the East Coast, just to check in and share a funny story—and boy does she have those from years of flying. I like to rib her that at five-foot-nine, she's too tall, but she always counters that I lied about my height on my baseball card, which is listed at six feet. In reality five-nine or five-ten is closer to the truth, but what the hey?

It wasn't at all unnatural when Tim went in search of someone who could care for me that he would turn to Jennifer. The challenge, obviously, was how she would manage her family and my health from opposite coasts. But she agreed to take a leave from American and move to Philadelphia for long stretches to manage my daily life, chart my progress or failures, talk to doctors, and serve as the clearinghouse of "Tug updates" to family and close friends. She became my driver, my cheerleader, my alarm clock, my cook, my filter for bad news, and my dearest friend. What she provided in conversational and emotional support you can't hire from some home-health-care agency.

I should have known that her knowledge of cancer—given her uncle's losing fight with brain cancer and her father's losing fight with liver cancer—should have made her the most skeptical of my friends and family. She probably had reason to be. She knew tumors grew "fingers," and while it is very possible to get the largest portion of the growth, those fingers can regenerate the body of the tumor, especially in an aggressive cancer like mine. She asked a few questions, but didn't kill the moment.

Tim, Cari, Daine, Denise, Sam, and Hank all practically cheered Dr. Brem's great news about the surgery. They were all shocked because what little they knew about brain tumors indicated the statistics weren't with me. Hank joked that you couldn't compare me to statistics, since so little in my life actually resembled the norm.

"We have confidence that we're ahead in this game," Dr. Brem said, making one of many baseball references. "Tug was right: 'ya gotta believe.'"

In the months after my surgery, my children and friends really stepped in to help. Jennifer helped me manage my life. Laurie stepped in and helped organize my life. It's one thing to be organized and it's another thing to be well managed. Tim stepped up and, through generosity I still can't explain, tried to help make me comfortable. He sent his right-hand man, Daine DeVillier, to Philadelphia, and, along with Jennifer, they rented a house for me to live in. I hadn't had a real home since leaving Diane two years earlier, so it was incredible of Tim to give Daine and Jennifer the green light to rent a place and then furnish it right down to the coasters. The two of them had only five days to pull it all together—they worked with Larry Bowa's wife, Sheena, to find the place; then Daine hired a painting crew to redo the place in two days while furniture started pouring in.

Hank came around to try his traditional family role, as he's done for the last twenty years, which is if somebody's sick, he'll be there for them. Everybody around me rallied, and that made things a lot easier.

The one thing I didn't do during all this was pout. I made a promise to myself that I would never sit around and ask the "why me?" question. Whatever happens to me, happens to me. If it's avoidable, I try to stay away from it. If it's unavoidable, I try to keep it from happening to me as long as possible. I'm not a "why me" whiner. Just go with the flow. Accept that fate doesn't play favorites.

The other thing I didn't do in the days after my diagnosis was pray. I haven't been a particularly religious guy over my lifetime, and I thought it was pretty disingenuous to reach out to God now. I'm sure there's a day coming when I'll make that call to God, but I wanted it to be some time other than when I was lying there staring death in the face. Even though I'm not religious, many of my fans are. Hundreds of them sent crosses, Bibles, prayer books, rosaries. There was even a "pillow lady" in Tampa who came to the hospital in her wheelchair to deliver hand-crocheted pillows made for me. And Father Victor had come to give me the sacrament of healing, not the last rites.

I've also read about some folks stricken with cancer who decided to break down their lives, looking for something they might have eaten or drunk, maybe someplace they lived where high-power electric lines near their homes caused their grief. Maybe I'm just simple, but I didn't do any of that. I didn't do anything that was that much different from other people. Some people get brain tumors; some don't. Live with it, die with it.

I decided while I was lying there in the hospital that I was going to live with it. I had too much to take care of in my life to let it end that quickly. Tim promised me he would make sure I got the best medical care available, and I promised I'd do my part—keeping hope and thinking positively.

As I was searching for optimistic thoughts, I remembered my father. Big Mac, as everyone called him, was one tough son of a bitch. He had always taught us boys the importance of not only being strong, but of thinking strong. His last few months on earth proved his point.

In January 1991, doctors told Big Mac he had stomach cancer and he would live no more than three months. The family all rushed out to California, and he told us not to worry. He said the doctors were wrong—even using a few strong words to tell the doctors how wrong they were—and he made us a promise.

"I'm turning eighty this summer," he said, seven months in advance of his birthday. "And I want all of you there for the party."

Big Mac did not want to die in the hospital. He wanted to come home. My brother Hank sat by his side feeding him, changing his IVs, and singing to him.

His birthday was July 24. Hank leaned over and whispered to him, "It's okay. It's your birthday. You can make it if you want to." Even though his last few days he slept nearly every moment and was largely incoherent when he was awake, he had willed himself to open his eyes every morning.

During the final hours Big Mac opened his eyes and said, "Oh, shit." Hank thought he must have opened his eyes and thought he was where he was supposed to be in the afterlife until he saw all of us still staring at him. Two hours later, at 8:11 P.M., after the sun had just set, he passed away. He looked peaceful. I sensed he just said, "See you later."

I was only fifty-eight as I was lying there in the Tampa hospital. I starting thinking positively and decided I wanted to check out like Big Mac.

On my eightieth birthday!

CHAPTER 3

Growing Up in Vallejo

I have always thought every family has a certain level of dysfunction. With the McGraws, our dysfunction has long been off the chart. Pick a social problem and I think we've had it. Mental illness, divorce, drug abuse, physical abuse, prison . . . you name it. In some ways, it is a wonder we are all still going—and talking to each other. The story of my family is the tale of three brothers who lived in a house of many uncertainties, a troubled mother who managed to destroy and damage those around her, and a father who struggled to create a good life for his kids. The three boys wound up taking three very different paths in life. The characters and subject matter are interesting and important enough that this could be a novel. It has all the twists and turns needed for great reading—love, fame, wealth, madness, jealousy, badness, loss, and murder. That sums the family up. But unlike a novel, it is all true.

My mother, Mabel McKenna, and my father, Frank McGraw, met in Carson City, Nevada, just outside Reno. They went out a couple times and my mother got pregnant with my brother Hank, which would become a recurring theme in our family. In 1942 that kind of thing wasn't supposed to happen, which meant my father had to marry her. My father wasn't drafted, as he had been classified 4F; he had a perforated eardrum from birth. So they had a quick little wedding to make things legitimate. I don't think they had a real smooth time of it from the get-go. I'm not sure if they were ever in love with each other, even at the beginning.

I was born in Martinez, California, on August 30, 1944. My brother Hank is about eighteen months older than I am. Martinez was a working-class port city hard on the Sacramento River, in Contra Costa County, which is in the Bay Area, about thirty-five miles northeast of San Francisco. While we were close to San Francisco, our area wasn't anything like the city. Nearby was the Concord Military Ocean Terminal, so that whole area was government housing and government workers. Refineries and shipping of a lot of grains originated in this area. Later we moved to Vallejo, which is in nearby Solano County and where I really grew up. If you look in the dictionary for the term *working-class blue-collar neighborhood with a* Huckleberry Finn–*like ambience*, you'll find a picture of Vallejo. The population then was about thirty thousand, and a lot of people in Vallejo worked for the military also, usually at the Mare Island shipyard. Decades later this area became a bedroom community for commuters to San Francisco. So there were lots of young couples and lots of kids. The city's population exploded while we were living there. During the 1950s the Eisenhower Interstate System was built, and all the freeways that connected the area to San Francisco made commuting even easier. The whole area—Vallejo, Fairfield, everywhere around there—grew almost overnight. By the time I left to play pro ball in 1964, Vallejo had a population of fifty thousand. Today it houses over 110,000.

We were a working-class family; my dad held a ton of different jobs when we were growing up. When he was first married he worked at a Union Oil refinery over in Crockett. He worked in the labs while he was going to school. Big Mac would moonlight as a butcher, where he'd lug beef. He was still doing that all over Napa Valley when we were kids. Every once in a while he'd take us to the killing floors, which is something that as a kid you never forget. Different places killed cattle in different ways. I remember one place where they had a .45-caliber military gun. The workers would push the cattle up the chute and we watched the guy who would try to shoot them on the unicorn, right above the eyes. Then another guy would straddle the chute with a sixteen-pound sledgehammer and try to bean them right on the unicorn as they came under him. He usually missed one out of three times and hit them in the eyeball or something. When that .45 would go off in there on the killing floor, it sounded like a bomb had gone off. Once the cow was dead the men would cut its throat and let it bleed, and they all would run down the chute to hook the carcass and put a chain around the back legs; then the guys would start whacking on them, and send them down the line. Sometimes the cattle would still be twitching and flinching, hanging out there, blood pouring out. Pretty cool shit, in a grotesque, awful sort of way. My Auntie Sis, my father's sister, told us the tales of my grandfather, Andrew McGraw, who was a world-champion sheep butcher. What made him so great was that he could cut with both hands at the same time!

Then for a while Big Mac was an independent trucker; he owned three trucks with which he would deliver lumber and basalt around the northern coast. He eventually lost his ass with the trucks. He decided it was time for a real job. But he never had benefits or health care as an independent businessman, and when you have kids you need those. Dad then went to work for the fire department for about five or six years. He liked being a firefighter, but then he got hurt pulling some guy out of a fire. His back was so bad he couldn't be a fireman anymore, but he didn't want to lose his bennies and so he stayed on with the department as an inspector. He did that while he was finishing school, where he studied to be a water-treatment plant operator/engineer. He left the fire department and switched over to Vallejo's water-treatment department. He worked there until he retired. My mom worked for a while when we were young too. She was a dispatcher for the highway patrol and for a trucking company for a while. She was a secretary at one point. Eventually, when she was trying to raise all three of us boys, she was a housewife.

My mother had a very difficult childhood in her own right, so I don't think that helped her any either. Shortly after the end of WWI, her father, Frederico, returned to Fresno from Europe. Mabel was a little girl, about three, and her dad died soon after, a result of his war wounds. It was tough for her growing up without a father. Her mother, Marie Suchauek, who was from Bohemia (present-day Czech Republic), stayed in the Fresno area after Frederico died. Marie was blind and a real mean woman. I never met her, but that is what I heard. Mabel's aunt Helen—Marie's sister—raised my mother. But her aunt, if you can believe this, was also blind, and by no means was she sweet either. There was just no love in the home, and by the time my mother was fourteen she ran away. She couldn't take it any longer. She came to San Francisco. Her older brother, Jack Turek, lived in Oakland. He was a cool guy who wore a leather jacket and rode a motorcycle back in the 1920s or 1930s. My mother later met my dad in Nevada. While my mother could see fine, it was apparent that the apple didn't fall far from the tree when it came to parenting skills. Despite my mother's upbringing, she and Dad would still take us kids to Fresno to visit her family every year.

Although we didn't own a home, we lived among happy families in working-class Vallejo. Not everyone may have had a lot of money, but this was still the good life. Which made our situation that much more ironic and proves that no matter how nice things look on the outside, how peaceful a home appears, you never really know what is going on inside. The closest I came to having that picturesque life experience was when I spent time with my Auntie Sis and her children, Dotia, Frank, and Neal. Auntie Sis was the most consistent female in my life and raised her family in a much more stable environment than ours. I loved being over there because life seemed so . . . normal.

I have always been proud that I grew up in Vallejo. I grew up in all four corners of the city because we moved around a lot, so I really felt like I knew everyone in the town growing up. The thing that brought the whole city together was sports. It was a big enough community so that you could still live in different neighborhoods and have different friends, but it was still small enough so that through sports, you played with a lot of the same people over and over again. Sports was the glue that held the community together. It was a real right-on sports town; I don't think any kid ever felt left out of sports. There was always room for one more; people were supportive, and they helped you along. The youth leagues, whether football, baseball, or whatever, were always well run. We always had really good, dedicated coaches. That is a big reason I made it in baseball.

While Vallejo wasn't a bad place to be as a kid, my home was a bit different. My parents never got along, at least as far as either Hank or I can remember. There was never a peaceful stretch between them. So unless it was blue skies and roses during the first couple years, when Hank was a baby, that marriage never worked out. One thing I remember about my parents is that they were always doing something—playing cards, big-band dancing, playing sports like volleyball together, and camping or hanging out with other couples. That's a marital trick though. If you are doing stuff with other people, then it saves you from having to be with your spouse and deal with real stuff. It's always fun to be with other people. It just isn't always fun to be with your husband or wife.

My mother was bipolar—the latest term for someone who is manic-depressive—not that we knew about that then. All we knew was that she was either in a great mood or she was in a really horrible mood. When she was in a horrible mood, she took it out on Hank. But on the other hand, when she was in a great mood, she embraced him. I think she really resented Hank because she was pregnant when she and Dad got married, and I think she held that against my brother. She lost control of her life and had to get married because of Hank. That, of course, is completely unfair, but that's my mother. I don't think she held it against my dad, because they had three more babies after that.

The thing that I believe sent her over the edge was our little sister. After she had my brother Dennis, she got pregnant a fourth time and gave birth to a girl my parents named Maureen. But our baby sister was born with some umbilical cord problem and it caused her to die a day or so after she was born. She never had a chance. It really crushed my mother, and everything went further downhill from there. We didn't see the warfare between her and my dad most of the time, but we could hear it even if they tried to keep it away from us. But then there were times when she would come after us. She was pretty quick on the draw, and she could just blow up at you in an instant. She'd punch you, hit you with something, just attack you. My brother Hank has always credited her, in a semijoking way, for making him such a good athlete. You had to be fast around my mother; you had to be able to escape out that door, or else you were going to catch a beating.

She was a natural athlete too, and played in some leagues in Vallejo—volleyball, tennis, and bowling. We credit her for our involvement and introduction to organized sports as well as yo-yo and marble tournaments. You had to be pretty speedy to "outquick" her. She was about five-foot-eight, and athletically built, although later in life she became a heavy old lady. And, as Hank knew too well, she could really hit hard. Hank was wary of her because she was big and had a short fuse. On the flip side, Mabel had a beautiful singing voice and played the accordion. Heck, she even had Hank singing in the city choir. He had a high-range soprano voice. His high notes disappeared when he started getting hair on his business and his voice changed. It would take a couple of years before he could sing decently again.

Being the youngest brother—until Dennis was born—I used to avoid the most severe beatings. While she was cracking on Hank, I used to sneak out, using him as a distraction. Or if something would happen I would just say it was Hank's fault, and she'd jump all over him. But that's what little brothers do, don't they? The old, "He did it." Then I would hope that she would vent her anger on him and be worn out by the time she got to me. My mother actually had a great sense of humor when she was happy. My dad too—he had a big sense of humor. It could be a lot of fun to be around them, but then my mother would get depressed and that was the end of that.

When things had been really bad between my parents, Uncle Ted and Auntie Sis would come and pick us up and take us to a movie or to their home in Napa. We would sometimes stay for weeks and play with our cousins Dotia, Neal, and Frank. We also spent a lot of time with Hank's godparents, my father's brother and wife, Henry and Edith. They had a place in Plumas County near the Feather River. They loved to pan for gold and had eight claims in the area. This was where we learned to trout fish, pan for gold, and camp out and sleep under the stars. Beginning in the 1970s, Hank would often return to this area. He loved to spend time there because of our relatives, friends, and even some old girlfriends. It was also a place for him to make some dough. He would buck logs for independent lumber mills. The Forest Service would mark off sections for clearing. He would come out with a good amount of dough, because they fed you and housed you.

After my parents worked things out, they would come and get us. We kids did not know they were trying to work out their dirty laundry. They did a good job keeping it from us. I credit my father for that.

In 1955 I was in the sixth grade and my mother was taken off to Napa State Mental Hospital. Dad became a single parent with custody of his children, unusual for the time. Dad tried to get us up to Napa Valley to see her fairly regularly at first so we would have some contact, but she would verbally beat up on him when he took us up there. Dad stopped taking us to visit her when she started getting shock treatments. She was there for three months.

The big change came when Mom was given a weekend pass from Napa State Hospital after she'd been there for a week in 1957. She came home and called up one of her girlfriends, and told my dad she was going to a movie—which was no big deal. Everybody went to the movies. So he said, "Yeah, go ahead and go to the movies; I'll watch the boys." But I think he thought it was a little weird that she got a weekend pass and then instead of seeing her family she went to the movies. But that was what she said she wanted to do. Well, I don't know if she went to the movies or not, but she didn't come back. Nobody knew where she went—she just disappeared. It was a plan she had put together, and that was the last time we saw her for about two years.

My dad was always working, so when we were very young it was hard to get to know him. Hank understood him better than I did. For me he was just a guy who, depending on what period of our lives it was, was always overwhelmed with the responsibilities of holding the family together. As we got older, he found time during the day to be with us. By the time we got to high school he was working the graveyard shift at the Water Department, so while we were sleeping he'd be working, but then he would be off during the day shift. That way he could help with the football team by driving the school sports bus. He could help chaperon dances. He was always involved in our school activities. Big Mac would even have a drink or two with the pastor and principal of our school.

Sports saved me. Two or three years after my parents got divorced, Hank got a scholarship to a Catholic school—St. Vincent Ferrer. Dennis and I would follow a couple years later. Big Mac thought the school would give us a little more discipline and guidance than he could supply. He thought the nuns would be decent authority figures for us boys, since we lacked a female role model in our family at that time. The school was in a convenient location for us—about half a block away. Dad worked night shifts at the water-treatment plant. At least sports was something I could pour myself into. There isn't a lot of joy in being young and emotional to begin with, and then seeing your parents split up. But I could get out on a ball field and all my problems would go away. The thing that kept my family together was sports, not sitting around a dinner table. We didn't have that kind of life.

My dad always encouraged us to play sports. He had been a good athlete himself, but he grew up in San Francisco during a time when not everybody had golf clubs or catcher's mitts or tennis rackets lying around. So he was good at all the stuff that didn't require expensive equipment. He was fast, quick, and power-oriented. He and his brothers were all boxers and football players, and they ran track—various distances in track and field. Or they threw the shot put and discus. He and his brothers were all the same in that they could all swim really well. They were obviously skilled. They were also great butchers, well known for good hands. They had skills, but not baseball skills. Big Mac never played any baseball.

However, Dad was a handsome guy in his day, and in the early 1930s he was spotted by a talent scout for the movies. He was sent down to Hollywood for a screen test, but unfortunately he got drunk and ended up in a fistfight, busting up a hotel. He was asked to leave. So much for becoming a movie star!

Finally, in 1959, when I was a sophomore in high school, we got Christmas cards from her. There was no return address but the postmarks were from San Francisco. Somehow through those Christmas cards we found her. She had left some clues, so in reality she wanted us to find her. I guess she felt as though the years away from us were enough to rehab her. By the time she wrote us the cards, she had done all the paperwork to be legally released from the hospital. Everybody was looking for her, so it was cool for us to go down to San Francisco and find her. By this time my parents were divorced by the state on grounds of abandonment. But Big Mac always encouraged us to visit the city and maintain a relationship with her. We started trying to visit with her again. She would eventually remarry and move to Hayward.

* * *

The person who was most affected by my mother's illness was Dennis, my younger brother. He is three years younger than I am, and when we were little kids he spent more time with and was closer to my mom. I can still remember her sitting in her rocking chair with Denny in her arms, for what seemed like forever. She would rock and rock and rock . . . crying the entire time. When she got sick, I think he felt a sense of loss. He didn't know which way to turn. I think he got really confused, and he tried to turn to Hank and me. We were already used to my dad being away because he had been a truck driver and fireman. When my mother disappeared, that made things kind of strange and weird, but we adjusted right away because we were always involved in after-school activities and sports. But Dennis was cut from a different cloth.

I wasn't a very good brother to him growing up. Dennis was kind of out there. When he tried to get in with me and Hank, I think he felt ignored. Mom was always coddling him—he was the only one she would be nice to—so I didn't see any reason for me to be involved with him. I thought he was fine. So while he hung out in his room, Hank and I were out running around doing stuff. Dennis had his own group of friends, so it never dawned on us to try to include him, and as a result neither Hank nor I spent enough time with him. He also wasn't into sports like we were. He tried to play but he was nowhere near the athlete Hank and I were. When Mom disappeared, he jumped into Little League and he tried to play football, but the talent just wasn't there for him. My brother Hank was an incredible natural athlete; he was six-foot-one, 185 or 190 pounds when he was a senior in high school. He was always cut, with great definition, and he had speed. He ran the 100 in 11.2 or something like that, which was pretty good for a white guy back then. Dennis, however, was pudgy. He just wasn't athletic.

He thought there was a place for him in athletics, but it turned out that there wasn't. He tried all the way up into his sophomore year in high school, and then finally he said, "The hell with this; this isn't me." The good thing was that in his junior and senior years he started getting good grades. While he was playing sports his grades were bad. He decided he wanted to get good grades and go to college, so he started studying. Hank never had to study; he got all As and Bs anyway. I was more like Dennis: I never did get good grades, but somehow made it through. Anyway, once he gave up on sports he started getting into music and his grades improved to honor-roll level. He became like Bob Dylan: He had the guitar, he had the harmonica, and he had the voice. He was doing great by doing his own thing.

Dennis wound up going to San Francisco State University in 1965. He majored in photography and philosophy and wound up driving a cab to work his way through college although he never quite graduated. He used to come over to Candlestick and see my games when I played with the Mets. For the most part, however, when he was in college he became really independent. He didn't share any of his school experiences with Hank or me. It was almost like, "You have yours; I have mine." He also started getting paranoid. Then he just disappeared and we didn't know where he was. It turned out he went up to Alaska to work on the pipeline for about six years. We didn't have any contact with him. He went off his own way, probably because there was some resentment with the family and he was still trying to figure things out himself. He just wanted to get away. He did—about seven thousand miles away.

After a couple of years, he showed up out of nowhere. His

appearance was different. His eyes were empty. He was a different guy—mean. Something had changed him dramatically. This new person was intense, just scary. Very macho. His reaction was always to fight. We felt bad for him.

A lot of things happened to Dennis up there. Exactly what they were, we really don't know even now. He would never talk about his experiences. The only thing we know for sure is he drove all the way back to California, to San Francisco, nonstop. He didn't sleep at all. That's a week's worth of no sleep. The only way you can do that is on amphetamines. But by then we knew he was doing some drugs anyway. I should have known sooner, like when he was in college, but at that time I wouldn't have recognized a drug user if he was standing right in front of me. If it was my little brother, he'd be the last one I'd suspect. So I never thought of drugs at the time. But somewhere in the mid-1960s, he started fooling around with them.

The thing about the drugs is that they really contributed to his mental condition. Drugs can bring you down and make you paranoid. When he got back to San Francisco after his years in Alaska, he tried to get straight but it didn't work. He was on cocaine for a while, and though I couldn't prove it, I was pretty sure he was doing some heroin. I wanted to help him, but he would get offended if anybody tried. The only time he tried to get any help was if somebody called the cops on him and they put him in rehab. But he never made it through an entire program. He actually lived for a little while with my mom, when she moved back to Vallejo for a bit. She called the cops on him and he went to jail. That was his first bout with jail, I think.

After he came back from Alaska, around 1977, Dennis was living with my dad, and he took a pop at Dad. My dad knew something was wrong with Dennis, and he thought it would be a good idea for Dennis to go live with my aunt and uncle in one of their cabins in Northern California. But then he bit—yes, bit—my uncle Henry, who was at that time nearly eighty and blind. Aunt Edith called the cops and Dennis moved away. Hank asked him why he would do such a thing. Dennis just blamed the family for his ways.

Later on, Dennis would have nothing to do with the family. He didn't want any contact from me or Hank, Dad—anybody.

Dennis had moved back to Vallejo and the guy in the apartment next door, thirty-one-year-old Jason Garfield, was harassing him. Dennis claimed that Garfield had terrorized him for months. He'd do things like play his music real loud. Dennis would call the cops and they would arrive and tell Garfield to cut it out. The music would stop and the cops would leave. As soon as the cops left, the music would start up again, with Garfield playing his music into his sink. It would go through the pipes into Dennis's apartment. Dennis called Social Services, but his complaints fell on deaf ears. His landlord wouldn't help him either.

Finally Dennis warned Garfield that if he didn't stop the harrassment, he would shoot him. Dennis went to Kmart and bought a .22 rifle and a box of shells. Then Garfield got him angry again—one time too many. Dennis shot Garfield in the head.

So on July 13, 2002, he killed the son of a bitch. Since nobody would help him, Dennis decided that was the only way he could get rid of Garfield. Dennis is just not all there. So he just plugged him. He shot him four times. On the first three shots the guy didn't die, and he was out in the street, lying there. At that point the cops had pulled up and saw the whole thing. But even though they were watching, Dennis shot him right in the head. Later the cops asked, "Why did you shoot him a fourth time? We were here." Dennis said,

"Because he would have been pissed. If I only injured him, he'd have just been pissed and come back and harassed me even more. So I had to kill him." Dennis really believed there was no way to get rid of the guy unless he offed him. When the story broke—"Tim McGraw's Uncle Kills Someone!"—a lot of my friends thought it was Hank! Needless to say, Tim has never met his uncle Dennis.

The sad thing is that I wasn't totally surprised that this happened. I immediately went into damage-control mode to see how we could get Dennis protected. I was embarrassed for what had happened. I worried for Tim and what my friends and business associates were going to think. No Mc-Graw would be convicted of murder if I could help it. I flew out for support, only to find that Dennis had told his lawyers he did not want family contact, although the lawyer did ask if the family could arrange to get Dennis some decent court clothes. I was afraid to go to the hearing out of fear that it might draw attention. I was there for only one day. The day I did go, Dennis never even saw me in the courtroom. Everybody told me not to worry. The court assigned a public defender to my brother who was supposed to be the best defense around. He was not the best. I wanted to do more to help my brother, but I was kind of blocked. There wasn't anything I could do.

Once Dennis had gotten back from Alaska, neither Hank nor I was involved in his life much. He reconnected with my mother and then my father, and then the police, and then Social Services. But not us. We tried to help him, but the Social Services people told us to leave him alone, to stay out of his life, and that if he ever wanted to talk to us, they would contact us. They said every time we got into his life, we disrupted things. I felt there was a certain amount of truth to that although I did wonder why they didn't ask for our side of the story. But they didn't. We might have been able to help him out a little bit, talking about our mom and some of the history of depression in the family.

At the time of the trial, Hank was not involved at all. Hank had been angry at Dennis for hitting Dad and Uncle Henry. Hank was always proud of Dennis because of his academics. It was shocking for all of us to see this different guy. If Dennis didn't want Hank and me to be part of his life, Hank didn't feel there was any need to force himself on Dennis. The truth is, Dennis did not want me in his world either.

When it came to stuff like the situation with Dennis, I wasn't assertive enough. I always left things like that up to Hank because he was older. During the whole Dennis mess, I always thought it was Hank's responsibility. I never looked at myself as the person who should be helping. We got reports on the trial from our cousin Frank Henderson, who sat through the whole thing. We just weren't very aggressive when it came to Denny's life. We never really understood Dennis very well, and I don't think he wanted us to. So we kind of accepted the fact that we shouldn't be in his life.

Well, in the end, the legal team he had didn't do such a hot job. They went with a cockamamie plea of self-defense because the guy had been badgering him. Needless to say, it didn't work. On December 9, 2002, my brother was found guilty of first-degree murder. In January of 2003, Dennis was sentenced to twenty-five years to life in California State Prison for murder, plus another twenty-five years for using a firearm in the commission of a crime. Under California law, Dennis must serve 85 percent of his sentence, or more than forty-two years, before he will be eligible for parole. He'll be ninety-seven then.

*   *   *

Sometimes I shake my head with amazement when I think of my family and how three very different brothers came from the same parents. One guy's in jail for life, one's a drifter, and then there's me. We're all broke. Dad ended up with a small pension; Hank's been broke for thirty years by choice. Of course, that's no excuse for my ending up broke after having millions of dollars slip through the palms of my hands.

As far as my own life, if it weren't for sports, I probably would have been in juvenile hall as a kid and maybe bunking with Dennis right now as an adult. I would have been in trouble. As a kid I could have gone either way, but it was my love for Hank and passion for athletics that made me want to stay in school and stay eligible for sports. I didn't want to go drinking and smoking and hanging out and exploring the dark side of my life. I would start that lifestyle in junior college. For me, leaving Vallejo was the best thing that ever happened to me. It was really my chance to blossom, to get out on my own and leave my family and all of that behind. But I don't hate Vallejo. I understand what it meant to me. I certainly wouldn't be what I am if I hadn't lived there. I just also know I wouldn't be what I am if I had never left.

CHAPTER 4

Hank McGraw

It doesn't matter how talented you are; if you want to be a professional athlete, you have to catch a break. My break lived right down the hall. My brother Hank wasn't just the greatest influence on me as a child; he was my role model as an athlete. And he gave me the break I needed to become a major-league ballplayer. While my mother and father both had a role in shaping me as a child, neither could compare to Hank, who was eighteen months older than me and was the big brother I idolized, mimicked, and followed around.

He was also the big brother who sprung me to the major leagues. Hank was an incredible athlete, not just a terrific baseball player—he played twelve years in the minors—but a great athlete in any sport. Coming out of high school he had scholarship offers from all over the country to play not just baseball, but college football and even basketball from some state schools. He was less than thrilled to play college football, knowing that the coaches wanted to make him a tight end, not a quarterback. In those day, tight ends were more like blockers. Hank felt he wasn't tough enough to make it as a tight end. A combination of the divorce, loans for Big Mac's failing business, and Mabel's medical bills, as well as the cost of keeping all three boys in private schools, had left Big Mac broke. But my family needed the money, so Hank wound up skipping school and becoming an original bonus baby with the New York Mets.

In 1961, all eighteen major-league teams—plus the Mets and the Houston Colt .45s, who would begin play in 1962—had come to Vallejo to scout him, and he could have signed with about eight or nine of them. But we all liked the Mets' scout, Roy Partee. Partee had been a catcher for the Red Sox and St. Louis Browns and had played in the 1946 World Series. Partee, then forty-four, was a handsome guy, and had once been offered a part in a movie. He was one of the best people I ever met in baseball, a real straightforward, honest guy. He was in his first year as a Mets scout. As an expansion team, the Mets were allowed to start signing players in 1961. Before Hank signed with him, he made Partee promise that he would make sure I'd have a tryout one day. At the time I doubt Partee thought the Mets would ever get anything out of giving me a tryout. By the time I graduated from high school I was about five-foot-eight and I weighed about 140 pounds—not enough to survive as an outfielder or a pitcher. Plus I was dumb. But the Mets wanted Hank badly, so Partee made the deal, Hank signed with New York, and that was that.

Unlike with Hank, the scouts didn't come and watch me play in high school. I was discouraged because I wanted to be like my brother, but the reality was that I wasn't then as good as he was. He told me to be patient and keep playing. After high school I attended the then–Vallejo Junior College, and during my sophomore year it was basically "put up or shut up" time. Hank had helped me the summer before my sophomore year to sign on with a team of college stars playing in Canada. I was still somewhat small, so I needed an experience like this, where I lived away from my family, worked out, and concentrated on baseball. The Canadian college league, which is much like the East Coast Cape Cod League, pulled talented players from California schools. My squad was coached by legendary Stanford skipper Ray Young, and I learned more during those two months than I could ever have imagined. We couldn't be paid to play because it would have cost us our eligibility, so they offered me cash to be on the grounds crew at the stadium. That summer set the stage for what turned out to be an amazing second season of junior college ball.

I was a good pitcher by that time, and the California junior college leagues were heavily scouted, but I was no guarantee to make it. We had a heck of a team that year, though—I was the undefeated star pitcher—and reached the state finals, where we met Mount San Antonio College down in L.A. I was the starting pitcher for that game and I choked. I pitched the worst game of my career. I got knocked all over the park and was pulled in the third inning and put in left field. Then I dropped a routine fly ball that allowed two runs to score. It was a total disaster, and not surprisingly major-league scouts didn't exactly mob me after the game.

When I got home I called Hank and related what had happened. He was disappointed for me, but encouraged me to call Roy Partee anyway. We were both hopeful that the gentlemen's agreement Hank and Roy had made a few years before still held and Partee would still give me every consideration. And that was where Hank gave me my big break: He called Partee and not only reminded him, but vowed to quit baseball if I didn't get a proper and fair tryout. He said, "If you don't give my brother a shot, I'm going home." While this may sound like an idle threat coming from some brothers, anyone who knew Hank knew he would do it. Roy Partee knew Hank well.

So Partee called me again and asked about what had happened in the state championships down in L.A., because he had heard bad things. I told him not to worry, that everyone has an off day. All he needed to know, he said, was that I could play. Well, lo and behold I was invited to Salinas, California, where one of the Mets minor-league teams was located. It was also the team Hank played for. I got to have a tryout with Hank. The whole roster was there. It was sort of a makeup exam for the game in L.A. The Mets had me pitch some batting practice and throw on the sidelines in front of Partee and manager Kerby Farrell. They thought I had some pretty good stuff. In 1961 my brother had gotten $15,000, which was a ton of money back then. I coyly said I didn't need that much. I'd gladly take $10,000. What can I say? I wasn't real sharp. They were a bit dumbfounded, considering I didn't have a single offer and that the only reason I got the tryout was because my brother threatened to quit the franchise if they didn't watch me pitch.

I realized pretty quickly that I was in no position to play hardball, so I backpedaled and told them I'd sign for anything. I just wanted the chance to play pro ball. That was enough to get a second tryout, up in Stockton, California, in front of the Mets coaches there. Hank and the Stockton team were on the road, but I must have impressed someone. Hank's manager, Kerby Farrell, told the folks in New York they should go ahead and sign me. All of a sudden I had a contract sitting in front of me, and it offered a $7,500 bonus! I think Partee offered a good recommendation because he knew I needed the cash.

I was so pumped that I didn't pay much attention to the fine print. I came to find out that the $7,500 bonus came with a contingency clause: If I didn't stay on a rookie-league roster for at least sixty days, I didn't get the money at all. I later learned that was a trick many of the major-league clubs used back then. On the fifty-ninth day, they'd either cut you or offer a low month-to-month deal and never have to deliver on their promised bonus money. This was a tactic used especially on pitchers, who were rolled into camps by the busloads. Those same buses were reloaded with guys getting cut, which definitely took its toll mentally on those left behind.

That contingency never came into play for me, though. The first day they threw me out on the mound, I pitched a seven-inning no-hitter. I followed that with another seven innings of shutout ball in my second game. They stroked me the check. Unbelievable!

Of course, I immediately spent the money on a used 1960 Chevy convertible—the beginning of my ingenious money-management decisions. Hank was happy for me—after all, it was because of him that I even had a chance. If it weren't for him, my ball career would have ended after that championship game in L.A.

It's not the normal way a player becomes a "bonus baby." In fact, I was extremely lucky. But it was the break that sent me on the path that made me a two-time world champion. Besides, when it comes to Hank's doings, nothing is normal.

I am not afraid to admit that I was a dumb kid. I just didn't think things through back then, and as a result I was constantly getting in trouble for really stupid pranks. When I was in fourth or fifth grade I was literally teetering on the brink of the dark side of life.

It seems like I was always in trouble. When I was about six, I got caught stealing mail out of a mailbox, proof that I would have been a bad thief. Then I used to write on the sidewalk right across from our school. When I was seven, I'd take chalk and I'd draw pictures of naked girls on the sidewalk. That got me called into the principal's office. That's how dumb I was. Rather than write on a sidewalk down the street or around the corner, I'd do it right in front of the school, so I was easy to catch.

When I was about nine my dad caught me smoking. I'm not sure exactly how he caught me—whether he smelled cigarettes on my breath or saw me do it—but he knew. What I used to do was walk down the street, down the hill on Ohio Street in Vallejo, and pick up old cigarette butts and then smoke those. Like I said, dumb.

Getting hooked on cigarettes in the fourth grade wasn't a very good thing, even back when smoking wasn't considered the taboo it is today. It sure is addictive, though. I finally quit smoking about three years ago. Dad knew I needed more guidance, but he was working two jobs and didn't have the time needed to straighten me out. So he sat me down and simply said, "I think you ought to spend more time with your brother." I guess he thought Hank would be a good influence on me. I listened to my dad. I started hanging around Hank more. How a younger brother gets in with an older brother isn't simple, and my dad did not convey a plan. He certainly didn't tell Hank I was going to be hanging around! My dad left it up to me to figure out how to stick with Hank. Naturally, my "in" with my brother was to learn how to play sports.

I was already playing baseball, but I was small. You have to understand that when I was a freshman in high school, I was four-foot-eleven and weighed ninety-eight pounds. I was real small. I didn't think I was ever going to grow. When Hank was a freshman in high school, he was five-foot-nine and weighed 160, and he was fast. I didn't see how I could ever compete with that. Especially in baseball.

The first team I ever played for was a rec-league team coached by Dick Bass, who would go on to be a halfback for the L.A. Rams. I had watched baseball on TV, and one of the things I loved was when the major leaguers slid into home plate. Well, I got a hit one day, and since we had no fences, if you got it between the outfielders you could just run and run until you had an inside-the-park homer. That's what happened, and as I was rounding third I thought about those majestic slides that the major leaguers had. My only problem was that I didn't know *where* to slide. So I hit the dirt halfway down the third-base line and immediately came to a stop in the middle of nowhere. As everyone laughed I crawled the rest of the way for a very red-faced home run.

Hank actually got me my first break in baseball back then, too. There was Little League in Vallejo but not where we lived. Ours was a thing called Peanut League baseball. If you were a real peanut (like me) you got into the Junior Peanut League. Hank was in the junior league too, until he turned twelve and one of the Peanut League teams wanted him. The coaches were a couple of police officers, Andy Myers and Mel Nickolai. My father was a fireman at the time. Dad told them that if they wanted Hank, they had to take me too—a two-for-one deal or no deal at all. They didn't want me, but since they were cops and dad was a fireman, they took me.

I basically followed my brother's lead for years after that. If he did something, I did the same thing. Fortunately for me, he stuck with baseball or Lord knows where my life would have headed. Hank also liked playing tennis and at one point considered giving up baseball for it. The baseball coach at St. Vincent's, our high school, was Al Endress. He was about six feet tall, really cut, looked good in a suit, handsome, with black hair and high cheekbones—just a good-looking guy. He coached varsity baseball.

Courtesy of Tug McGraw

Big Mac and Mabel. On the courthouse steps in Carson City, Nevada, on their wedding day. Hank is there too, but Mabel isn't showing yet. I look a lot like her.

Courtesy of Tug McGraw

You dirty rat... Big Mac was a handsome guy, reminiscent of a young Cagney in profile. But a drunken brawl blew his shot at Hollywood.

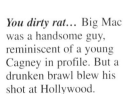

Ozzie and Harriet? Not! Denny, Tug, and Hank, in the early 1950s.

Something to do after baseball season. Hank (right) and I played together on the high school football team—the St. Vincent's Hilltoppers, 1960. Hank helped lead us to a 9–0 record.

Courtesy of Tug McGraw

Courtesy of Tug McGraw

Courtesy of Tug McGraw

Courtesy of Tug McGraw

Like father, like son. Me and Big Mac at his seventy-fifth birthday party.

Courtesy of Tim McGraw

Betty. She did a great job of raising Tim, and she had been right all along—I was his father.

Louis Requena/MLB Photos

The Youth of America. Legendary baseball sage Casey Stengel imparts his half century of wisdom to the wide-eyed twenty-year-old Mets rookie in 1965. Note the World's Fair patch on my uniform sleeve.

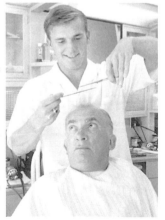

Photo by Bob Moreland, The St. Petersburg Times

Just in case the baseball thing doesn't work out... Tug "The Barber" McGraw cuts the hair of a skeptical customer.

AP/Wide World Photos

No, Delilah, I need my hair for my extraordinary pitching strength! Phyllis is trying to give her protesting husband—me—a rinse and curl.

Tom Gallagher, New York Daily News

A man who wears two hats. Mets VP Johnny Murphy signs Marine Pfc. McGraw to his 1966 contract—for $9,500, more than Uncle Sam paid. And the chow was better in the big leagues too.

Courtesy of Tug McGraw

Yes, sir, who do you want me to shoot, sir? Marine boot camp in Parris Island, South Carolina.

Courtesy of Tug McGraw

Good morning, Vietnam! I went overseas to visit the troops for the USO with pitcher Denny McLain of the Tigers (right) and White Sox infielder Pete Ward (left). Not exactly Bob Hope with Ann-Margret…

Courtesy of Tug McGraw

Groovy outfit, baby! Bobby Heise and I—clean-cut Marine reservists and members of the Mets AAA Jacksonville Suns—say good-bye to our mod and stylish wives before reporting for duty in 1968. That's Phyllis (right).

And you should see what I can do with my left arm…. One handed push-ups are great for impressing the guys in the clubhouse, but not so great for getting batters out on the field.

Dan Farrell, New York Daily News

Bill Meurer, New York Daily News

You say Pucci, I say Poochie.... Me and Phyllis with the dog, no matter how you spell it, in August 1969.

New York Daily News

Honey, you're sitting in the sink. Tight quarters inside the camper we bought for the honeymoon we never had.

Have a Rheingold, Mr. Grant? Celebrating the 1969 World Series win with catcher Jerry Grote and chairman of the board M. Donald Grant. It was Grant's speech about the front office still believing in the club during the '73 season that helped solidify "Ya Gotta Believe!" into the Mets' rallying cry.

George Kalinsky

Hal Mathewson, New York Daily News

Now you know where Tim gets it from. The Amazing Mets belt out "(You Gotta Have) Heart" from *Damn Yankees* at Bellsound Studios on West 54th Street for our Buddah Records album. Front row, left to right—Art Shamsky, Ken Boswell, me, Ed Charles, and Ron Swoboda. Behind us are pitchers Gary Gentry, Jack DiLauro, and Cal Koonce.

Corbis

Thanks, guys. Glad I could help out. I receive congrats from Joe Morgan of the Reds, the Pirates' Manny Sanguillen, and Ron Santo of the Cubs for getting the win in the 1972 All-Star Game in Atlanta.

Courtesy of Tug McGraw

Where's the fire? Usually, it was on the pitcher's mound when I was called in to a game. By 1973, I'd built up a nice collection of toy fire trucks sent to me by the fans.

Corbis

Ya Gotta Believe! I was on the mound when we clinched the NL East on a rainy Monday, October 1, at Wrigley, the day after the regular season ended. That's third-base coach Eddie Yost behind me.

Frank Hurley, New York Daily News

And the crowd goes wild. We've just beaten the Big Red Machine to capture the NL pennant on October 10, and I had to elbow and hurdle my way past the fans to make it to the safety of the dugout with my hat, uniform, and glove intact. I guess playing football as a kid finally paid off.

Here, roomie, have some champagne! Sometimes ballplayers drink the stuff. But Ed Kranepool and I agree that winning the pennant isn't one of those times.

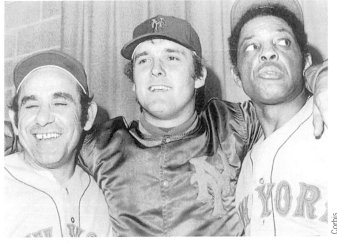

Surrounded by Hall of Famers. Yogi, Willie Mays, and I celebrate the Mets' wild victory in Game Two of the '73 Series. I pitched six innings—in relief! Man, I thought that game would never end.

Corbis

Corbis

Corbis

Don't try this with a mustache. Top A's reliever Rollie Fingers keeps his waxed handlebar away from my giant Bazooka bubble before the first night World Series game in New York.

Yeah! I've just fanned A's pinch hitter Billy Conigliaro to nail down a 2–0 Met win in Game Five of the '73 Series. We were up 3 games to 2 over Oakland, but couldn't get that final win on the road.

John Duprey, New York Daily News

A screwball signing Screwball. Writing a book was one of my many off-season jobs that kept me away from my family.

Anyone seen John Denver? Phyllis was right—the image of the happy family that we projected was a lie, and was damaging to Mark and Cari.

Yeah, he's a screwball, all right. The Phillie Phanatic and I help the cast of my comic strip, "Scroogie," come to life.

Ed Clarity, New York Daily News

Swing, batter batter batter . . .
My two-year-old son Mark tries to drive in a teammate at the family-day game at Shea on July 11, 1974. I tried to put on a good show, with the help of bullpen coach Joe Pignatano behind the plate.

AP/Wide World Photos

You're playing with the big boys now. Mark, age seven, tries to bunt on me after the catcher, six-year-old Aaron Boone, has called for the scroogie at a Phillies family-day game on May 20, 1979.

Courtesy of Tug McGraw

My own personal Hall of Famer. Matthew, age seven, my pride and joy, is my companion on this 2002 trip to Cooperstown. The only way I get into the Hall of Fame is by buying a ticket.

Prentice Cole, *Philadelphia Daily News*

And people thought I had long hair. Hank, Mark, and I work out at the Vet, in one of the only photos of Hank and me in uniform together. People looked at Hank's ponytail and forgot that he was a heck of an athlete.

Courtesy of Tug McGraw

Grandma Mabel. Mabel is backed up by three of her grandchildren—Mark, Cari, and Tim.

Courtesy of Tug McGraw

The Three Amigos. Hank and I begin to bond with Tim at a baseball camp he worked at with his friend Lance in the mid-1980s.

Courtesy of Tug McGraw

Well, if you insist. Tim coaxes me to the mike at one of his concerts in July 1998. I'm sure it wasn't because his fans wanted me to sing!

Coach Endress decided to lobby my brother when it was time for him to decide between tennis and baseball. Hank was a freshman then, but Coach Endress knew he was good. He said, "Look, I want you to play varsity baseball."

My brother said, "I've already made the varsity tennis team."

Coach Endress tried to get Hank with the macho thing, throwing out lines like, "Girls play tennis." You know, that kind of thing.

Hank was resolute. He said, "I'd rather play tennis."

And Coach Endress said, "Well, I want you on my baseball team." My brother wasn't budging, though, so Coach Endress said, "Only one freshman has ever played on the varsity here. I want you to be the second freshman on the varsity team."

That did it for Hank, the chance to face a real challenge. He became the second freshman ever at our high school to play on the varsity team.

I have often wondered what would have happened to me if Coach Endress hadn't been so persuasive and my brother chose tennis over baseball. I was such a follower of Hank's that I probably would have never played baseball. I might have a much better forehand, though!

Growing up wasn't easy in the McGraw household, but what I went through was nothing compared to what Hank faced. My mother's illness made her violent, and we just never knew what would set her off. Because Hank was the oldest, he took most of Mom's beatings, often because I blamed everything on him. She started losing it with my brother when he was little, when he was just a little toddler. She would get a wooden coat hanger out and whack him until he bled. She would hit him hard. He still has marks on his legs. That's tough stuff for a little kid.

But when she was around my brother took all the beatings, and he's still not very relaxed about his life because of it.

I'm the one who never got beaten up. I never had to bob and weave. I wasn't really afraid of my mother like he was because I never got hit to the point where I was bleeding. I never had to take any of that kind of stuff, so I wasn't angry all the time. I really think that shaped my brother. He might be a little bit like my mom in a sense, only he has more control over it than she did. He definitely doesn't handle authority very well, though. In fact, few deal with it worse.

As I mentioned, my brother was a great ballplayer and an incredible natural athlete. There wasn't a scout out there who didn't say he'd be the best McGraw of all. Despite all that talent, he wound up playing twelve years in the minors and never made it to the bigs. His career was a series of peaks and valleys, peaks and valleys. He had some real hot streaks and then something would happen. The reasons were simple—attitude and injuries. Injuries and attitude. At any given time it was one or the other.

Hank's first big adjustment to the game came in 1961, when he was playing for the Mets' farm team in the Western Carolina League. The lights in a lot of minor-league parks were pretty dim then. This was also his first introduction to sliders. He had to adapt both to catching and hitting the slider.

His first injury happened in 1964, when he was in the California League. The Salinas Mets were playing the Bakersfield Phillies. Hank and six other players were standing on the right-field line, just tossing the ball and getting loose. Then the batter in the cage hooked one. Hank didn't even see it coming. Bam!—right in the eye. He was out for a few weeks and was not allowed to do any physical activity, for fear it would hemorrhage. It just really badly bruised his eyeball. For a long time, that pupil wouldn't dilate with the other one, so it made it hard for him to see. He still had a pretty good year, but he really had to battle that eye problem. It prevented him from improving his stats.

His most famous attitude problem is part of baseball lore. He didn't make the majors because he wouldn't cut his hair, or so the story is conveniently summed up. What happened was that Hank was a utility man, catching and playing infield for the Phillies' AAA team in Eugene, Oregon. It was 1970 and Hank was doing great under manager Bob Wellman, having a banner year. He was leading the team in hitting, batting over .300, leading the Pacific Coast League in home runs and RBIs, and he was on a real hot streak. But the team was in last place.

So Wellman was fired from his position and moved to another part of the organization because the team didn't belong in the cellar. A new manager, Lou Kahn, was brought in. After a couple weeks, while the team was in Hawaii on a road trip, he decided to shake things up. Lou wanted the guys with muttonchops to cut them, no sideburns below a certain point, and for their hair to be above their shirt collars. He wanted the team clean shaven and to be able to see their ears. He pointed to six or eight guys, including Hank, and told them that they needed grooming. Hank's hair wasn't any longer than normal; in fact, it was short for that period. It was 1970, for God's sake, and guys wore their hair long back then. Hank's hair was bushy, but it didn't even extend past the collar. It wasn't bad at all—at least in my opinion. But the manager was an old, crotchety, fat, tobacco-chewing, WWII-era son of a bitch. He wasn't comfortable with the way the younger generation behaved, hated the fact that Hank would do beadwork, making necklaces for the teammates and their wives. That same night as Kahn's announcement Hank had gone to talk to Kahn in his office and asked if it was an organizational or a personal problem. Kahn told Hank he would talk to the Phillies that night when he made his report. Hank did not challenge him; it was a pleasant conversation between coach and player.

The next day Kahn walked in and announced Hank's suspension—the other guys had all cut their hair. Hank at that point figured he was done with baseball. If they weren't going to call him up when he was hitting .900, they were not going to call him up ever, so what was the point?

Kahn told him he would receive no pay while he was suspended, and to clean out his locker after the team took the field and so on. Hank was finished. So he left Hawaii and retreated to Lake Oswego, near Portland, Oregon. Hank didn't care about the suspension; he seemed all right. He thought he had given a baseball career a good shot. It was now time for him to start thinking about doing something else.

Well, as luck would have it, just before all this happened, the Phillies catcher at the time, Tim McCarver, took a foul tip and it split one of his fingers open. Then, in the same game, Mike Ryan, the bullpen catcher, took a foul tip and split one of his fingers open. It's a rare injury and it just isn't supposed to happen to two catchers on the same team in the same game. But it did. So all of a sudden the Phillies were in desperate need of a catcher. One story has it that the Phillies front office called Eugene to tell Lou Kahn to "get McGraw up here; we need a catcher." Lou said, "I don't know where he is. I suspended him." The Phillies couldn't believe it. "You suspended him? For what?"

"Well," Kahn said, "he wouldn't get a haircut."

They said, "Why didn't you call us first?" In reality, the Philadelphia people would have supported Kahn's discipline; that is the way baseball works. But the Phillies had already called up a couple of other catchers—Larry Cox and Del Bates—so it was a moot point.

The Sporting News was following Hank's hair story. Reporters were claiming to have talked to him, and even quoted his reactions. Hank laughed when he finally saw the articles, because no one from the media had ever spoken to him! Then the story made the national wires. As unusual as it was, and considering the political state of our country then with Vietnam and all, it was run in papers all over the nation. Poor Hank got letters from all over expressing outrage, not too many saw him as a man standing up for principles. *Go home,* they said. *Stay away from baseball, you commie bastard!* Someone suggested he needed Jesus. One mother blamed him for her daughter's running off and marrying some long-haired freak.

Not that Hank knew too much at the time of the controversy. He was in his tony summer home, waterskiing, kicking back, and enjoying life. About all the good he could claim, from a baseball career standpoint, was that he still had his hair.

Hank finally got hold of me and I told him that Marvin Miller—the head of the major-league players' union—had been calling to see if he could help straighten out the situation. Marvin could not represent Hank because he was a minor leaguer. However, his private law firm could represent his case. Hank's girlfriend, who was a stewardess, stowed him away on one of her flights from LAX to JFK for his meeting with Marvin Miller in New York.

Hank ended up getting a big raise after Philadelphia traded him to the Hawaii Islanders, an independent minor-league team. He had two great years, leading Hawaii to the Pacific Coast League championship. Despite the raise and his success on the field, the trade had essentially taken him out of baseball's feeder system to the major-league teams.

There's a line in baseball's minor leagues when you go from being a prospect to being suspect. Hank had crossed that line a couple of years earlier. He never did look at himself and think that he might have been part of the problem. That just isn't Hank. He wouldn't compromise; he was always proud as hell of himself as a ballplayer. If you looked at it another way, he was too stubborn to make any compromises. I mean, all he had to do was get a haircut. But he doesn't look at it that way. He says that if the same thing happened today, he would react the same way. He's a stubborn son of a bitch. But, to Hank's credit, he doesn't hold a grudge against baseball. He figures he got a fair look for twelve years. If he were good enough, he would have made it. And back then, with fewer teams, it was more competitive. He had some problems with individuals in the organizations, but not with the system itself. After all, it's not just about talent—you need to know how to be a professional.

The ironic thing was that two years later, the Oakland A's won the World Series and half the team grew Afros, handlebar mustaches, muttonchops, beards, and long hair—and were paid bonuses by the team's owner, Charlie Finley, to do it.

Which ought to tell you what Lou Kahn knew.

Hank's branding as a rebel started early in his career. Right after signing with the Mets in '61, he was sent to their minor-league team in Lexington, North Carolina. The team was on a road trip and, to Hank's surprise, three black players on the team couldn't go in a restaurant to eat. That wasn't the way we were taught in Northern California, so Hank decided to make a point. He went back to the bus and sat with the black players. His manager told him that attempting to take a stand like that would cost him if he wanted to make it as a pro. Hank basically told him to kiss his ass. Racism was something he wouldn't allow to go on without taking a stand.

Hank ended up always sitting with the black and Latino players in the back of those minor-league buses, and they'd make it a point to sing and laugh whether the team won or lost. Managers hated that. It is ironic that the when the Mets held their first spring training in St. Petersburg, Florida, in 1962, they made an organizational decision to fight racism and not to stay in any hotel that would not accept their black players. They became the pioneers of integration in St. Pete.

So I would say that Hank was right to take those stands. But, just as he does today, Hank made sure you knew his position was righteous, and if you disagreed you weren't really worthy of his attention. Management didn't ever grow to accept the way he showed his difference of opinion, whether you labeled it rebelliousness or nonconformity. And Hank just kept thumbing his nose.

You might think that during those years when I was with the Mets and the Phillies that there would be some jealousy between us, what with me, the younger brother, making the majors and Hank, the older brother, never getting out of the minors. But honestly, there was none whatsoever, and Hank will tell you the same thing. Both of us were very comfortable at the levels we achieved. Athletically we were great together; we never had any problems with each other in sports. Funnily, he says he couldn't have been the athlete he was if I hadn't been there to compete with him. I never believed that, but he says it. He also has long said that when he saw me on the mound during major-league games, he felt like he was there with me, as if we were one.

It wasn't until after I retired that some serious friction

emerged between us. Our up-and-down relationship took a few dips when he had to cover for me when I was cheating on my first wife. It took years and years and years for that rift to build up. But a bigger wedge between the two of us was my decision about Dad's funeral. Big Mac had told us he did not want to have a "God and Jesus service." I did not honor our father's request. I had a Catholic service—priests and all. And that really pissed Hank off. Hank has never really forgiven me for that.

I did honor my father's other request—that is, how to handle his ashes. He wanted his ashes baked into loaves of bread and fed to the seagulls at the pier so they could shit all over the city and his remains would be spread all over San Francisco.

Looking back, Hank had sometimes been a mean big brother when we were kids. Not really mean, just kid mean, bully mean.

Some of the difficulty is easy to understand. He went from being Hank McGraw, the best athlete in the Valley, to one day becoming Tug's brother. Then, just as he was getting used to that, he became Tim McGraw's uncle. That's a lot for one of the greatest athletes I've ever known to absorb.

Down deep, I always understood that Hank cared for and about me. In a family where my mother was really not a mother, Hank assumed that caretaker role. He's handled it for years. For reasons like that, Hank was my hero back then and still is to this day. There are times he can really stress me out, though. Sometimes it is tough to be with him because he's so angry. To me, it seems he's just looking for things to be angry about.

My brother is a hippie now. Has been for years and years. We call him the Happy Hippie from Napa Valley. Nobody can figure out what he is or what he does. He's held every odd job in Northern California. He's tended bar, sung in bars, made leather goods and ceramics. He's been a handy-man at a hotel, coached felons in a rehab school, worked in factories, panned for gold, was a UPS deliveryman, and even was asked to join my son Tim's concert tour, and was billed as the tour guru. For a couple years he even coached at our old high school in Vallejo, but only as an assistant. He had no desire to be the head coach. And he really made a splash there when he showed up at the Catholic-school homecoming wearing a shirt that read, *Legalize Weed*.

A lot of people refer to Hank as an underachiever. In 2002, *Sports Illustrated* did a big piece on him. Their great writer, Gary Smith, found him in the guesthouse of a friend we'd known since junior high. The story was called "The Uncommon Life of Hank McGraw." You can't argue with that title. I've been on his ass about underachieving for a long, long time. His response is based on his politics. He's an anarchist—he wants it all torn down and rebuilt, so everyone can start with a level playing field. In his opinion, governments are established so that the proper crooks have a license to steal. He believes in life, liberty, and the pursuit of happiness. And that is about it. He isn't going to compromise anything for anybody. I look at him and say he's not made the most of the gifts he was given. He looks at me and says I've compromised so that I can live a "better" life.

I know it doesn't make a lot of sense for me to still consider him a role model, but I just admire his independence. It's a paradox. I admire his tenacity, the way he'll stand up to his beliefs. I've often compared him to the forward scout for the wagon train. He went out ahead of the rest of us, blazing the trail and willing to fall off a cliff so the rest of us would know when to turn back. In the last couple of years, I've started to realize that when he doesn't have a supply of at least some money—and if he doesn't have a supply of at least some pot—his life breaks down.

But that doesn't mean I don't appreciate what he stands for and continues to stand for. Or that when it comes to the person I am, Hank was key to my development. People thought I was a freethinker, a screwball. They just didn't know Hank!

CHAPTER 5

Riding the Elevator

Though Hank was able to use his influence and reputation to open pro baseball's door for me, I had to take that opportunity and prove I could make it to the majors. If you think back to that time in the mid-1960s, there were only five hundred guys in the world who were major-league professional baseball players. But there were thousands more like me who were, as we used to say, riding the elevator—working our way through the dozens of rookie-league and minor-league teams scattered all over America.

After my poor showing at the Junior College State Championship game, my elevator started in the basement—actually it was the subbasement! When you get on most elevators you pick which floor you want to get off on, but oftentimes it makes other stops and can even go down when you thought it was going to go up. The same is true for playing baseball. You start out on one floor and then end up on many others before you either head back down or get to ride to the top. The trick, however, is staying on that top floor when you get there and not being put back on the elevator unexpectedly—which happened to me a lot.

After my first tryout in Salinas in 1964, I didn't start with the Mets until a month or so later, when they sent me down to the rookie league in Florida. They had enough left-handed pitchers that they didn't need me, but I didn't care. I had signed my first pro baseball contract with the Cocoa Mets, and was headed for the big leagues—or so I thought. I played in Cocoa Beach with a host of other rookies for manager Ken Deal. When I first arrived we were put into a dorm-style building built by the Houston Colt .45s with two to a room and an adjoining bathroom that we shared with two other guys. That was not exactly my idea of a swinging pad, so a few other guys and I decided to get an apartment in town. Deal, who would soon earn the nickname "Super Sleuth" from us, was not real hot on the idea of our getting our own place, but there was nothing in the contract saying we couldn't, so we did.

We came up with a group of five guys for our "off-campus" apartment: Gary Enserti, Jim Lampe, Kevin Collins, Fran Raley, and myself. We loved the apartment, mainly because we were not living in dorms with the rest of the team. Deal insisted on our keeping the midnight curfew the rest of the team had, and even personally enforced it. Every night, Super Sleuth would drive into town to check on us—every night. No matter what the excuse—which we always had—for blowing the curfew, he would greet us with the same line: "That will cost you fifty." He was relentless and a real pain in the ass—even though he never took money from us.

Whether we were up airing out our apartment after causing a smoke fire from cooking a postgame meal, or just sitting around talking, Super Sleuth was always there to catch us. One night in particular, my little brother, Dennis, drove into town about two a.m. and Super Sleuth showed up while I was helping him unpack. He issued his usual admonishment—"That will cost you fifty"—before jumping into his Cadillac and driving off. So in typical Tug McGraw fashion, I got pissed and took off after him. We were racing down the highway, me behind his big Caddy and Deal speeding up to outrun me. When I finally got him to pull over and stop, I explained my excuse for still being up and he once again told me that he didn't accept any excuses and to get my ass in bed. Obviously my propensity for mischief carried down to Florida.

Other times Super Sleuth got mad at me for getting badly sunburned at the beach after being told the beach was off-limits, and for showing up at the end of a game that I thought had been rained out. Now I am not saying that I didn't deserve most of his admonishments, but it's not like I was looking to get into trouble. With me, it just happened.

All in all my time in Florida was fun and eventful. Who wouldn't love living near the beach and getting paid for playing ball? What a life!

At the end of that summer of 1964 I asked Denny and a friend, Pete Badarraco, to drive my car out to Florida from California. They were only juniors in high school at that time, so when I offered to pay for both of them to drive across the country they jumped at the chance. However, as soon as they arrived, I was called up to the Mets class-A team in Auburn, New York, so I flew to Buffalo, and Denny and his friend drove to Auburn. Once we got to Auburn the club left for a road trip, so I sent them to Niagara Falls. It turned out to be quite an adventure for them, and needless to say my new car had quite a few miles on it when I finally got it back. They ended up flying back home to California.

While with the Auburn Mets, I actually hit my first home run in the pros—in a play-off game, no less—and we were the first Mets minor-league team to win the play-offs. The organization had been in existence only three years, so they hadn't had much time to accumulate talent or wins. Still, it was a special moment for those of us who would go on to stay with the club for many years. The best part was that Hank had flown in from California to watch.

Most pitchers spend their time in the minors developing a more diverse repertoire. Everyone can throw a fastball and a curve. The pitchers who eventually make it to the big leagues come up with those extra pitches—a slider, a knuckler, or even a screwball—downstream from the majors. While I was in Auburn I worked hard to develop a third pitch—the palm ball—so while I had to watch us win the play-offs from the bench, I picked up a few tricks while I was there. At the time, I had a so-so fastball and a good breaking ball. My big positive was that I had good control of both pitches. In those days the hitters could lie back for my fastball and really jump on it, so I needed a new pitch. It would take me a few years, but I finally found it.

After I finished that season in Auburn, Hank and I decided it was time for a vacation, so we traveled to Niagara Falls and then to New York City. We had hoped to catch a Mets game, but they were on the road, so we went to a Yankees game. It was our first time in Yankee Stadium, and we saw Mickey Mantle hit his 450th home run. We watched a rookie pitcher named Mel Stottlemyre, who later became the pitching coach for the Mets and Yankees and helped both teams win pennants and the World Series. Dean Chance had pitched for the Angels. He won twenty games that year, and, in 1970, he briefly became a teammate on the Mets. For a young guy like me, it was an awesome duel.

Once that game was over, we headed back to California. When we finally arrived home, my dad met us at the door wondering where we had been. "You both belong in Florida.

The Mets have been trying to get hold of you. If you would've called I could have saved you some driving time." In those prehistoric days before cell phones and pagers, folks like Hank and me could be out of touch with the world for weeks. The Mets had been calling my dad, wanting us to play winter ball, so he put us on a plane headed for Florida.

After winter ball ended, we found ourselves back in California waiting on word of where we would go next. Hank was a few years ahead of me—he had played A ball in the California League that year—so naturally we were expecting word to come about him first. We were very surprised when a letter came for me. Obviously we all thought they had made a mistake. How could this contract with the words *National League of Professional Baseball Clubs* on top of it be for me, not Hank? It took a while for it to sink in that this was a big-league contract and that I was now on the express elevator to the top floor.

The contract was for a salary of $7,500, and though it was the major-league minimum, it was quite a step up from the $400 a month that I had been getting. Hank and my dad were so happy and proud of me that Dad broke out the Irish whiskey. Dad couldn't believe one of his sons was going to get the chance to play ball and earn a living doing it. Of course, he reminded me of his motto that the sun was going to come up whether we made it or not—so we might as well make it.

It was February 1965 and I was heading down to Florida for Mets training camp. It was unbelievable for me. I was now headed to the bigs! No one had any idea what an impression I would make on that ball club. Back then the Mets were known for their crazy players—Marvelous Marv Throneberry, and Jimmy Piersall, who ran the bases facing backward when he hit his one hundredth career home run, for example—but they were about to see what crazy really was.

Most days I had to pinch myself. I was a twenty-year-old professional baseball player joining a club that was starting its fourth season and had already lost more than three hundred games in the first three. This ball club was known for its oddities and follies. The Mets had always been described as a circus, and they were about to get another clown!

The day I arrived at the Colonial Inn, I was so excited and nervous that I wondered if this was all a dream. I didn't even know I was in the right hotel until I woke up the next morning and recognized Al Jackson, the Mets' top left-handed pitcher, in the dining room. Jackson invited me to have breakfast with him, and I thought that was awesome. We talked about the team and how I'd been working out every day since I got my contract. "In a few years, you won't be doing that," Jackson told me. "I haven't thrown a ball all winter." I was shocked.

Later that day I went out to the ballpark and met manager Casey Stengel and all of the coaches. I had always thought that Stengel was old as dirt, and while he didn't look as old in person as I had expected, he still looked like a museum piece. We had a who's who of baseball coaching us. Warren Spahn, who once asked me how I got to the majors with a hat rack for a head, was a pitcher/pitching coach; Eddie Stanky was sort of an all-purpose coach; Yogi Berra, who had been fired as the Yankees manager after losing the World Series to the Cardinals in seven games, was the first-base coach; and a guy named Jesse Owens—yes, the famous Olympic runner Jesse Owens—was our track coach. A pretty famous crew of leaders, huh?

I will never forget the sight of Stengel standing in the middle of the field that first day, hollering to no one and everyone, "Yes, sir, come see my amazing Mets."

I was wide-eyed about the whole experience, even if nobody else was. I went outside and decided to act like a baseball player. They had a batting cage near the clubhouse. I walked over and saw Larry Bearnarth, a big right-handed reliever who had already spent the '63 and '64 seasons with the Mets, taking his cuts at the balls being thrown by the pitching machine. I watched for a few minutes before coolly asking, "Who's next?"

"You got to get a number," Larry said. Larry was a native New Yorker and had a wise-ass sense of humor. He knew he had me when I asked, "Where do I get it?" He said, "In the clubhouse." So I went back into the clubhouse, where I saw Nick Torman, the equipment manager. He seemed to be the guy in charge. He always had a grumpy expression, and the younger players were always afraid of the guy. Somehow I mustered up my courage and said, "Hey, Nick, I want to hit. Bearnarth says I need a number for the batting cage."

Nick knew I was being played, and he played right along. He said, "Okay, I'll find it." About twenty minutes later he was still checking out equipment, looking at papers, doing whatever it is equipment managers do, every so often pretending to look for a number, just to keep me on the hook. I finally couldn't take it anymore and ran back outside to the cage and yelled, "Goddamn it, I want to hit," to Bearnarth, who was still hacking away. When I showed up again, he was laughing so hard he could hardly stand up.

Bearnarth had me. I was his fish that day. I couldn't stay pissed long, because it told me I had really made it. I was there—and being paid!

My entire first year as a pro ball player was a blur, but one thing I do remember was that I was more dedicated than ever. I was certain that I didn't belong there, so I tried to work harder than everyone else to prove to them—and to me—that I belonged. Every day I would run a mile up and down the beach before getting to the park by eight-thirty. I wanted to be the first one there and be the fastest on the field.

Soon it was time for some of us to get cut, and I was nervous as hell that I would be one of the rookies to go. I knew that the contract between the owners and the union said that if they sent me down to a farm team I would be able to move to another major-league team. I didn't want that. I wanted to be a Met. Obviously the Mets didn't want that either, since they kept me and three other rookies—outfielders Ron Swoboda, who became my roommate, Danny Napoleon, and pitcher Jim Bethke. I was relieved to be heading up to New York with the rest of the team, but I knew in the back of my mind that I was probably kept only to be protected—so that no one else could snatch me up.

That season in New York we all got a chance to play. It was often said that if you were the twenty-fifth guy on a twenty-five-man Mets roster, you still got called to play, since it sometimes took twenty-five New York Mets to play nine guys on any other team. My first time in the game came in a doubleheader against the San Francisco Giants on a cold Easter Sunday. When I stepped out on the field at Shea Stadium for the first time, I thought it looked like a giant birthday cake just for me, with a slice taken out of the outfield. I came into the game with one out and a guy on second and third. Orlando Cepeda was up to pinch-hit, and I remember thinking how loud the fans were when he came up. I was scared shitless. All I could see was his bat—it looked huge. My knees were shaking, my palms were sweating, and my stomach was in knots. But I struck him out looking.

I was so excited that I started jumping up and down and hollering like a fool. I know everyone around me thought I was nuts, but I didn't care. I was pitching in the bigs and had just struck out Orlando Cepeda! I had made it. After I got out of the inning and returned to the dugout, I was so wound up that I spilled a hot cup of beef broth all down the front of my uniform. The trainer, Gus Mauch, gave me a tranquilizer.

The tranquilizers relaxed me, all right, but after taking another one before my start in the second game of a doubleheader in Chicago, I decided not to take them again while
trying to pitch. Those damn things had me so wigged out
that all I could focus on was the piece of pie I'd eaten during
the first game. I didn't even make it through the first inning.

We didn't do very well that season, losing 112 games and
finishing forty-seven games out of first place, but I did win a
game that would put me on the map. On August 22, I pitched
seven innings against the Cardinals and recorded my first
win, but the big game for me came four days later. I started a
game against the Dodgers, opposing Sandy Koufax. All
Koufax did in 1965 was go 26-8, with a 2.04 ERA, twenty-
seven complete games, eight shutouts, and 382 strikeouts!
The Mets had never beaten Koufax, but that losing streak
was about to be broken. With the Mets ahead 3-2, Wes
Parker hit a triple in the seventh off the right-centerfield
fence in front of the big scoreboard to put the tying run on a
third with two outs. Jack Fisher, the Mets' ace starter, was
called in to relieve me and struck out John Roseboro. In the
eighth, Ron Swoboda and Joe Christopher hit back-to-back
home runs for the win, 5-2. Koufax and I were taken out of
the game at the same time. I was already back in the clubhouse when the game ended, and needless to say I was jumping up and down and screaming at the top of my lungs. Hey,
you would have too if you'd just outpitched Koufax. This
time no one was looking at me like I was loony. Some of
them thought of me as an annoying kid looking for attention.
They were beginning to either accept my strange ways or just
ignore me.

That summer I finally got a chance to see Hank again. We
were in Williamsport, Pennsylvania, for an exhibition game
against the Williamsport Mets, the Eastern League farm
team that Hank had been playing with since I made the par-

ent club. The local papers had built up the "showdown" between the McGraw brothers, so Hank and I cooked up a show. I had told reporters that I was going to knock Hank on his ass, and while he was expecting me to do it, the ball got away from me and I really did knock him on his ass. I was worried at first that I might have hurt him or pissed him off, but he shook it off and nailed a double off of me the next time up. I am sure some people thought I handed him that pitch, but the truth is, he could just flat-out hit.

As that summer was coming to a close, I would finish out the season with another first for my career in the bigs—the first time I was thrown out of a game. It was September, and the last game before I was leaving for boot camp with the marines. I had received my notice for selective service in my fan mail—go figure—and decided that I would get into the reserves before they had a chance to draft me. I first looked into the navy reserves, but they didn't have the program I wanted, so I narrowed my choices down to the army, the National Guard, and the marines. I'd love to claim I put a great deal of thought into picking a branch of the service, but the truth is that the marines had the shortest line at the recruiting center, so I picked them. Most of the young guys didn't want to go into the marines because of horror stories that were circulating, like the one about the drill instructor leading a group of guys into a swamp at low tide and then getting them stuck and drowned when the tide came in. But that didn't faze me—I just didn't want to stand in line and figured this baseball thing would end sooner rather than later, so I'd better be prepared for what was next.

So I was pitching my last game before heading off to be a "pickle" for Uncle Sam; Hank was in the stands, and I decided I was going to pitch a no-hitter, since it had never been done in Forbes Field in Pittsburgh. The first three innings I was doing great. Nine up. Nine down. Then everything went to hell. One of my teammates booted one for an error, breaking my streak. I walked the next guy, and then Roberto Clemente hammered a ball off home plate, high into the air, and beat out my throw for a single. And then Donn Clendenon came up. Clendenon was the Pirates' big first baseman, on his way to batting .301 that year. Four years later, he would be my teammate and the 1969 World Series MVP, belting three homers and batting .357 against tough Baltimore pitching. But now he knocked the hell out of my curveball. He whaled it right through my legs, almost castrating me, right into center field. The ball headed right for Jim Hickman in center, who overran it and then chased it as it rolled out to deep center. Center in Forbes Field was so deep that the batting cage was stored on the field! The ball rolled all the way to the cage. The whole thing was so comical that Clendenon was laughing his ass off as he rounded third and slid home. Three errors, four runs, and one hell of a shitty play later I was really pissed. I started jumping up and down and cursing up a storm. While my tirade wasn't aimed at anyone in particular, the umpire thumbed me out of the game. The Mets coaches didn't seem to mind—they never understood me. On the way back to the visitors' clubhouse at Forbes you had to exit through the Pirates' dugout. They were having a great time at my expense. They thought it was such a riot that a rookie left-hander blew his top, so Clendenon asked, "Who were you cussing?" As if he really cared.

"Not him," I said, motioning to the umpire.

"Who did you mean?" he added.

"You, you son of a bitch!" I responded. And with that I got scared and took off running. Clendenon later told me that nobody was coming after me because they were all rolling on the dugout floor laughing.

Each off-season, while my major-league career was still not a sure thing, I had taken time to start learning some other career. I just never believed I would last in the major leagues, and I knew I had to be ready for the fateful call that the jig was up. One year I attended barber school. Another year I trained to work in the hotel and restaurant industry. But this off-season I was destined for the career training that nearly changed my whole life.

I spent the next six months in boot camp pretty much undoing all of the talent in my pitching arm. One handed push-ups and chin-ups are great, I suppose, for hand-to-hand combat, but it does a number on your ability to throw a curve. My time with the marines wasn't too bad, but it did make me realize that I preferred playing ball for a living instead of being screamed at and bossed around by a drill instructor. They once made us go three days without peeing, and one of the guys actually used a plastic bag to go in and then put it in his pocket. When the DI slapped his pocket to see what was in it, it broke all over both of them. I think that poor guy is still doing push-ups down in South Carolina.

I will admit that I did learn a lot while in the corps. I dedicated myself to being a good marksman, even though I was forced to shoot right-handed despite being a lefty. I barely qualified, but I made it. This was the first time I had really concentrated on being good at something other than baseball. I also learned how to be by myself. This was the first time I didn't have my brothers or teammates around, and it forced me to get to know myself and find out what made me tick. Toward the end of my boot camp service, one of the commanding officers approached me about staying in the corps. I'd even qualified for Officer Candidate School. I actually gave it some real thought, even going so far as to tell my brother, who had driven to Camp LeJuene for a visit, and my father that I might be making a life change. The Vietnam War was hot, and I knew from my experience there that the marines were in need of pilots. I was determined that if I could get into flight school in Pensacola, I'd leave baseball and go serve my country. Big Mac wasn't too pleased, but he was willing to stand by my decision. Hank, on the other hand, went nuts. When he had received his selective service notification, he was classified 4F like Dad—he also had a perforated eardrum. I think that was the beginning of Hank's turn to the far left. He had become a peacenik, and the idea of heading to war was bad enough. But he kept pointing out that I had already been fortunate enough to get a taste of the bigs—a taste he had yet to have—and he wanted to see me chase the dream the two of us had shared as boys.

After a couple of weeks of going back and forth, a marine instructor finally leveled with me and admitted that flight school was only a remote possibility. That sealed the deal. I was headed back to baseball, though I would now be three weeks late to spring training.

In March of '66 I headed back down to Florida as a busted-out pickle and a trained killer—or at least that was what the marines called me. Friends closest to me have said I came back from my marine experience a changed man. Some said that that the idea of holding a live hand grenade helped me put holding a baseball in perspective. The confidence I gained from having made it through marine boot camp gave me a pride in myself that even my athletic accomplishments at the time couldn't match.

My arm was very stiff from all the push-ups and chin-ups, but I assumed that I could loosen it up and be right back to where I was before enlisting. Boy, was I wrong. I was afraid to tell anyone that my pitching arm was hurting out of fear that they wouldn't want me, so I kept on as if everything was how it used to be.

After we opened in New York and I pitched a few games, my arm got worse and I started to get worried. During a game in May I heard something snap and just knew my arm was finally done. The team doctor said I had tendonitis, gave me some pills, and told me to ice my arm. But I still couldn't throw the next game and was put on the disabled list. That first year after the corps was my worst on record. I pitched in only fifteen games, started twelve, and finished one. I won two and lost nine. Definitely not one for the books, and my elevator was about to go back down a few floors.

After the 1966 season I participated in the instructional league for new rookies and major and minor leaguers who needed some help. There I had the good fortune to meet Ralph Terry, the onetime Yankee pitcher who had been picked up by the Mets. Terry, who had gone 23-12 with two World Series wins in 1962, was working on his knuckleball and his golf swing at the same time, trying to figure out whether he wanted to keep playing baseball or play golf. Later he decided to go play pro golf. It was the right decision.

While we were down there, Ralph and I were out playing golf one day and were talking about my need for an "out" pitch. I had a fastball that I could cut and a nice big curveball that nobody could hit very well—when I threw it right. The palm ball was coming along. But I still needed a go-to pitch, a changeup, and hadn't been able to find it. While we were on the course, Terry told me he had long tried to develop a screwball, and showed me his grip using a golf ball to show me what he was talking about.

The next day we were warming up at the ballpark and I tried Terry's grip for the screwball. It worked! In the pepper game the next day, whoa, there it was! I stuck with it, and the next thing I knew, I had my pitch. I had a hell of a screwball. You try to teach that to people now and they're not into it. They just don't want to learn it. Maybe I was just lucky—a lucky screwball with a great screwball. I finished in the top ten of the instructional league that winter, before heading off for a month of active duty in the marines. That was the beginning of a lot of good breaks for me.

In 1967 they sent me to Florida to play for the Jacksonville Suns and try to rehabilitate my arm. That year proved to be better for me, and my rehabilitation time helped. While in Jacksonville, I started twenty-one games, pitched fourteen complete games, and had a 10-9 record. While you will later see that this season, personally, changed my life—it also professionally put me back on track and on the map. The manager for the Suns at the time was Bill Virdon, who'd just finished up a respectable eleven-year career as an outfielder with the Pirates. He taught me a lot about handling myself and being a better player in general. So when I was called back up to the Mets at the end of the season, I was ready. Ready to ride back to the top and hopefully stay there.

I returned to New York in August of '67. The Mets hadn't moved very much since I left. They were still in last place and Wes Westrum, the old New York Giants catcher who replaced Stengel as manager when Casey broke his hip in 1965, was now fighting to keep his job. Wes didn't like me very much and even warned me when I got back to watch myself, since things were now done differently under his watch. He was a real shit. He started me in a game in L.A., and I was doing great for the first four innings—then after I'd loaded the bases with a walk, a hit, and an error, he pulled me out. Needless to say I was pissed and let Wes know it. He didn't like that and decided to get even. For my next start, in the Astrodome, where the Mets always struggled, he kept me in the entire game after I'd given up eight runs by the fifth inning. I would like to say that my talk with him helped, but I know it was his way of making me suffer. He knew I wanted out but made me stay in. We kept losing games, and Wes finally lost his job, getting canned with eleven games to go. He was replaced by Salty Parker to finish out the season.

They were tough days, but they would prepare me for a long career at the highest floor the elevator reached. Soon I'd be pitching with a World Series trip on the line and the Mets about to make history.

· CHAPTER 6 ·

Drugs, Women, and Booze . . .

My days in baseball were the best days of my life. Of course, it goes without saying that I had a blast playing ball for a living and spending time on the field with some of the greatest guys in baseball. But some of the most memorable moments took place off the field. I may have made it to only two All Star games, but I was known as an all-star in the "neon league" for almost all of my nineteen years in the bigs.

When I was with the Mets and the Phillies, off the field culture was about 75 percent booze and tomatoes, and 10 percent drugs and other recreational treats. Tomatoes, for future reference, are women. Many years ago, I heard Clark Gable refer to the ladies as tomatoes in some movie and it stuck with me. Hank came home one year having heard the same phrase used in Reading, Pennsylvania, where he was playing in the minors. Pretty quickly the term spread throughout our friends and family.

After games and on free nights I could often be found at the local hot spot of whatever city we were in—with a drink in one hand and a tomato in the other. Over the years I was often asked how we knew where to go in each town. But the truth is, no one ever told us. It was as if the ballplayers who were there before us had left word on where to go. I still don't understand it—but some things you don't question, and this was one of them. I guess you could say it was one of the legends of the league. Of course, there were some legendary places, but none of them lasted forever. The locations would change, but the athletes and groupies would always find each other, no matter what state we were in.

Each town had its own distinct nightlife and groupies, and some towns were better than others. For example, Houston seemed to be a bad place for Tug and the tomatoes. For some reason, even though there were young women hanging out at our hotels in Houston hoping for a tryst, I never did well there. Now, I'm not trying to sound like Wilt Chamberlain, but I usually did all right in the tomato department. When it came to that type of produce, I was always able to pick one out of the bunch. Let's face it, the girls knew where we hung out and would go there looking for us. We were there for the offering, and they were too. Some of them would play slightly hard to get, while others would just walk right up and say, "How about you come back to my place?" To which I would generally reply, "Lead the way!"

I have no idea how it is today—though I doubt it is much different—but in the sixties and seventies none of the athletes or groupies thought too much about one-night stands. We were all young and invincible, and disease or pregnancy never even came up when we were doing the mating dance. "Sexual liberation" and "Free love" were the mottoes, and I never heard anyone complaining.

I always wondered what made us athletes so special to the tomatoes and why it was so easy to hook up. I suppose part of it is "celebrity by association." Or maybe it's because we were a sure thing. I never played on a team where less than half of the guys—married, engaged, or otherwise—weren't players when they were on the road. Nobody knew how to say no.

Each town was a new adventure and a new party scene. In Pittsburgh we would frequent a place called Market Square. It wasn't far from Three Rivers Stadium at, as Hall of Fame Mets broadcaster Bob Murphy used to say, "the confluence of the Ohio, Allegheny, and Monongahela rivers." There was a bunch of places around the square with four or five bars you could bounce around to and pick up a buzz and a tomato.

One night in Pittsburgh after I gave up a grand slam in *both* games of a doubleheader while pitching for the Mets—that was a mark in history I'd love to forget—I was just trying to get back to the hotel to hang my head and drown my sorrow. But we had an off day the next day, so I changed my mind and decided to go drinking. I got so smashed that I voluntarily walked into the police department and asked them to lock me up. The desk sergeant said he couldn't put me in jail because I hadn't done anything wrong. I told him that if they didn't lock me away I was going to go out and do something that would earn me a night in jail. I guess they knew I was serious, because they found a place to keep me for the night, though I don't believe it was a cell. I can't remember, because I woke up with the worst hangover of my life and two losses to my credit!

L.A. was a bitch of a town to go out partying in because it was spread out all over the place. One of the places we used to go to was Whisky a Go Go. It was famous from movies in the fifties and sixties, so we would always go there and were sure to have a hell of a good time. They had dancers wearing bikinis, and that was fertile ground for young ballplayers.

New York was also quite the place to be if you were a professional athlete looking for a night out on the town. I used to go out with Jets quarterback Joe Namath, ol' Broadway Joe himself, and his teammate Pete Lamans. We'd end up at Namath's bar/restaurant, Bachelors III, and women knew we would be there. We'd go to Mister Laffs, a bar owned by former Yankee Phil Linz—Phil was briefly a teammate of mine on the Mets in 1967—and known for its famous baseball and football player patrons, as well as Toots Shor's and lots of other swinging places. Every one of those hot spots was dark, noisy, and full of prospects.

I want to make it clear that this was a two-way game. Most of the women I met over the years had no interest in a relationship that lasted longer than that evening. Some of them were married, and none of them cared whether we were or not. There was no question that many of us were pigs. To complete the analogy, I guess these women were sows.

But the good times weren't just relegated to bars and hotel rooms. We were known for getting a buzz on even during games with the help of some pills and a shot of "Listerine." Back then it was different; you could get your treats from the trainers, and it wasn't like you had to sneak them. It was frighteningly easy. Amphetamines, red juice, and tranquilizers—they were all readily available. Red juice was a liquid amphetamine that you'd take by the capful from a Listerine bottle. We'd put trainer's tape all around the bottle, several layers, so we could put it in our kits and not have to worry about it shattering—at least, that is what the tape was supposed to do. You didn't want your uniform to get wired or waste any of the good stuff.

I was never on anything when I pitched for the Mets other than that one time that I took a tranquilizer before a game to calm my nerves and didn't make it out of the first inning. I'd say I pitched wired only 1 or 2 percent of the time I was with the Phillies—around half a dozen times over ten years. But some of the guys pitched better when they were wired. It seemed to make everything crisper and clearer. Of course, they had to know how to pitch straight before they could pitch wired. If you sucked sober, you sucked high.

Now, one great pitcher I played with could go out without being wired and be a pretty damn good pitcher. But when he did get wired you couldn't beat him, and if you did you were damn lucky. A couple of guys even tried to emulate him. We had a California kid, a left-hander, who everyone said was going to be the next big thing, and he believed it. He was tall and skinny, but dumb as dirt. He was one of those guys who read his press clippings and believed he was a star in the making. He threw a couple of good games, but never even approached a lofty status. He knew that some great pitchers took amphetamines, so he figured he needed to do the same. It just didn't work for him. The rule is that you have to know how to pitch before you can learn how to pitch wired, and he never learned.

After the Phillies won the 1980 World Series, I was invited to appear on the David Letterman show, which had just started airing after the *Tonight Show* on NBC. The Phillies drug scandal had just surfaced. Dave wanted to talk about drugs in baseball. I told him there was no way that I was going to discuss drugs in baseball on national TV. If he wanted me as a guest, we would talk baseball, not drugs. Dave's people agreed. Come showtime, from the moment I sat on the couch, Letterman was coming at me with all sorts of questions about drug users in the game, and whether I saw any of the players popping pills. I was so pissed that he brought the topic up. We had a deal. So I leaned into him and said, "You know, now that you mention it, I do remember some guy in the World Series."

Letterman came unglued. "You really saw him? What did the drug look like?" At this point Dave was on pins and needles.

I said, "It looked like a brown capsule."

Dave looked to the band to see if they knew what type of drug a brown capsule could be. Everyone looked puzzled. Dave pleaded, "Who is it?"

"George Brett." The house came down.

Dave said, "You actually saw him swallow it?"

"No, he didn't swallow it," I said. "It was a suppository. He had a hemorrhoid." They went to a commercial break and I walked off the set.

I wouldn't say everyone partied all the time, but we did have our good times on the road. When we were at home, most of us had to get home to our families. We played eighty-one games on the road and sometimes spent a couple of weeks on the road at a time. That's plenty of opportunities to drink, believe me.

But players understood you had to pace yourself to some degree. If you played every day, like Schmitty or Bowa, you had to pick your party spots. You couldn't play every day and party every night and have a fifteen- or seventeen-year career. As a reliever, I had a little more leeway. I could stay out partying all night and would need the red liquid to get ready for the game. Then, after the game, we would go back out. It was a cycle, and you had to keep the ball rolling, so you just kept on.

Players today get paid a lot more than we did, but I can't imagine they're having as much fun. The press is more adversarial now—the beat writers don't drink or hang out with the players today—they couldn't afford to! But nothing is swept under the rug anymore, either. And the groupies and the hangers-on want players for more than sex and celebrity—often they're in it for the money. The whole country has changed. Back in the sixties and seventies it was a different time, a great time to be a professional athlete, and I rode it for all I could.

CHAPTER 7

Meeting Betty

As a young, carefree adult in the sixties, I found it easy to forget or ignore the fact that the choices I made could have real and future consequences. As a young man playing ball I never thought too much about partying, drinking, and sleeping with different women. After all, I was having a good time, and wasn't that what really mattered? Over the course of my baseball career I lived in many cities and states and met many young, pretty women whom, after a few dates, I would leave behind for a new team and new town and, of course, new women.

Living this lifestyle of continuous booze, traveling, and women, I always understood that one of those dates or one-night stands could lead to fatherhood. This topic came up often amongst ballplayers, so I shouldn't have been shocked when the call came to me. The call was from the mother of a young girl I met while in Florida when I was almost twenty-two, and it was to tell me that I had gotten her daughter pregnant.

Back in June of 1966 I was doing a stint with the Jacksonville Suns rehabilitating my arm after my winter hitch with the Marine Corps. I wasn't surprised when I hurt it shortly after returning, feeling something pop while pitching to Tommy Harper of the Reds during a night game in May.

I was in my third year of pro ball, struggling to stay with the Mets. I probably should have taken everything more seriously, but that's a hard thing to do when you're a whiskey-drinking, testosterone-driven young athlete. While with the Suns I lived with some other ballplayers in an apartment complex across from Jacksonville University called University Apartments. University Apartments was known for its heavy population of female baseball groupies who were not shy about getting around. They knew where most of us lived and came there to see us. Hey, it was the sixties, baby, and that was just how it was—you never heard us complaining.

During the hot days of that Florida summer, my teammates and I could often be found playing football or spending time by the pool. When we weren't on the road or practicing, we liked to have a good time, which usually meant hanging out with tomatoes, other ballplayers, and throwing parties for our friends and new neighbors.

One day in particular, I was hanging out with some of my ballplayer friends, Tom Seaver—who had also done a stint in the marines—catcher Greg Goossen, and some others by the pool, when we noticed a group of young girls sunning themselves near our apartment. As I had done many times before, I saw some young ladies who sparked my interest.

Of course, we decided that we had to say hello, so we used a pickup tactic that is well known amongst most young men—toss the football around with your friends and see where it lands. There were five or six of them, so I don't know why Betty D'Agostino caught my eye, but she did. She was a cute girl in a tiny bikini, so I made sure my ball landed right near her, and was eager to introduce myself when she came over to return my football. Her petite frame and brown hair sparked my interest. Arrogantly, I figured she was there to catch my eye. A lot of the local girls from Jacksonville would come to this apartment building just to hook up with baseball players, so I had no reason to think that she was any different.

"What's your name?" she asked.

"Tug," I replied, thinking she had to have known who I was, or at least have known that I played baseball.

"Excuse me?" she said with a puzzled look on her face, as if she thought I was kidding.

"T-U-G, Tug," I answered. "That's my name."

Betty giggled and went back over to her friends. I would later learn that she was not all that impressed with my baseball stats, nor was she a groupie. In fact, she didn't care much about the game.

Later that afternoon, after my roommates and I had come back to our apartment and were getting ready for that night's game, I realized that we were out of bleach to clean our uniforms. Even though we were at the highest minor-league level before reaching the majors, we still had to wash our own uniforms. I remembered seeing Betty going into the apartment right above ours. So, being the direct young man that I was, I decided to take the handle of a broom and bang it on the ceiling to get her attention. After all, I couldn't go to my game with a dirty uniform. Betty heard my banging, and we shouted back and forth to each other from the balcony. She agreed to share her bleach with me, even though I really did not give her a chance to say no. By the time she came back onto the balcony to tell me to come up, I was standing at her front door with my empty bleach cup.

"I've got to wash my baseball uniform," I explained.

"Aren't you a little big to be playing baseball?" she asked.

"I play *professional* baseball," I boastfully replied. We

talked for a few more minutes, and after she turned down my invitation to do laundry with me, I left.

It was a couple of days before I would see Betty again. She was doing her wash in the Laundromat when I came in one afternoon. We spent most of the afternoon talking about our lives and families. Betty told me that she was eighteen, worked at a radio station in town, and had just broken up with her boyfriend. I learned early on that age and availability were two important questions to ask. This helped me keep from getting beaten up or thrown in jail.

That night my roommates and I were having a party, so I told Betty to invite some of her friends and come by. She accepted my invitation and came by with a friend—of course, I reminded her to make sure that her friend was eighteen. That night Betty and I talked for a while, looked at my baseball trophies and photos, walked out by the pool, and drank beer. We made out a little, and I guess that was considered our first date.

A couple of days later I invited her and some friends to one of my games there in Jacksonville. She said she would come, even though she really wasn't into sports. I left tickets for her and three friends at the gate and made sure she would be seated right above the dugout. During the game I noticed Betty and even gave her a wave, but I was really more focused on trying to look cool out there on the mound. Forget about the baseball career—let's look good for the chicks!

The next day the Suns headed on the road for a few days, but when we returned I began seeing Betty again. One night, while I was sitting outside by the pool with some friends, Betty came out and I could tell she had been crying. She told me that her father had shown up at their apartment and that her mother had left for a while with her boyfriend. She didn't get along with her father very well and had gotten into an argument with him that night. Betty's parents were headed for divorce, and being from a divorced family myself, I could relate. We spent most of that night outside talking about family and friends and swapping stories about our lives.

That would be the beginning of the evening that would change both our lives forever.

After a few hours, Betty asked if she could use my apartment telephone to call a friend for a ride. We were sitting on the couch talking and drinking a soda when one thing led to another and we began engaging in the national pastime—and I don't mean baseball. Afterward Betty seemed embarrassed and quickly said good-bye. I did not know it at the time, but I was Betty's first. I tried to talk to her later that night, but she never answered her apartment door. The next day I tried to contact her again, but she never responded. After a few days of yelling to her from my balcony or leaving messages at her mom's house, I decided to just give up. I assumed she didn't like me or had just moved on. After all, I had only known her for a little while and really hadn't become emotionally attached. To be honest, I am not sure if I could've become emotionally attached back then. It just wasn't me.

Betty moved out of the apartment complex about a month later, and I was called back up to the majors to play for the Mets. I had pitched several great complete games in a row for the Suns, and the big guys in New York wanted to see what I had. I never heard from Betty again until the day her mother, Annie, called the Mets front office a few months later and left a message for me to call her. Betty was now living in Louisiana with her parents.

"Tug, I guess you know why I am calling," Annie said in a very stern tone.

"I have no idea," I told her.

"Betty's pregnant and you are the only one she has been with," she said.

"I do not mean any disrespect, but how do you know that it's mine? There were a lot of ballplayers staying in that apartment complex," I exclaimed. Her mom told me that Betty had been a virgin and reiterated that I was the only one she had been with.

"So what do you want me to do?" I asked.

Annie told me that she wanted Betty and me to get married, for the baby's sake. In 1966 a child born out of wedlock would be deemed illegitimate on the birth certificate, and she did not want that to happen to her first grandchild. I told her that I needed to talk to my father, my brother, and my manager and would call her back. I always outsourced or subcontracted all my problems. This time was no different.

At this point I would like to be able to say that I had no experience dealing with these types of things, but this was not the first such call that I received. Back in college, I met another young tomato who later called to tell me she was pregnant and that the baby was mine. I knew for a fact that she had been with quite a few of my friends and fellow ballplayers, but I still gave in when she called and ask for money for an abortion—which was then illegal. I sent her the $250 she asked for and prayed that nothing went wrong.

I have since realized that Betty was different and was never in this for herself, only her son. But I barely knew her, and how did I know that I was really the only person she had been with? That apartment complex was full of baseball players and I just assumed that if she slept with me then she must have slept with one of the other guys. I didn't know this girl enough to trust her version of the story. By this time I was back in the majors. For all I knew she could have been calling me for money, too.

In the big leagues, I heard countless stories of players getting women pregnant, but no one ever seemed to panic. I knew I could call on the Mets for help, and that was what I did.

I called Johnny Murphy, who was the team's farm director at the time. He had been a terrific relief pitcher for the Yankees in the 1930s and 1940s, and was part of the old Yankee trio of Casey, George Weiss, and himself that took the Mets from losers to champions in seven years. Johnny was my guy, and I knew that he could help me. Over the years he had constantly reminded me to call him when—never if—I got in trouble. Now was that time. Either he had a sixth sense about me, or he said that to all the young players with the team.

Johnny told me to just keep pitching and he would take care of everything else. I never asked what that meant, but I was led to believe that the Mets had a law firm to take care of this sort of thing. A few years ago I did try to find out what the Mets had done, and found no records for me or Betty. According to Betty, neither she nor her mother was ever contacted by the team. Johnny Murphy has since passed, so I may never know what "just keep pitching and we'll take care of everything" meant.

After a few days of talking with my father and Johnny, it was decided that I would deny that Betty's pregnancy was my responsibility. I didn't actually believe that I was the father of her child, and I did not want to be trapped into something like this when my ball career was just starting to go places. I called Betty's house in Louisiana and told her mom that the baby was not my responsibility and that this sort of thing would be bad for my career. I tried to explain to her mom that the timing was simply not good for me and that the world of baseball really wouldn't understand this sort of "situation." I told her that I wanted nothing to do with the baby or Betty and never to contact me again. It sounds pretty harsh, reading these words today. Betty's mom obviously thought so too, because before she hung up she told me that she would see me in court and that I would regret my decision to deny her grandchild.

Almost one year after I met that young, petite brunette in Jacksonville, Florida, I received a call that Betty had given birth to a son on May 1, 1967, after a long and at times grueling delivery. She named him Samuel Timothy McGraw.

CHAPTER 8

The Team at Home

Just as chance meetings and wild evenings had changed my life so many times before, a night in December of 1967 at a New York bar set the stage for another chapter. The story of meeting my first wife, Phyllis, entails two stewardesses, a dog, an alleged kidnapping, and a lot of beer. That sounds like the makings of a great story or joke, but in fact it is just another part of the life of Tug McGraw. Crazy and unbelievable at times—but true.

It was shaping up to be a great night at Mister Laffs. I was doing what I did best—after pitching, that is—drinking and talking with tomatoes, when a young stewardess introduced me to her friend who flew with TWA and was from California. She was a very pretty brunette named Phyllis Kline, and right away I liked her. She looked like Katharine Ross from *The Graduate*. We spent most of the night drinking and talking about California and what it was like back home. She was from Santa Monica and had been going with a guy there. They had just split up, and I acted sorry for her. Inside I was loving it. She was working in New York while waiting for a transfer back to California. She was homesick and wanted to move west as soon as possible, and was expecting word of her transfer in the next twenty-four hours—she was third on the list.

By the time the bar was closing, Phyllis couldn't find her roommate and had no way to get home. Her roommate, also a stewardess with TWA, was quite the partier, more than Phyllis, and we weren't sure if she had gone home with somebody or had taken someone back to her place. So I offered to drive Phyllis home to the apartment in Manhattan where she was staying with three other girls—one from England, one from Greece, and one from Florida—even though it was out of my way. Once I got Phyllis in the car, a marine-green Pontiac, I told her she had to come to my apartment in Queens and meet my dog, Poochie, who at the time was a puppy. Phyllis wasn't too hot on the idea of my taking her to my house; after all, she had just met me, and I'd had a lot to drink. As a young guy I could drink a lot, but it would hit me like a ton of bricks all at once. And I did hit a chain-link fence with the car that night—no one got hurt, though. When she told me that she didn't want to go to Queens, I sped up. Phyllis later told me that she so was terrified she even thought about how she could get out of the car. She told me that as we pulled into the underground parking garage of my building in Lefrak City—right off the Long Island Expressway—she was certain that she had gotten herself into a bad situation. She later joked that I practically kidnapped her, since I wouldn't take no for an answer on her meeting my puppy. But once we got to my place she met the dog, who started scratching Phyllis on her thigh-high boots after I'd drunkenly tossed her on the sofa. After all this craziness, I drove her back to her place.

By now I was getting really tired, and my night of partying was beginning to catch up with me. The apartment in Manhattan Phyllis was staying at was miles from my apartment—Lefrak City wasn't too far from Shea. All I wanted to do was get there and crash. By three a.m., the alcohol had completely kicked in. I never minded sleeping on people's floors, and in fact had done it quite a few times in the past. When we got to Phyllis's place, one of her roommates let us in and let me pass out on a studio couch. The next morning I wasn't sure who I had been with—Phyllis or her friend. In fact, I had no memory that I'd taken Phyllis at my apartment. I guess I'd had so much to drink that I'd blacked out.

At eight o'clock that morning, Phyllis got the call she had been waiting for. Her transfer back to California came through, and she had ten days and two flights before she left. I really liked her and felt a connection to her, maybe because she was from California like me, so I asked her if I could spend some time with her before she left. Somehow that first night didn't faze her, and I took her to the airport and picked her up from her flights that week and even asked her to go to a Mets team banquet with me. Phyllis loves to tell the story of my asking her to the banquet and her being worried about what she should wear. She was classy and never wanted to show up somewhere inappropriately dressed, so she made me take her to Macy's to buy a black dress that came down to her knees. When we got there, all of the other players' wives, Nancy Seaver, Ruth Ryan, and some others, were all dressed in miniskirts—the same clothes Phyllis had in her closet. So she felt a little dowdy and silly, since she went out and bought new clothes when what she had would have worked better.

After Phyllis left for California, I began writing her long letters—ten pages on legal-size paper, sometimes three letters in one day!—telling her how much I missed her and how much I had enjoyed our time together. And I hate writing letters. Yet for her I was pouring my heart out. I called her a few times and found out that she had a friend she was going to be visiting in St. Petersburg, Florida, in March. I told her I was going to be down there for spring training and would pick her up from the airport, since she was coming in on the red-eye. Evidently Phyllis wasn't too sure about me at that point, and even asked her friend to pick her up at the airport so that I wouldn't, but her friend told her to ask me, since her plane was landing so early in the morning.

Phyllis was down in St. Pete for a little over a week on that trip, and we spent some great times together at the beach and at her friend's house. She even got to meet Hank when he and I came to a party they were hosting. That night was Phyllis's first taste of what I was like when I *really* drank too much.

I was on muscle relaxers that night because of recurring pain in my shoulder, and the combination of pills and beer turned bad. Phyllis had to drive me home, and she even had to have Yogi Berra help her get me out of the car and into my room. Amazingly, I woke up in the morning and found that she hadn't abandoned me.

The next day she brought my car to the ball field and had been sitting in the stands watching Duffy Dyer—thinking he was me—for almost an hour when I walked up to say hi. She jokes that that was her first lesson in baseball: Learn the numbers so you can know who you're watching. She wasn't much of a sports fan. She had a lot to learn about the life of a ballplayer—but I didn't care. All of my buddies were either married or getting married, and I really liked Phyllis, so I figured—Why not? After all, I was twenty-three now. So after four dates and two drunken stupors, I asked her that week to marry me.

She didn't answer me right away, so I told her the question was still there and to just let me know when she had an answer. A few days later, while we were at Ted's Hideaway in St. Pete with Ron Swoboda and his wife, Cecilia, she told me yes. We were engaged on our fifth or sixth date. I wanted to get married right away, by the end of the season in October, but Phyllis thought she needed more time. I got worried, figuring that the better she knew me and my crazy family, the less likely she'd be to stick around. I pressed her to make sure she didn't back out, and we got married in Jacksonville, Florida, a few months later.

I had been sent back down to the minors in Jacksonville after a spring training incident with Pucci—Phyllis respelled the dog's name after the fashion designer—and Joe Pignatano, the Mets' bullpen coach. Pucci had already gotten me into trouble when she dug up the flower bed outside of Johnny Murphy's door at the executive cottage at Huggins-Stengel Field. When Pucci got out of my room and ended up taking a dump in front of Pignatano's door, my number was up. Pignatano—an old Dodger catcher and a member of the '62 Mets who ended his career as a player by grounding into a triple play—walked out of the room barefoot and stepped on Pucci's log. Those two events, combined with my bad spring because I was banned from throwing screwballs, meant that Pucci and I were headed to Jacksonville.

My wedding to Phyllis wasn't exactly a spectacular event. She took a one-year leave of absence from her job with TWA and flew to Jacksonville to get married and live with me there. She took only a one-year leave because she expected that I'd be back with the Mets soon and she'd still be able to fly for TWA based out of New York. We decided to get married at a church down the street from our apartment complex, which, ironically, was just a couple of blocks away from the complex I had lived in a year earlier where I met Betty. Just before we had hooked up, Phyllis had broken off her three-year relationship with a jet-setter in L.A. My $13,000-a-year salary was a big comedown for her.

We decided to get married on a day that I was pitching in one-half of a doubleheader. Kevin and Linda Collins were supposed to stand up for Phyllis and me, but he had been called up to the majors and couldn't be there. Phyllis asked Lynn McAndrew (the wife of Jim McAndrew, a pitcher on the Suns) to be her maid of honor, and I asked Larry Bearnarth (now the Suns pitching coach) to be my best man. Yes, the same Larry Bearnarth who pulled that gag about needing a ticket for the batting cage my rookie year. The ceremony was quick, Catholic—even though Phyllis wasn't—and simple. No guests, no family—a strange ceremonial beginning for two people who barely knew each other and weren't even sure if they actually loved each other. Phyllis had taken care of all the wedding details with Lynn. I knew I really liked Phyllis, and she seemed to like me, what she knew of me anyway, but we really didn't know each other or our families and had no idea whether this marriage was going to last.

After coffee and doughnuts with the few folks there, Phyllis got another taste of the type of chaos that Tug McGraw was going to bring to her life. As we were leaving the church I got pulled aside by a reporter asking me about an accident that our second baseman, Jack Tracy, had gotten into the night before. Jack was driving Kevin Collins's car—a new Camaro that Kevin had asked me to take care of after Kevin had been called up to the bigs. I had loaned it out to Jack the night before, even though Phyllis had warned against it. Jack had a bad game that night and took off across the Jacksonville Bridge in Kevin's car and slammed into a stalled car, nearly killing himself and totaling Kevin's car. After that, Kevin and I weren't too close anymore, and only minutes after we were married Phyllis was looking at me like, "What were you thinking?" Like I said—I bring chaos to people's lives.

Between games we went over to the big white tent, set up for the buffet dinners before and during the games, for what would serve as our reception. We did the handshake thing and everyone congratulated us on our marriage. As we were leaving, Clyde McCullough, the general manager of the Suns, gave Phyllis the thumbs-down sign—asking her to go easy on me, since I had to pitch that day. She was just learning the ropes of this baseball thing and took everything very literally.

It quickly became a family joke that something would always get in the way when we tried to have some kind of a honeymoon. The next day the club left on a road trip, so Phyllis began married life as a baseball widow.

Phyllis and I never did take that honeymoon. Considering the fact that she had been a stewardess it must seem odd that we were never able to travel somewhere together—just the two of us. But baseball or family obligations always cut that off. We had planned to take some time alone during our drive home to the West Coast after the season. First we planned to stop in Reading, Pennsylvania, to visit Hank— the two of them hadn't really had a chance to get to know each other. We found out that Hank had burst a blood vessel in a freak baserunning accident—he actually came close to dying from internal bleeding. We drove up to Pennsylvania and picked him up at the hospital, and, since he was freaked out by all of this and not yet ready to fly, we decided to take him home to California. Our romantic trip across country turned into Phyllis in the backseat of my new Grand Prix with Pucci and me up front with Hank.

When we got to California, Phyllis was anxious to finally meet my family; she really wanted to get to know Mabel. Phyllis felt bad that my mom was all alone without her three boys and that she had just lost her second husband to a heart attack not long after they married. But she got to meet only my dad and Dennis. She didn't think much of them. She saw Dad as a man's man—he lived in a man's world and was the type who would pat a waitress on the butt. And she could tell Dennis was taking LSD. She didn't think he was playing with a full deck.

That fall we bought a truck with a camper attachment to drive back to Florida for spring training in 1969. It was attempt number two at a honeymoon. This time Phyllis wanted to invite my mom, whom she hadn't met. She didn't want Mabel to be lonely and sad, so there we were once again, on a trip that was supposed to be a romantic twosome, with another McGraw along for the ride.

When we finally got down to St. Pete that spring, things started falling into place and life seemed to be going well. I had a new wife, a new shot at the majors, a new pitch—my screwball, which manager Gil Hodges and his coaching staff gave me the green light to throw—and a new job on the field. In order to make the big club, my days as a starter were over. The bullpen behind the right-field fence in Shea Stadium would be my new baseball home.

Phyllis and I even worked out a system so that I could acknowledge that I'd seen her in the stands without management thinking I didn't have my head in the game. She told me that I had tipped my hat to too many other girls and she wanted a special signal just for her. Even though she now knew my uniform number—45—she said that in our uniforms we all looked so alike and that she still had trouble spotting me. That's why I would slap my right leg with my glove as I was running out. She never mistook me for Duffy Dyer again!

An event in 1970 really made me think about my family, and whether I wanted to start a new one with Phyllis. While we were in San Francisco to play the Giants, I had arranged for a party in my hotel room for my father and relatives on his side of the family, as well as a bunch of old high school buddies. It was after a Saturday game and my plan was to get together with my mom on that Sunday, since my parents just didn't mix well. I even had to make sure that they didn't sit near each other during the games. So that night we were all partying up in the hotel suite that my new roomie, Ed Kranepool, and I had upgraded to. Krane was the only Met left who had played in the 1962 season—he grew up in the Bronx and had signed with them right out of high school. He was having a rough season and would end up getting sent down to the minors. Although he never lived up to the expectations—few do—he'd developed into a solid first baseman, and after his stint in the minors he rebounded at the plate in '71. Krane would become one of the top pinch-hitters in the game toward the end of his career.

My mom was having a drink by herself in the hotel lounge, near some of the Mets coaches. One of them called up to the room to tell me that she was getting drunk and was becoming belligerent, so I invited her up to the party. I didn't feel like I had a choice, really. She knew we were all up there having a good time, and I didn't want her sitting downstairs by herself.

My dad had his girlfriend and her mother up at the party, and at first they both played it cool. When my father's girlfriend and her mother left the room, my mom went over to sit down next to my dad. I knew the sparks were going to fly if this wasn't broken up soon, so I started going around telling people the party was over; we had a team curfew and had to play the next day. When I got to my mom she got it in her head that I was only telling her the party was breaking up so that she'd leave. I tried to explain to her that everybody was leaving, not just her, and that the party was not going to continue after she left. She wouldn't hear of it.

The next thing I knew, my dad's girlfriend walked in

from the next room, saw me trying to reason with my mother, and tried to help. "Now, Mabel," she said. "Tug's got a game tomorrow, and he is trying to get us to go home. If you really love your son and want him to pitch well tomorrow, you'll leave too." Well, that wasn't such a good idea, especially the condescending part about looking out for my well-being.

Mom became furious and popped my dad's girlfriend right in the mouth! The girlfriend's mother jumped in and it was a donnybrook. Krane, at six-foot-three and 205 pounds, managed to keep my dad from getting involved, but those three ladies really threw down. I hustled my mom out of the hotel and into a cab, and went back upstairs to finish off a bottle of booze.

The whole scene made me so depressed and upset that I told Phyllis I didn't think we should have children in case the crazy gene ran in the family. I didn't want crazy kids. The next day I felt horrible. I was hungover and just wanted to be left alone. I was both laughing and crying in the clubhouse. The Mets thought I was having a nervous breakdown after the incident. Someone in the front office contacted Phyllis to tell her to fly out. But Gil called on me in the clutch and I somehow saved the game, striking out Bobby Bonds with the bases loaded in the bottom of the eighth. Even though I pulled myself together, the night of the hotel room brawl affected me personally and professionally and would stay with me forever. Every time I got depressed or bothered, I found myself having visions of that scene and wondering what kind of family I had come from—and, after Mark and Cari were born, what kind of family I was creating.

The traveling circus of my life that I thought would settle down after marrying Phyllis only got crazier. Our marriage seemed to have ten seconds of normality and twenty years of insanity. My cheating began practically right after I got married—that winter at the LaCosta Spa in San Diego. I'm not sure that getting married, for either of us, was anything more than two people doing what everyone else around us seemed to be doing at the time. My drinking got worse and my flightiness never calmed. It seemed that Phyllis and I never really talked, and she took on the role of baseball widow, housewife, and de facto single parent. As bad as it was, it took years for us to split up. Phyllis was insecure and did not have a support system in place that would allow her to leave. Her family was three thousand miles away. And something always came up—never giving us time to think about going our separate ways. Talk about chaos—we lived in three states a year the first nine years.

Phyllis had a miscarriage in 1971 and was going to fertility clinics in San Diego and Los Angeles the first few years we were married. She didn't know she was pregnant when we almost split up in 1972. I had stretches where I wouldn't come home and Phyllis wouldn't know where I was. She begged me to talk about it with her, but that just wasn't me. I didn't talk about it with anyone. I would make up lies—my car broke down, or I had drunk too much and had to pull over on the side of the road, et cetera. Many times she had to call my teammates to find out where I was. One day in 1972 she came to me with the evidence that I'd had another woman in the apartment—a pair of dirty underwear. When she confronted me, I fell asleep. I soon woke up to a flurry of uppercuts. Phyllis said she couldn't live like this and that I was either here with her or gone. I didn't know what to say. I wanted to assure her that things would get better, but I also had concerns about my own sanity.

With that said, she disappeared, although I later found out she went to St. Louis with Art Shamsky's wife. Art is from St. Louis, and the Shamskys had an apartment there in the off-season. But until I found out, I went crazy not knowing. I even tried to get Art drunk to get him to tell me where Phyllis was. When we finally spoke I asked her to come back home. She told me that she didn't want to be with a yo-yo. It was then that I found out she was pregnant. For all this weirdness, we decided to try to make our marriage—and now our family—work.

I really wanted to be there when Mark was born, on May 12, 1972, but in true McGraw fashion, even that got screwed up. Phyllis was at North Shore Hospital on Long Island and I was at our house in nearby Manhasset. She called and told me when to be there, but it turned out the clocks in the hospital were wrong due to construction. I had gone out to walk the dog, and when I came back to the house I fell asleep. Obviously I arrived at the hospital late. I walked in, ready to go through the delivery with her, but she already had our boy in her arms. She was disappointed, but she knew that I had been trying to do the right thing. She also knew that being anywhere on time was always an issue for me. I was so bad with time that I had long ago given up wearing a watch, since it did me no good.

When I was with the Phillies, I once ran into my teammate Larry Bowa in the lobby of the hotel where we stayed in Chicago, before there were lights in Wrigley Field. I was just stumbling back in after an all-nighter on Rush Street, when I tried to request an eight a.m. wake-up call. The desk clerk pointed out it was already eight-fifteen.

Whoever said having a child changes you was right. Mark represented a new stage in our lives and in our marriage. But, as in most things concerning my personal life, I probably handled this life change badly. Instead of turning inward, I started worrying about setting us up financially. I had a bad habit of buying things before the paychecks arrived. And I guess seeing how my dad had worked like a dog to make ends meet when I was a kid really preyed on my mind. In addition to my "day job" as a major-league baseball player, I did appearances, speeches, wrote an autobiography entitled *Screwball* with Joe Durso of the *New York Times* after the '73 season, and after I was traded to the Phillies I created and was a contributor to a syndicated cartoon strip—"Scroogie." All these outside challenges limited my family time, putting more pressure on Phyllis.

I loved playing with Mark, doing everything a father should with a young son. There's something special about being an athlete and having a son. Immediately you start planning for him to be the next great version of whatever you are. Mark had gloves, hats, and balls from the moment he was born. When he got a bit older, after I'd been traded to the Phillies, we loved going to the ballpark together. It was great getting to watch him pal around with sons of teammates like Ryan Luzinski, Brett and Aaron Boone, Pete Rose, Jr., and Garry Maddox. But Phyllis used to get pissed off when I handed off the kids to the Phillies' hot-pants girls.

About a year and a half after Mark was born, Phyllis and I went to Las Vegas with some friends and, as happens so often in Vegas, we conceived our second child. We weren't really planning on another child at the time but also didn't really think too much about birth control, since it had taken two years of fertility treatments for us to get pregnant with Mark. I guess the odds had swung back in our favor in Vegas! The result was a beautiful daughter, Cari Lynn, born on September 1, 1973, in the heat of that crazy pennant race.

Cari was a real rascal from the very beginning. I used to call her "Opposita," which I pretended was the Spanish word for opposite, because she did exactly the opposite of whatever we told her to do. She was a little doll. I worried that she'd end up running into guys like me when she got older—every father's worst nightmare!

Both kids were born while I was playing for the Mets and

every game was an adventure. The season after Cari was born I'd started experiencing shoulder trouble, and I wasn't sure that I still had a future in the game. I remember in the months after each was born that I'd go out to pitch with a new sense of urgency. Even though there weren't money problems yet, on the way to the mound, I'd tell myself, "You'd better get this right tonight. There are new mouths to feed."

Unfortunately, my close connection to the kids didn't last much past the diaper stage. The distance between Phyllis and I was growing, and it left me less and less interested in being at home. My career had gotten exciting, and I was more interested in being center stage at the ballpark, without any issues to worry about. At home there were obligations. One manifestation of this was that I had a lot of one-night stands. At the time Phyllis never worried about my developing a serious relationship with another woman. As a result, I was out of the house most of the time Mark and Cari were growing up. Phyllis was not a party girl, and she basically raised them by herself.

I guess like a lot of celebrity families we put on a show in public that left the world thinking we were living the dream. When I was with the Phillies, Phyllis, the kids, and I did commercials together, always smiling and slugging 7UP. Phillies fans loved it when I blew kisses to the kids. Phyllis warned me about selling ourselves as that family next door, albeit one with a World Series trophy on the mantel. I wish all that happiness had been more real than show.

When I actually started getting paid big money—well, for those days, anyway—for my work on the field, my fears grew that I could get cut and lose it all. I became a workaholic. In the off-season I would always do paid appearances and work other jobs—afraid that if I didn't we would end up broke. Looking back on it, I probably could've and should've just stayed home during the off-season, but Phyllis and my manager would tell me to stop spending. I was a chronic overspender on the road—$200 to $300 bottles of wine and dinners at Morton's Steakhouse add up very quickly, along with the $600 phone bills. Could've, should've.

My busy life did come at a price to my family. When we lived in Philadelphia we had a seven-bedroom house on a big estate with a pool and a massive twenty-two-foot barbecue pit that Phyllis helped build. Big Mac, Hank, Phyllis's mom, and her niece all lived in the house with me, Phyllis, and the kids. I was supporting all of them. While you would think that Phyllis would have plenty of help with all of those roommates, it was completely the opposite. Phyllis's mom helped her with the kids, but my dad and Hank probably added to her work. She was always on the go, taking care of everyone, and I was rarely there to help. And when I was there I was either working, on the phone, or heading out the door. It wasn't the formula anyone would pick for a successful marriage.

My schedule was so busy that Phyllis would have to tell my secretary what days to mark off on my calendar for the kids' birthdays and other events so that I wouldn't schedule anything on those days—though I still would. One time I had to rent a helicopter so I could make it to a school party for Mark and a commercial appearance in northeast Philly on the same day. Other times I would be late or miss the entire event, which would really steam Phyllis and disappoint the kids. I kept telling myself I was doing it all for them and that they needed to be more understanding. In reality, I did not like the responsibilities at home. I didn't get to be the hero there. I wasn't the clubhouse clown—I was grumpy, and not very fun to be around.

I know Mark and Cari knew that I loved them, but I don't

think they ever really understood why I was always so busy. I know it was particularly hard on Mark to be Tug McGraw's son while living in Philadelphia. He told me one day that he didn't want to play Little League baseball because there was too much pressure on him to be like me. He may have been right, but deep down inside it bothered me that he didn't have the passion for baseball that I did. Mark changed to swimming and soccer and never really played baseball. Mark also had attention deficit disorder, and that made school difficult. He dropped out of public high school and enrolled in a private school for kids with learning disabilities. Once he got into private school, he did better and started to find himself.

Mark was always pushing the envelope. When he was six he nearly burned our garage down while he was playing with matches in the attic. The landscapers had left the matches and Mark was lighting them and flipping them. Fortunately, my mother-in-law saw him running to the attic with a Tupperware cup of water and asked him what he was doing. She followed him and saw smoke billowing out of the room. That house had been built in the 1800s—if the fire wasn't put out quickly it would have gone up in flames. She called the fire department. Maybe that's why he works with the fire department in Eugene, Oregon, now!

Cari pushed the envelope even farther. She was a real cutie, but, as I feared, she started hanging out with the wrong crowd in junior high school. She started screwing around with drugs—pot, acid—when she was thirteen, around the time I left Phyllis. Cari later said there was nothing she wouldn't put in her mouth. She ran away from home, and called the ballpark to tell me so. Phyllis told me there were a few places she could be. We had to go in and physically pull her out of the basement of a house. I took her home and whipped the hell out of her, and she fought back hard. Phyllis intervened, telling me that she thought we had made our point. Then I had to leave to go to an appearance that night. Again Phyllis was left with Cari by herself. Phyllis stayed up the rest of the night with her, and the next day we took her to a counselor. Cari spent eight weeks in rehab and I did not go to her meetings.

To her credit, Cari's stint in rehab, at the age of thirteen, fixed her early, and she has never relapsed. Back then it was thought that if you did drugs you had a self-esteem problem. So we enrolled her in private school with Mark. She did well in private school and ended up graduating and blossoming into a great young woman.

At one point Phyllis forced us to go to a family therapist, who told me that my kids acted out to get my attention, to try to find a way onto my radar screen. I had missed that one completely. I was so absorbed in being liked by fans that I missed giving love to my own children. In one of the great truisms of my life, I focused too much attention on those who barely knew me and screwed up the relationships with those who needed to know me. It was a lesson I learned far too late.

Mark never really benefited from being my son; in fact it probably hurt him more than it helped. When he was in college he was accused of a crime—for which he was later acquitted—that drew a lot of media attention in Philadelphia because he was my son. Any other young guy wouldn't have ended up in the news. That was a downside of having the last name McGraw.

Mark once told me that it was obvious I had a hard time leaving Tug McGraw the baseball player on the field to be Tug McGraw the dad at home. He said he and Cari thought the family lifestyle was just too boring for me, and I must admit that he was probably right. While I loved my kids very much, all I really knew how to do was play ball and work and party. Our very complicated home life wasn't always enjoyable.

Not long after her stint in rehab, Cari even wrote me a poem, cutting me wide open with this one. . . .

"My Feelings"

I feel like shit,
I just want to quit,
Everything!
I want to get high,
So high I can float in the sky.
I need love.
Love from above.
I'm scared of people.
People who care & feel,
For me.
Me Cari McGraw!
Not Tug McGraw's daughter,
But Cari McGraw.
I care about people I don't need.
My drug dealers
Who give me speed.
Why, why, do I have this wall.
It won't let me bawl!
I want to cry!
But I have no feelings,
And not one teardrop from my
Eye.
How can I open up.
Break my wall.
Or just jump.
Jump over the wall!
Help me, help me

Break it and bawl!
As I said before,
Me Cari McGraw
But how can they
Who is she?
Is she a whore?
What should they like her for?
Is she a spoiled bitch?
Only to talk to and then get ditched?
Who am I?
Someone tell me.

Cari has always loved writing poems, even though they were sometimes dark. She writes a lot of her poems from her inner pain. Unfortunately I have been the source of some of her best work.

Now that they're grown and gone, I know I should have been more of a father. I gave them what I knew—remember that my father worked multiple jobs to keep food on the table for me and my two brothers. I just wish I had done more.

CHAPTER 9

Those Amazing Mets

In July of 1969 the biggest story in the country, or maybe the world for that matter, was the moon landing. President Kennedy had challenged America to put a man on the moon and safely return him to earth by the end of the 1960s, and so here we were, going for it. Everyone was riveted to the developments. It seemed practically impossible then; no one was certain it could even be done. And as we all know from the more recent disasters with the space shuttle, spaceflight is still incredibly dangerous.

In late July the rocket holding Neil Armstrong, Buzz Aldrin, and Michael Collins took off. The Mets were in Montreal for a four-game series with the Expos. We were "only" eleven games out of first place at the time, and while we were having a tremendous season by previous Mets standards, we still weren't expected to do much, just like every Mets team since we entered the National League in 1962. But with the addition of Montreal and San Diego, and the splitting of the National League into two divisions, we had only five division rivals to beat out, not nine other teams, as before. The Mets had a ton of good young pitchers, and the reality was that during two series with the first-place Cubs, we won four of six. In late May and early June we had strung together an eleven-game winning streak. We had a little confidence. We knew we were pretty good, but most of us didn't think we were good enough to really threaten for a pennant or anything. I guess you could say we didn't believe. Yet.

On the last day of the Montreal series, July 20, we split a doubleheader to move to 53-39. This was the latest any Mets team had even reached the .500 mark, and here we were, fourteen games over! After the game we were at the Montreal airport waiting to fly home, and everyone was watching the lunar landing on some of the TVs in the terminal. It was amazing, just awe-inspiring stuff. Who wasn't glued to the footage? Especially when Armstrong got out and declared he was taking "one small step for man, one giant leap for mankind." Well, as we were watching the news footage, someone—I think it was a sportswriter who was with us— said, "You know, if they can put a man on the moon, the Mets ought to be able to win the pennant."

It sort of caught us dead in our tracks. All of a sudden the boys were looking around and saying, "You know, maybe we could." And then, "Why not?" And then, "Let's do it!" It was true: We had been looking at an eleven-game hole and a late-July calendar and saying it was impossible. Well, for thousands of years they thought it was impossible to put a man on the moon, and yet it was happening. And this was just baseball! Whether we were inspired by the moon landing or not, all of a sudden we caught fire. Our bats got hot. Our pitching got even better. We started making all the little plays, doing all the late-inning things that separate winners from losers. Basically, we believed. We overcame that eleven-game deficit in August. By the second week in September, we were in first place.

It was incredible. All of a sudden we went from being the amazing Mets, lovable losers, to the amazing Mets for real—the Miracle Mets. We ended up winning one hundred ball games that season. Then the next thing you know, boom, boom, boom, we swept the Braves in the first-ever National League Championship Series, and then—world champions. We took off like a rocket ship!

To fully appreciate how unlikely this was you have to realize what the Mets represented in the spring of 1969. About to start their seventh season, the Mets remained the laughing-stock of the league, more comic relief than pennant con-tender. It had been that way since 1962, when the team came into existence to give New York a National League presence after both the Brooklyn Dodgers and New York Giants headed off to the greener pastures of Los Angeles and San Francisco.

For the job of building those first years, the Mets hired Casey Stengel, a former star player with the Dodgers and Giants in the 1910s and 1920s, who became a great manager with the Yankees from 1949 to 1960. Poor ol' Casey couldn't believe what he had gotten himself into. That first spring training—playing on a field named after Stengel and Miller Huggins, two of the greatest managers in Yankees history— was something out of a situation comedy. The Mets were ter-rible, stuck picking up whatever castoffs, has-beens, and never-would-bes they could find from other teams.

It wasn't a surprise when the Mets lost their home opener that year 4-3 to the Pittsburgh Pirates, followed by the next eight games straight. Nor was it a surprise how they did it, thanks to a dropped lazy fly ball that resulted in a run-scoring triple and three wild pitches that caused two more runs. Stengel figured he had seen it all, but he hadn't. The

Mets would go on to lose 120 games that year, a major-league record that stands to this day—although the 2003 Detroit Tigers gave it a run, losing 119 games. Roger Craig was the ace of the pitching staff. He lost twenty-four games that season and twenty-two games—including eighteen in a row—in 1963.

Needless to say I didn't have any delusions of grandeur when the Mets invited me to training camp in 1965. I pretty much knew about the circus I was joining. Stengel was still the manager, and while New York had improved, it wasn't by much. In 1963 the Mets improved and lost only 111 games, and in 1964, playing in their new home next door to the World's Fair, they got even better and lost a mere 109! But I just wanted to be a big leaguer, so who cared? The worst franchise in the majors was fine with me, because at that point I still wasn't convinced I was good enough to get big-league hitters out. When I was invited to spring training that year I got to the team hotel, the Colonial Inn, in St. Petersburg, and, looking around the lobby, I didn't recognize a single player. They had about fifty guys at camp that year, and when we would all line up to run sprints in the outfield it really did look like a circus. But that was the Mets, though. They were the worst for a reason.

At spring training of 1969, there was actually a little optimism about the season. In their first season under new manager Gil Hodges, the great Brooklyn Dodger first baseman in the 1950s, the Mets had gone 77-89 in 1968, easily the best ever for them. In his rookie season, Jerry Koosman went 19-12 with a 2.02 ERA. He lost out being Rookie of the Year to some guy named Johnny Bench. Tom Seaver, who had been Rookie of the Year in '67, had a good sophomore season, going 16-12. We weren't terrible anymore—

just mediocre. But we also weren't conditioned to think we could be great. All that losing, all of the jokes about the franchise had worn us down. Even with our improved record in '68, the Mets were still cellar dwellers, finishing ninth, one game ahead of Houston.

When Gil predicted during spring training in 1969 that we would win eighty-five games and a division title, I don't think we even knew he was talking about us. At that point, all of us young guys were too busy fighting for our job, fighting to prove we belonged in the major leagues, to even consider fighting for a pennant. But Hodges wasn't the only one predicting greatness. In fact, one person went so far as to say, out loud, that he liked our chances to actually win the World Series. It was our catcher, Jerry Grote. No one took him seriously. We figured it was just the positive vibes of spring that made everyone think they had a chance. But maybe we should have listened. Grote—one of the best defensive catchers of the sixties and seventies, had caught our staff the season before and knew the kind of pitching we had, especially with our two great starters, Seaver and Koosman. When you threw those two out there every five days you had a chance to be really good.

That season turned out to be Seaver's first great year. He'd win the Cy Young that year, and he deserved it. He went 25-7 with a 2.21 ERA. He pitched 273⅓ innings with eighteen complete games, struck out 208 batters, and walked only eighty-two. He was dominant, the superstar the franchise desperately needed to make fans—and indeed the players—believe. I was in awe of Seaver—a fellow Northern Californian and a fellow marine. I looked up to him so much that my son Mark would later be given the middle name of Tom, in his honor.

Seaver was a fun guy. I always thought he got a bad rap from some people who thought he was distant or too cool to talk. Not true, especially in the locker room, where he was the prankster frat-boy type. It was just that there were other times that he was more mature, a little calmer than the rest of us. Besides, the demands on Seaver were immense. Dealing with the fans is a challenge for all major leaguers, but it's something most of us truly enjoy. But when you get to Seaver's level, it is an entirely different ball game. And playing in New York on a winning team multiplied that exponentially.

Seaver wasn't our only star pitcher that year, though. Koosman wasn't far off of his 1968 pace. He wound up 17-9 with a 2.28 ERA, whiffing 180 and walking only sixty-two in 241 innings, with sixteen complete games. Those were good enough numbers to be the ace on most staffs most years. The rest of our rotation—twenty-two-year-old rookie Gary Gentry; Don Cardwell—a thirty-four-year-old righty who'd been in the league since 1957 with the Phillies, Cubs and Pirates; and Jim McAndrew in his second year in the bigs—was strong also. All of them had ERAs under 3.50. The bullpen was terrific too. Ron Taylor—who'd been to the World Series before with the Cardinals in 1964—was our right-handed relief ace and he finished with a 9-4 record, a 2.72 ERA, and thirteen saves. In my first year as a reliever I turned into the Mets' left-handed ace, with nine saves, a 9-3 record, and a 2.24 ERA. Cal Koonce added another seven saves and six more wins. We also had a guy by the name of Nolan Ryan out there who could throw it a little too. He was used as a spot starter and for long relief. I think Nolie still might be pitching for some team even now—after all, he's only fifty-seven!

At the plate, center fielder and leadoff hitter Tommie Agee slugged twenty-six homers while hitting from both sides of the plate, while left-fielder Cleon Jones hit twelve and nearly won the batting title with a .340 average. We picked up my old rookie season nemesis Donn Clendenon from the Expos for four players to supply some right-handed power and anchor the infield at first base, and we had a lot of guys who chipped in, putting up good numbers even though they were platooned. Art Shamsky smacked fourteen homers and hit .300, sharing right field with Swoboda.

But our greatest strength down the stretch was our attitude. We were used to being mathematically eliminated by mid-August, so to us there was no pressure. The longer we stayed alive the better. No one in the stands or in the press thought we could win it, so there were no expectations. People were just happy if we won at all. This contrasted with the Cubs, who had built the big lead early, going 16-7 in April and 16-9 in May. But as the season got along, the pressure to live up to the expectations of all of those long-suffering Cub fans seemed to become too much.

We really got hot in August and that loose feeling just took over. That month, riding our moon-landing "why not?" attitude, we went 21-10 to make it a real pennant race. The rest of the way we turned up even more, finishing on a 24-8 tear. By mid-September we had taken over first place from the fading Cubs, who basically melted down. Chicago went just 8-17 in the month of September, one of the worst collapses in baseball history. Things tightened a bit when we were swept in a three-game series by the Pirates and the Cubs started climbing back into it, but then we reeled off a nine-game win streak to clinch it, actually taking the National League Eastern Division by eight games. All of a sudden the Mets—*the New York Mets*—were in the play-offs. We wound up going 100-62 on the season, meaning that after Neil Armstrong took one giant step for mankind, we went a torrid 47-23 (.671).

We faced the Atlanta Braves in the National League Championship Series, and it remains one of the greatest thrills of my life. I can actually still remember the moment I knew I belonged in the major leagues. It was also the moment that I was no longer the kid brother of Hank McGraw. I was Tug McGraw, major-league pitcher. It came in the second game of the NLCS. We had won Game One, 9-5, and it was a tough win. Seaver, our ace, had started, and the Braves had knocked him around a bit. Both Hank Aaron—Tom's childhood hero—and Tony Gonzalez had hit home runs, to give the Braves a 5–4 lead in the bottom of the seventh. But we managed to score five big runs in the top of the eighth on four hits, a walk, and two errors. Atlanta threw the ball around like the Mets of old. Coming into the series almost everyone thought this was where our nice little fun story was supposed to end. The media and many fans didn't give us much of a chance. Many people felt that we had gotten lucky and stolen the first game.

But the Koos pitched three shutout innings to start Game Two and we jumped all over Ron Reed, Paul Doyle, and Milt Pappas, with Agee and second baseman Ken Boswell hitting homers, and the Braves making more errors. It was 9–1 heading into the bottom of the fifth and we were feeling good. But then the Braves struck back. Aaron hit another homer as they chased Koosman. By the end of the fifth it was 9–6. We got two more in the seventh on a two-run homer from Cleon Jones, and Hodges brought me in to replace Ron Taylor, who had put out the fire. But now it was up to me to keep it that way. I pitched a scoreless seventh, and then, in the eighth, along came Aaron, and there were fifty thousand people screaming and yelling inside Fulton County Stadium, fully expecting this great home-run hitter to hit one of this no-name's feeble pitches out of the park. Aaron was as frightening a hitter as you can face in October. Hammerin' Hank, Bad Henry, you know? Well, there were two outs and Jerry Grote was catching. We called him "Game

Face" Grote, because if you didn't throw what he wanted, where he wanted it, and when he wanted it, he'd get pissed and fire one back at you. Jerry was a fiery Texan who demanded excellence from the pitchers.

Against Aaron I quickly worked the count to 0-2. Aaron was looking for a screwball away, and Grote put down screwball away. I shook him off. I figured that if I came inside, which is what pitchers are taught to do, then I had options. I could change his world a little bit, brush him back, or at least come in tight, and that would tweak his thinking, make him consider that I was not afraid to throw it in there. And then I could go back outside or I could stay in. So I went inside, and the in thing worked. It was a ball but it stopped him from swinging. Now it was 1-2 and Grote called for the screwball. But I came back in again and I froze him with a fastball for strike three. Unbelievable. We are talking about Hank Aaron here. I remember thinking, "Damn, I can call these games; I'm ready for this. I just struck Hank Aaron out in the play-offs, and Hank Aaron never strikes out!" That was a great moment for me. I started as a moderate relief pitcher with no confidence but good stuff, and I jumped right up to the top of the league. Not only was there no way I was ever going back to the minors, but right then I began thinking, "There's nobody going to be any better than me now." Confidence is such a big thing. Striking out Hank Aaron and pitching three scoreless innings in the NLCS to save Game Two and put the Mets one victory away from capturing the NL pennant gave me that confidence, the confidence I would ride for the rest of my career.

We went back to New York for Game Three and won 7–4, with Nolan Ryan getting the victory after coming in as a relief pitcher in the third inning and finishing the game, allowing only a two-run homer to Orlando Cepeda in the fifth in seven innings of stellar work. Tommie Agee and Ken

Boswell both homered for the second game in a row, and rookie third baseman Wayne Garrett even got into the home-run act. The power-light Mets actually outslugged the heavy-hitting Braves. We were going to the World Series! The fans at Shea—including Pearl Bailey, Jackie and Aristotle Onassis, and Mayor Lindsay among 53,195 or so others, went crazy! They rushed the field and tore up chunks of turf. Baseball had never seen anything like it before.

Much like the NLCS, or the regular season for that matter, we were the underdogs in the Series. The Baltimore Orioles represented the American League, had home-field advantage, and had a lineup full of some of the biggest bats in the game. There was Boog Powell (thirty-seven HRs), Frank Robinson (thirty-two HRs), Paul Blair (twenty-six HRs), and Brooks Robinson (twenty-three HRs). It was enough to make a pitcher nervous. We sent Tom Seaver out for Game One in Baltimore, but on his second pitch of the game Don Buford took him out of the park. Baltimore went on to win 4–1. A lot of people wrote us off, figuring this was the end of the line for this scrappy team.

But Jerry Koosman started Game Two and threw a masterpiece when we really needed one—throwing a no-hitter for the first six innings. He came up big in the clutch—and turned out to be a hell of a big-game pitcher. As he was locked into an old-fashioned pitcher's duel with the O's Dave McNally, the score was 1-1 with two outs in the top of the ninth. Then our veteran third baseman and clubhouse poet Ed Charles singled, Jerry Grote drove him to third on a hit-and-run single, and utility infielder Al Weis came through with yet another single to give us a 2-1 lead. Jerry wound up with the win on a two-hitter, getting some ninth-inning help from Ron Taylor for the final out after walking the dangerous Frank Robinson and Boog Powell to put the tying run in scoring position. We headed to New York for the next three, and at this point the city was going nuts. It seemed like everyone was behind us; our team had captivated the attention of New Yorkers, who couldn't believe our transformation from lovable losers to pennant winners.

One interesting thing that people often ask me is how it was being a Met in the home city of the Yankees. But personally, I didn't know enough about the history to really think of that. I didn't ponder on it very much. As far as I was concerned, we had the World's Fair, we had Shea Stadium, we had Brooklyn, Queens, Long Island, parts of Manhattan, whatever part we picked. It wasn't even a territorial issue. I didn't even realize until recently that the Yankees had twenty-seven world championships; it never occurred to me. If you're a fan, it might be true that rooting for the Mets is a second-class-citizen kind of thing these days. But not then— since losing the '64 Series the Yankees had finished fifth, tenth, ninth, fifth, and fifth again. This was the middle of a bleak period for the Yanks in the years they were owned by CBS, before George Steinbrenner bought the team and made them into winners again in 1976. New York was a Mets town in 1969. We got the love from our fans; nobody could tell me that we were second-class.

The city was jacked up for Game Three, and we delivered. Gentry and Ryan combined on a four-hit shutout, and Tommie Agee practically took care of the rest. He and Ed Kranepool homered off of Oriole pitcher Jim Palmer in the first, and then Agee made two spectacular run-saving catches in center field to help the shutout. We won 5-0.

Seaver was back in Game Four and he was determined to get a win this time. He was locked into a pitching duel with Mike Cuellar, who had beaten him in Game One. The Mets took a 1-0 lead into the ninth on Clendenon's second homer of the series, but the Orioles scratched for a tying run on a couple of singles and then a line drive to right center that Ron Swoboda caught, somehow, while he was horizontal and airborne. I've seen it on TV over the years, and the catch still looks impossible. The funny thing is, Ron used to practice this type of catch. What a time to finally make it! It's got to rank right up there with Willie Mays's catch off of Vic Wertz in the 1954 Series. Anyway, a run scored and the game went into extra innings. Seaver stayed in and pitched the top of the tenth, shutting down Baltimore. Then, in the bottom of the inning, Jerry Grote led off with a bloop double to short left to put the winning run on second. Rod Gaspar pinch-ran for Grote. After Al Weis was intentionally walked to set up a double play, our third-string catcher, JC Martin, pinch-hit for Seaver, who now could only sit in the dugout and watch. Martin laid down a sacrifice bunt, trying to advance Gaspar to third. But O's reliever Pete Richert threw the ball to first and hit Martin in the wrist. The ball caromed into right field, and Gaspar flew home with the winning run. Even though JC really should have been called out for running on the wrong side of the base path, the umps missed it and the run scored. More Met magic!

Now we were up three games to one. The mighty Orioles were stunned. In Game Five, Baltimore jumped out to a 3–0 lead off of homers by pitcher Dave McNally and Frank Robinson off of Jerry Koosman. But Koos shut the door the rest of the way and went on to pitch a complete game. We had it tied in the seventh—courtesy of a two-run homer by Donn Clendenon in the sixth and a solo shot by the light-hitting Al Weis for his only homer at Shea all year! We got two more in the eighth thanks to doubles by Cleon Jones and Swoboda and a Baltimore error, to take a 5–3 lead. Koosman walked the leadoff batter in the ninth but then closed things down to clinch it. When Cleon Jones dropped to one knee to catch Davey Johnson's fly ball, the Miracle Mets were world champions.

Even though I never pitched in the World Series, I did warm up a couple times, which was good enough. Just being in the World Series was an incredible thrill. Besides, I went through a whole season of incredible thrills. We had a great bullpen and I was still a work in progress. So for me it was often warm up, sit down; warm up, sit down. Just because it was the World Series, nothing changed. I had to have a practical approach to these things; I couldn't get all lathered up. I sweated, I stayed ready, but I knew that when we did need relief, we were going to the veteran Taylor. And even then, in the Series, that wasn't often. We had Seaver and Koosman starting four of those five games, so you had everything you needed up front. Our whole bullpen pitched only a combined five and two-thirds innings the entire World Series. Besides, this was a different time too. We weren't into matchups, lefties and righties. And the teams didn't play each other during the season, or scout each other much, so there wasn't a wealth of computerized stats to use to make decisions. It was always, "Whose turn is it?" In the World Series, Taylor was well rested. I never got in there, but the reality was, I wasn't needed. And I was fine with that.

But I was a World Series champion, enjoying the greatest ride of my life. And thanks to that NLCS appearance, I was convinced that I was not only a viable major leaguer, but one who could excel in the future. Everything changed for me in 1969, the year we turned out to be goddamned amazing, all right.

As champions, the players got to do some fun stuff. On September 25, the day after we clinched the NL East, the Buddha Record label got us into a recording studio on West 54th Street in Manhattan to record an album of songs, including, "(You've Gotta Have) Heart" from the musical

Damn Yankees, "Take Me Out to the Ball Game," and even a version of "East Side, West Side" adapted by third baseman/poet, Ed Charles. After the Series win, there was a ticker tape parade up lower Broadway that was bigger than the one the Jets had for winning Super Bowl III and the one the Apollo 11 astronauts got for landing on the moon. There were receptions at city hall, a luncheon at the exclusive Four Seasons restaurant, and parties and banquets all winter long. The best may have been our appearance on the *Ed Sullivan Show*, where we sang "(You've Gotta Have) Heart." And there I am, in the middle of the pack, in my mod high-lapelled double-breasted suit with a belted jacket and shiny belt buckle, bouncing around and singing my heart out. Nolan Ryan kind of forgot the words, and elbowed Tom Seaver when Tom leaned over to sing with him. It was a blast.

CHAPTER 10

Ya Gotta Believe!

I suppose one reason why the 1969 season remains so magical to Mets fans is that we weren't able to build off of it. Perhaps if we went on to win two or three World Series in a row, it wouldn't stand out as it did. But that isn't what happened. As good as we were down the stretch in '69, we were just an okay team the next three seasons when we finished third in the NL East each year. Individually, however, I took my newfound confidence and developed into a real-deal major-league pitcher.

In 1970 I saved ten games and posted a 3.28 ERA, getting better as the season went on. In 1971 and 1972, I put together two of my best seasons, with a 1.70 ERA both years. In '71 I shared closer duties with Danny Frisella and saved eight games while going 11-4. But in '72 I became the Mets' prime relief pitcher. I was throwing hard and confidently and it showed. I could hardly wait for the bullpen phone to ring during tight games. I struck out ninety-two batters in 106 innings and allowed just three home runs the entire season. I saved twenty-seven games that year, my single season high.

I even made my first All Star game appearance (one of just two in my career).

Playing in the All Star game down in Atlanta that year was a thrill. Our NL team was loaded with stars, guys like Hank Aaron, Joe Morgan, Johnny Bench, Willie Mays, Willie Stargell, Joe Torre, and so on. The AL had Yaz, Reggie Jackson, Rod Carew, and Brooks Robinson, among others. The starters were Jim Palmer versus Bob Gibson. Pretty impressive. I was excited just to be around all of these guys. The AL had won the season before, so we actually took it seriously. The NL wanted to win. We were trailing 3–2 in the top of the ninth when I got the call to come in. I got through the inning without a run scoring, and then in the bottom of the ninth we scratched for one to tie it up. I worked the top of the tenth fine also, and at the bottom of the inning Joe Morgan drove in the winning run for the National League. I pitched two full innings, allowing just one hit and striking out four batters, and was credited with the win. It was an incredible experience.

Outside of my immediate family I don't think anyone has meant more to me than Gil Hodges. He was the manager who made me believe in myself, made me believe I was a major leaguer. Gil wasn't some rah-rah guy. He was a man of few words, and he always knew which words would be most effective. With a single look he could convey an entire message—just about any message. He wasn't a manager who was easy to classify. He was neither a disciplinarian nor a player's coach. He could be tough and he could be your friend. He would let some things slide, but he knew when to rein you in. He had a great feel for people. Lucky for me, because I wasn't the easiest player to coach—I could make a royal mess out of just about anything.

There were times he was gentle and fatherly with me. And there were times he would push me to do things I didn't think were possible. Most of all he was the immovable rock in the clubhouse, the one person I could always turn to and get what I needed. As a young major leaguer playing in New York City, I found that invaluable. He could make an insane situation seem sane. I was hardly the only player who felt this way about Gil.

Which was why the spring of 1972 was so difficult for us all. Just before the season began the Major League Players Association voted to go on strike. There were some important issues that had to be worked out. Remember, back then there was no free agency, salaries were comparatively low, and the game was as popular as ever. Owners were raking in the cash, and while none of us was in the poorhouse by any means, we felt we weren't getting a fair share.

Everyone knew there was no way the owners were going to concede anything unless they were forced to. A strike was the only way. So for the first time ever, the start of the season was delayed. Strikes in sports have become so commonplace since then that they hardly generate the same kind of outrage or frustration, especially if they take place early in the season. The 1994 baseball strike was different because it canceled the World Series. But usually a strike happens, the fans complain, and then the strike ends. Everyone sort of realizes that they are needed every once in a while. But back then it was so new and so defiant that there was great anger against the players. It was somewhat traumatic for all of us, who believed in what we were fighting for but had a difficult time explaining how being a major-league player was such a raw deal. It wasn't like we were mining for coal.

With the strike on and nothing to do on Easter Sunday, Gil went out and played twenty-seven holes of golf with his coaches in West Palm Beach, Florida. Afterward he collapsed and died of a massive heart attack. He was just forty-seven. I was twenty-six. And all of us Mets, in the middle of this contentious strike over money, had to attend the funeral of the boss we adored. Even though Gil had had a heart attack in 1968, and was told to quit smoking four packs a day, his sudden death completely rocked our team. When the strike finally ended we hardly knew which way to turn; that was how much Hodges meant to all of us. And to this day, his death sticks with me. Yogi Berra was named the new manager. As much as I loved Yogi, and I appreciated his using me as the main closer, I still missed Gil.

The 1973 Mets had a lot of potential. We had a million-dollar payroll—huge for that day—and a good number of players who had won it all in 1969. But injuries crushed us early and we were just 12-10 heading into an early home weekend series against Houston that would change my season (and perhaps the team's). We had a 4–1 lead late in the game when they called to the bullpen and said my three favorite words: "Get McGraw ready."

When I got in, though, I wasn't ready. I walked the first batter. Then the second. I couldn't believe it. I buckled down and struck Lee May out, but then promptly walked the next two, forcing in a run. I was reeling by this point, and by the end of the inning four runs had scored off of me and we were en route to a 9–5 loss. The performance rocked me. I had been pitching pretty well and hadn't had any control problems up to that point. For a relief pitcher, there is nothing worse than walks. It is one thing to get hit hard, but four bases-on-balls in one appearance? I immediately let it get to my head. Two games later, when Yogi called me in again to face the Astros, instead of just pitching, I was worrying about walks. It was everything you were not supposed to do. I got shelled.

I was officially in a slump.

From there, things went from bad to worse. I overanalyzed every pitch. I started getting a little nervous entering a game. I even referred to my slump as a "slump," a defeatist attitude. Because I was walking guys, I started aiming the pitch. But I got no velocity on it and hitters started hammering me. Then the coaches told me to stop aiming and just rear back and throw it. But my timing was off, my confidence was shot, and everything I threw got knocked around the park. So I tore up the clubhouse, but all that did was piss everybody off and make the coaches worry that I'd hurt myself. My teammates sympathized, but they didn't like it any more than management.

Well, the Mets unfortunately followed my lead. In part because of the injuries we just weren't very good. We quickly fell below .500, then into last place. Just four seasons removed from winning the World Series we were terrible again. We entered a July Fourth weekend series in Montreal with a 33-41 record, twelve or thirteen games out of first, and me in a slump. They sent me out in the series opener, which was a close game—at least until I got in there. I had never felt worse on the mound. I had no feel for the ball. I had no idea what to do. It was surreal. I was the fireman, sent in to save the game, and instead gasoline came pouring out of my hose. I got drilled for seven runs in a single inning. We were now 33-42. I didn't tear up the locker room that night; I just sat there, despondent. I simply could not believe I was pitching so poorly. I was in perfect physical condition, but I had lost it. I doubted everything about myself.

When we returned to New York I decided to go see a friend of mine named Joe Badamo. He was an insurance guy on Long Island and had been a close friend of the late Gil Hodges. Joe was also a motivational speaker, a guy who always saw the positive possibilities in a subject. Nowadays teams have sports psychologists who speak to the players to try to get them to achieve at the top of their game—and make those zillion-dollar-a-year salaries seem worth it. But thirty years ago it was just Joe. We used to talk once or twice a week; often he'd come down to the ballpark and we'd sit in the players lounge and discuss things. He'd go over some of the sales points he was using for insurance. I would convert them to baseball. He would elaborate, and I would elaborate. The next thing I knew, we would have a motivational session. We had these three-by-five cards, and we would write notes on them. Later on we'd get more sophisticated and he'd type notes out and then I would handwrite my little additions to them. Then I would post them up all over my locker. It helped us both. Although sports psychology and motivational speaking weren't big things then, they were big for me. I knew Joe used to do the same thing with Gil in 1969, which was why I had such trust in him. Gil could do no wrong as far as I was concerned, so Joe was okay, too.

Joe and I met that day not at Shea but over lunch near Manhasset, New York, which is where we both lived on Long Island. I needed Joe that day; I needed help getting my confidence back. I had just forgotten how to pitch—at least, how to pitch well. Joe kept saying, "You've got to *believe* in yourself." If I didn't believe, I could never do it. I had to stop worrying, start thinking positively. "You gotta *believe*, Tug," he said. "That's it, I guess, you gotta *believe*."

Sitting there that day I knew I didn't have a hell of a lot choice. I was out of tricks. "Okay," said, "I believe. Because you gotta believe."

It was a catchy saying, which was one reason it seemingly overtook New York the rest of that summer. Who doesn't like, "Ya gotta believe"? Eventually it took on a life of its own, but that afternoon as I drove to Shea in the little white 1969 Mercedes I had bought with my World Series bonus, I was the only one saying it. But I kept saying it and saying it, slowly buying into it. When I got to the park there was a whole group of fans waiting for autographs and to catch a glimpse of the players. They were yelling, "Yo, Tugger!" and stuff like that. I just kept shouting, "Ya gotta believe! Ya gotta believe! Ya gotta believe!" over and over. They'd say, "Hey, Tug, what's wrong with the Mets?" and I'd say, "Nothing! Ya gotta believe!" I parked and signed a couple autographs and went on into the clubhouse and started running around changing clothes, yelling, "Ya gotta believe!" to everybody I saw. I think they thought I had finally gone off the deep end. But it didn't stop me. I went out and did my early work, and kept yelling it out there. I was a maniac that day. I was off the wall—much more so than normal, even. It might have been one of those days where I was on the high end of things. I don't know if it was biorhythms, or anxiety—there are all kinds of things out there that describe those highs, so I'm not sure which one this was.

But there was definitely a buzz, and by the time we got back into the clubhouse and everyone settled down, I was still bouncing off the walls, saying, "Ya gotta believe!" It was all really a joke to my teammates. Everyone was just laughing about it. It wasn't supposed to be serious; it was just supposed to be something different, something that might shake people out of their slumps. Plus, it was fun to say. At that point we were losing and in last place, so we might as well have some fun doing something.

Back in the clubhouse we were told that the chairman of the board of directors of the Mets, M. Donald Grant, was coming in to have a team meeting. He was close to seventy, tall, distinguished-looking, with gray hair, bushy eyebrows, a martini guy. He wanted to come in and say to us, "Relax, we love you guys, we understand there have been a lot of injuries, you wouldn't be here if we didn't. We still believe in you." He just wanted us to remain calm and know that the front office didn't think we were a last-place club and wasn't about to do anything drastic. Just play ball. It was a good talk. The problem was that it took twenty minutes for him to say what should have taken five. I didn't know if it was halfway through the talk, or if he was getting toward the end—I didn't know where he was with all of this—but when he said, "We believe in you guys, every single one of you," that's when I couldn't contain myself anymore.

I just shouted out, "Aaaaahhhh, ya gotta believe!" Real loud. It stopped the speech in its tracks. I jumped up and ran around to a couple lockers, grabbing guys and yelling, "Do you believe? Ya gotta believe!" Some of the guys were laughing, some were afraid to laugh, but one person who wasn't laughing was M. Donald Grant. His face just went blank and he stormed out with his entourage of suits behind him. Honestly I wasn't trying to mimic him or make fun of him; I just reacted.

My roommate, Ed Kranepool, came over right away, and he said, "Hey, that boy's pissed."

I said, "What are you talking about?" I was so naive I couldn't even tell. In hindsight, I should have known, but at the time it didn't seem like a big deal.

Krane said, "You'd better get your ass up to his office and explain to him. He thinks you were making fun of him. You have the support of most of us down here, because we'll tell him that you've been that way all day, but I think you've caught him off guard. Why don't you go on up and do your thing?"

I couldn't believe it. I said, "You think?"

And Kranepool said, "You're damned right I think."

So I got myself upstairs and I did the Marine Corps slap

on the bulkhead, just to take some of the tension out of things. I went into Grant's office and said, "Reporting, sir."

And he said, "Come in, McGraw."

So I stood in front of his desk, he didn't say, "Sit down" or anything. I said, "Let me start off with an apology. I didn't realize how offensive I was being. I thought the 'gotta believe' was a real positive thing and I didn't see how you'd be offended by it."

He said, "Well, I was, and the only thing that will keep you here is if we start winning some ball games." And he wasn't laughing. He meant business.

I knew that. So I said, "Yes, sir."

He said, "You're excused."

Now I had two problems. The chairman of the board wasn't too happy with me, and, despite my newfound catch-phrase and state of mind, I was still in a slump. Yogi came up with the idea that I should try to start a game. He figured that what I needed was confidence, a chance to get back into a groove, and you just can't do that as a relief pitcher. Almost every time you come in the game is on the line, and you pitch only an inning or so anyway. He didn't say when I might start; he just batted it around.

We went to Atlanta in mid-July, and in a game on July 16, our starting pitcher was struggling. The bullpen phone never rang for me that game. It was very discouraging. I thought Yogi had lost all confidence in me.

When I arrived at Fulton County Stadium the next day, July 17, there was a new baseball sitting in my shoe in front of my locker. That's baseball shorthand for, "You're the starting pitcher today." I tried not to act too surprised, but I was. It is rare that a pitcher gets to the park and then finds out he is starting that game.

I didn't feel good warming up, didn't feel comfortable on the mound or holding the ball. So I gave myself a pep talk:

"Fight your way through this; starting is no different from relief work. Get a hold of yourself; the end of the slump starts right now." So what happened? Ralph Garr mashed my first pitch over the center-field fence. Nice, huh? At that point I just said, "Screw it. It can't get any worse than this, and it is just an experiment. The team stinks anyway, so just pitch." I gave up ten hits and seven runs in six innings, and three of the hits were homers. Although the stats weren't great, for the most part I actually settled down and just pitched. After I got pulled we came back and scored seven runs in the ninth and won 8–7. The guys were fired up at the comeback victory. After the game in the locker room I was on my chair yelling, "Ya gotta believe!" One of the reporters overheard it, I think, and it made the papers. It became our fans' mantra. We had a big celebration in the clubhouse that night, everyone drinking beers, and then we all went out on the town. I think there was a feeling that we needed to do something to spark ourselves, and maybe this was it.

I wound up starting again against St. Louis and did pretty well: five innings, a couple runs allowed, but five strikeouts and, most important, no walks. We didn't win—I was still zero for 1973—but Yogi decided that the starting experiment had worked well enough that I should go back to the bullpen. My first appearance out of the pen after that came in San Francisco. It was a wild game and I was brought in late. I wound up pitching five or six hair-raising but scoreless innings. But in the thirteenth I walked a guy, let someone else get on, and then Wayne Garrett blew a potential double-play ball while playing short, but got the out at first, so there were men on second and third with one out. Yogi had me walk a rookie so we could set up a force at home or a double play to end the inning. But that brought up Bobby Bonds. Just as was his son Barry, Bobby Bonds was a dangerous hitter anytime he came to the plate. I disagreed with

Yogi's strategy, but I did get Bonds to hit it on the ground. Too bad it rolled between third and short and won the game for the Giants.

But I had pitched well. I knew it. And on the road, no less. If you can pitch well in those situations then you can pitch anywhere, anytime. Despite the loss, my confidence was now back. I was a major-league pitcher again. The old Tug. Another thing that had happened was that during the All Star game the Dodgers' Jim Brewer told Tom Seaver that he had watched me on television and thought I was opening up on my delivery too quickly. Basically my delivery was coming in too high, which kills velocity on the fastball and makes the screwball stay high. He told Tom that when he was in slumps it was usually because he did the same thing. Tom related the comment to me and I worked on it. Jim Brewer was right. I started pitching better right away.

By mid-August another thing happened: We got our injured players back. I swear, the clubhouse looked like the set of *M*A*S*H* until then. Look at this list of the injuries we had that year:

- John Milner, 1B—pulled hamstring
- Jerry Grote, C—fractured wrist *and* fractured finger
- Cleon Jones, LF—strained wrist, hit by pitch on left elbow, bad feet
- George Theodore, RF—dislocated hip (one of the freakiest on-field injuries I've ever seen)
- Willie Mays, CF—bad right shoulder, fluid on the knee
- Bud Harrelson, SS—fractured hand *and* fractured sternum
- John Matlack, P—fractured skull (from a line drive to the forehead by Marty Perez of the Braves)

It was as if someone had tossed a grenade into the club-house!

But now we got solid up the middle. Grote and Harrelson were now 100 percent, and Don Hahn, who came to us in the trade that sent my pal Ron Swoboda to the Expos, took over for the forty-two-year-old Willie Mays in center. Since no one in our division was setting the world on fire, there was some postseason bonus money there for the taking. Whatever it was, everyone on the team started to realize the power of positive thinking by mid-August. Everyone kept saying, "Ya gotta believe!" After almost five miserable months, we all learned how to win again. Suddenly we had a reason to believe.

The first goal was getting on the good side of .500. We had been in last place for two months, so once we got it going it was exciting. We literally took it one game at a time. We'd win a game and then forget about it. On August 22 I finally got off the schneid for the year. We were playing the Dodgers in Shea and trailing 3–2 when Yogi brought me in for the eighth and ninth. I got through both innings, and in the bottom of the ninth we scratched for two off the Dodgers' screwball pitcher, Jim Brewer, to take the game. So there it was in the box score: "Winning pitcher: McGraw." I had finally won a game in the 1973 season. I went nuts after the game, screaming, "Ya gotta believe!" over and over. George Stone, who came to the Mets with Felix Millan in the trade that sent Gary Gentry and Danny Frisella to the Braves, had been the starting pitcher en route to a 12-3 season. He came up to me and said, like I was a rookie or something, "Well, Tug, the first one is always the toughest." Then Duffy Dyer, our back-up catcher, cracked, "Yeah, even if it comes at the end of August."

I hardly cared about the teasing. I was not going to go zero for 1973.

By this point our division tightened up. We had moved up to fifth place on September 1, but were only five and a half games out of first. No one ahead of us seemed to want to win this thing. St. Louis, Pittsburgh, Montreal, and Chicago all were in it, although the Phillies were pretty much out of it. Any one of those teams could win it, even us. In the NL West, Cincinnati and Los Angeles were both playing great; it would take the Reds 99 victories to win the division, beating out the Dodgers, with 95 wins. But in the East, a .500 record—81-81—might actually be enough. The Mets went 18-14 in August, our first winning month since April. But even beginning to play well, we were still nine games under .500 at 62-71 as we headed into September.

But after I got the win against the Dodgers, I got hot. Red-hot. And so did the rest of the team. Our injured guys came back ready to play, and we went on a tear. And best of all, because of the way the schedules were made in those days, we played only our Eastern Division rivals the rest of the way, so we could make up a lot of ground fast. We started winning games late, started winning wild ones, started doing the crazy things that are the difference between a playoff team and a floundering club. We still did stupid things, like score nine runs one night and then lose 1-0 the next. On September 9, Stone shut out Montreal 3-0—he was on an eight-game winning streak—to move us three games out of first. On September 12, lefty Jon Matlack (the 1972 Rookie of the Year who was in the middle of a five-game winning streak), beat the Phillies 3-2 to put us only two and a half games out, even though we were still in fourth place. I told you it was a tight race! We'd moved ahead of the Cubs, but were still behind Pittsburgh, St. Louis, and Montreal. On September 19, we moved up to third, only a game and half out, beating the Pirates behind George Stone. We were sweeping a crazy series with the Pirates, and two days later, on September 21, Seaver put us in first with a 10-2 win in front of more than 50,000 screaming fans at Shea. Our record stood at 77-77—the first time we'd reached .500 since May 29! Then the Cards came to town and we swept them, too. We ended up winning seven in a row and wound up going 19-8 for the month of September. I had wins or saves in seventeen of the last twenty-five Mets victories, with an ERA of 0.88.

The final weekend of the year saw what was almost a five-way tie for first. Everyone had some kind of mathematical chance. We had a four-game series with Chicago—games on Friday and Saturday and a doubleheader to finish out the season on Sunday, but it was raining and raining. St. Louis was making a charge, winning its last five. Meanwhile, we got rained out on Friday, but the Pirates lost. St. Louis beat the Phils. And then we got rained out again on Saturday, Pittsburgh lost again, and the Cards won again. Now we would still have our Sunday doubleheader in Wrigley, and a makeup doubleheader on Monday, after the season had officially ended.

We lost the first game of the Sunday doubleheader, with Matlack getting outdueled by Rick Reuschel 1-0. But Jerry Koosman, who won six of his last seven starts, beat Ferguson Jenkins 9-2. The Cards finished the season at 81-81, and we were now 81-79. The situation was this—if we lost both games of the Monday doubleheader, there would be a play-off with St. Louis. If the Pirates won their makeup game with the Padres and we lost both games, there would be a three-way tie for first place!

As Yogi said about the 1973 pennant race, "It ain't over 'til it's over," and he was right. But we believed that we would wrap up the division. Tom Seaver would face the Cubs in the first game on Monday, going up against Burt Hooten. Seaver wound up 19-10 that year with a 2.08 ERA, led the league with 251 strikeouts and 18 complete games, and would win his second Cy Young Award. He was tired toward the end of the season, but there was no one else we wanted on the mound. We were ahead 6-2 going into the bottom of the seventh. When Rick Monday belted a two-run homer off Tom in the seventh, Yogi had seen enough. It was time to go to work.

It was cold and drizzling that day at Wrigley, and only 1,913 fans showed up. It was miserable but I was hot and fired up. I ended the inning in order and then worked a perfect eighth—thanks to a great defensive play by second baseman Felix Millan. In the ninth Ken Rudolph got a single, but I struck out Dave Rosello with a screwball and then got Glenn Beckert to hit a soft liner to John Milner at first and he doubled up Rudolph. That was it! We got up to that little clubhouse in Wrigley and all hell broke loose. We had somehow, some way clinched the division title. We didn't start drinking though because we were scheduled to play a second game, even if it was meaningless. But it didn't take long for the umps to call that game due to rain, and then the booze started flowing.

Who could have thought this was possible a couple months ago? As the story goes, I wound up on top of one our equipment trucks, gripping a big bottle of champagne, screaming, "Ya gotta believe!" over and over. Well, you do have to believe. We had just won the NL East with an 82-79 record, a .509 winning percentage. To this day, it's still the lowest winning percentage of any division winner or pennant winner in baseball history.

I'm not sure how many people really believed in the Mets when the hangover of the pennant race wore off. Let's face it, we were barely above .500 and our opponent in the best-of-five NLCS was the Big Red Machine that had won the pennant in 1970 and 1972 and would go on to win the 1975 and 1976 World Series. Cincy, led by Sparky Anderson, won 99 games to outlast a terrific Dodgers team that would win the pennant in '74. The Reds had all these great players: Pete Rose, Joe Morgan, Dave Concepcion, Johnny Bench and Tony Perez—the last two being 100 RBI guys, which was a big deal before all the hitting stats started getting inflated in the 1990s. Starting pitchers Jack Billingham and Don Gullett won nineteen and eighteen games, respectively. This was an excellent team. We were . . . well, we were this fun, funky group without a .300 hitter, led by first baseman John Milner's 23 homers and Rusty Staub's 76 RBIs. On paper, it was a terrible mismatch.

One of the great flaws of the Mets during the early and mid 1970s was not supporting a starting pitcher when he had a good outing. We would lose a game 2-1 and then the next day win 3-2. It was frustrating. Our starters sometimes felt like they had to toss a shutout to win. In Game One of the NLCS in Riverfront Stadium we did it again. Tom Seaver, who could have won another fifty games if he'd pitched his whole career for a heavy-hitting team, pitched beautifully, throwing seven scoreless innings. But all we had done is scratch for one run in the second, with Tom smacking a double to drive it in. I guess he figured that if no one else was going to do it, he'd have to do it himself. In the eighth Rose got a hold of one and hit a solo shot to tie the game. We did nothing in the ninth and then Bench hit a walk-off homer to win it. Seaver had thrown a six hitter, setting a league playoff record by striking out thirteen, but we had managed just three hits off Jack Billingham.

Jon Matlack got the ball the next day and one-upped Billingham by giving up only two singles to Andy Kosco. Rusty homered in the fourth and we cruised to a 5–0 win, evening the series. We headed back to Shea for the final three games, feeling great about our chances. Our pitchers had snuffed out the vaunted Reds offense. Man, with this kind of pitching, I'd never even get into a game!

Jerry Koosman was the Game Three starter and he too pitched great. The bats came alive—Rusty hit two more homers, and we were clobbering the Reds 9-2 after four innings when the excitement really began.

In the top of the fifth, Pete Rose—who would be my future teammate on the Phillies—was on first when a slow grounder was hit to Bud Harrelson at short. Bud picked it up, stepped on second for the force out, and had just tossed the ball to first for the double play when Rose slid in hard, attempting to break it up. The two wound up nose-to-nose, and then they started pushing and shoving, and then they started throwing punches. Now, Buddy is the kind of guy who had to put on extra weight in the off season because the heat of the summer would just melt him down to nothing. He was a skinny guy, and Pete easily had thirty or forty pounds on him. If this was allowed to go on, we all knew how it would turn out, and Buddy was the glue of our infield—we couldn't lose him again to injury. Of course, I was way out in the bullpen, watching it on television, and all the relievers and bullpen coaches could see was this scuffle. We didn't really know what was happening. The big crowd started to roar, and both benches emptied. I jumped up and ran toward the bullpen gate and saw it was a fight. I started sprinting in. Generally, when there is a fight, the guys in the bullpen don't get involved much. By the time we get there the fight is broken up. This time, however, I got there and it was still pretty wild. I helped rip Rose off of Harrelson while the umps tried to get everyone separated.

A lot of people thought Pete was an asshole no matter what uniform he was in. He played hard and played clean and his idol was Ty Cobb. Even though Bud Harrelson was also a Phillie in 1979, the subject of the brawl in '73 never came up.

Just when it looked like everything was under control, the Reds bullpen came rushing in. All of a sudden, Reds reliever Pedro Borbon raced in and blindsided Buzz Capra, one of the Mets' young relief pitchers. Then Duffy Dyer knocked Pedro down and the brawl was on again. Then it got kind of funny, at least from my viewpoint. Borbon finally got up and, probably because he was still dizzy from Duffy's punch, picked up a hat and started to leave the field. Somebody pointed out to him that he was now wearing a Mets cap—which turned out to be Buzz Capra's. That threw Pedro into a rage. He bit the cap, tore the thing apart with his teeth, looking like a wild man. Then he flung it on the ground and stomped on it. I'd never seen anything like that before.

In the bottom of the fifth, Rose took his position in left field, and the Shea Stadium crowd let him have it. They started screaming at him and heaving debris at him—food, cups, garbage, cans, you name it. Rose just picked some of the stuff up and threw it back. When a whiskey bottle buzzed him, though, he decided that he'd had enough. He ran into the dugout, and Sparky called in all of the Reds from the field. The NL president, Chub Feeney, was at the game, and he came into the Mets dugout and said we might have to forfeit the game if we couldn't get our crowd under control. Hell, there was no way we wanted to lose a game we were winning 9-2, but this was not easy. The Mets fans loved Buddy, and they didn't want anyone messing with him. Well, Yogi decided to walk out to left field with Willie Mays to plead for calm. Tom Seaver, Rusty Staub, and Cleon Jones joined them. It worked. Peace was restored and we won the game.

Game Four was another nail-biter, and I finally got in. Up

until this point our bullpen hadn't thrown a single pitch. Once again, George Stone was good, pitching six shutout innings before letting the Reds tie the game 1–1 on a homer by Tony Perez. I got the call to end the seventh inning and got us out of trouble. But their staff was pitching great too, getting a solid five innings from Fred Norman and then another four from Don Gullett, who had pitched only five innings in Game Two. I pitched very well that day, proof that I was a completely different pitcher than the guy who couldn't throw strikes a few months before. I held the Reds scoreless for $4\frac{1}{3}$ innings, from the seventh to the eleventh, but unfortunately we couldn't get anything across the plate. And one of my pitches in the eleventh ended up flying to the wall. Rusty, who wasn't exactly a speedy outfielder, made a terrific catch, but crashed into the wall so hard he injured his right shoulder and couldn't swing a bat or throw. He saved the game, but it may have hurt us in the long run.

Harry Parker, who was in his first full season in the majors, replaced me in the twelfth. Who should come up but Pete Rose. Pete was now on the Shea enemy list and would be for the rest of his career. The fans were going crazy booing him and screaming at him. It was a zoo. So you had to give Pete all the credit in the world when, with his team's season on the line and 50,000 plus looking to kill him, he drilled a homer over the right field wall and then ran around the bases pumping his fist in the face of the fans. Then, to rub it in, Pedro Borbon came in for the twelfth and got the save. At least he wore a Reds cap.

Although we'd blown a great chance to win the pennant in Game Four, it was okay. We had Seaver starting in Game Five. The Mets bats finally gave Tom some support, and we knocked out Billingham in the bottom of the fifth. Ed Kranepool, my roomie, knocked in two runs with a single in the first to get the ball rolling. We pounded out thirteen hits, and when Yogi called for me in the ninth, we had a 7–2 lead. But I wasn't worried about the Reds; I was worried about our fans. The scene at Shea was out of control, in the same frenzied way that it had been back in 1969. In the seventh inning the game was delayed when fans started pushing toward the field, and the temporary wall of some of the VIP box seats were knocked down. You could hear firecrackers going off in the stands. It was nuts. John Milner fielded a grounder and tossed it to me when I covered first, and I just kept running. I didn't celebrate—I just sprinted for our dugout, right past the orange-coated ushers who couldn't keep the fans from running on the field. I was like a linebacker breaking tackles, elbowing and shoving the guys who were trying to make souvenirs of my hat, my glove, the ball, and my uniform. After the fans poured on the field, they started tearing the place apart. They took all the bases—including home plate and the pitching rubber and even some of the outfield fence. That still baffles me—what do you do with a piece of outfield fence? It was a mob scene; the police had no control. Then again, they were probably just as ecstatic as our fans were.

Our opponent in the World Series was the defending champion Oakland A's—the mustachioed, Swingin' A's of Reggie Jackson, Joe Rudi, Sal Bando, Gene Tenace, Bert Campaneris, Rollie Fingers, and twenty-game-winners Catfish Hunter and Vida Blue. The Series wound up going seven games, some of them pretty crazy in their own right, but after the intensity of the pennant race and the playoffs, the World Series was almost a letdown. I did get into five of the games, however. I made my first ever World Series appearance in Game One and pitched $2\frac{2}{3}$ scoreless innings, but we lost 2-1 anyway. Matlack had started against Ken Holtzman. The 1973 season was the first year the designated hitter was used in the American League, but it was still not allowed in the World Series. In his first at bat of the entire season,

Holtzman doubled and came around to score. Rusty Staub was too banged up to play.

Rusty was back in the lineup in Game Two, but had to throw sort of submarine style to get the ball back in from right field. Jerry Koosman, who had been so incredible in the '69 Series, only lasted 2⅓ innings, and he was followed by Ray Sadecki and Harry Parker to get us to the sixth. I inherited a 6-3 lead but gave up a run in the seventh and two in the ninth to blow the lead. Yogi kept me in though and I pitched a scoreless tenth and eleventh. Then in the top of the twelfth we got four runs, courtesy of two errors by Mike Andrews, the A's backup second baseman, and there's a whole story there all by itself. I was supposed to finish the game off but I gave up a triple to Reggie Jackson and finally Yogi got out to the mound and asked if I was tired. I had pitched eight innings the last two days, so I said, "You bet." George Stone came in for the save. And I got my first ever World Series victory.

Game Three was the first night World Series game in New York—the beginning of a long tradition of great games that end so late that nobody on the East Coast can stay awake to watch them because they have to go to work or school the next day. Seaver took the hill back in Shea, and even though we scored two in the first off of Catfish Hunter to give Tom a rare early lead, that was all we'd get for the rest of the night. Tom pitched eight innings, and I wound up pitching the ninth and tenth innings with the game tied 2-2. In the eleventh, the A's got a run off of Harry Parker when a passed ball by Jerry Grote let Ted Kubiak, who had walked, advance to second and then score on a single by Bert Campaneris. A's manager Dick Williams brought in Rollie Fingers and his 1890s handlebar mustache for the save. We were down 2-1 in the Series and we needed to take these next two games at Shea.

With Matlack on the mound shutting down the A's on

three hits through eight innings, we exploded for thirteen hits and six runs in Game Four off Ken Holtzman, who lasted only a third of an inning, giving up a three-run homer to Rusty Staub. Rusty, as banged up as he was, went four-for-four, adding three singles with five RBIs to go with his homer. Ray Sadecki pitched the ninth for the save.

Then, in Game Five, Jerry Koosman and I combined to pitch a three-hit shutout for a 2-0 victory. The Amazing Mets, the team in last place in August, was about to pull off another miracle. We had the A's number, and our pitching had really done a number on them. It was going to be fun to win the World Series in front of my hometown fans.

We headed back to Oakland needing one game to win it all. Yogi made the decision to start a tired Seaver on three days' rest instead of going with George Stone and holding back Seaver for a possible Game Seven. Yogi wanted to close it out right there. Some Mets fans with long memories are still debating this move. Once again, we didn't get Seaver any runs in Game Six. Reggie Jackson knocked in runs with doubles in the first and third to put Oakland ahead 2-0. Tom left after seven. We scored one in the top of the eighth off of Catfish Hunter and Darold Knowles to make it 2-1, but Rollie Fingers came in to put out the fire. Then I came in and gave it right back in the bottom of the eighth, and we lost 3-1.

Now it was nail-biting time. This was the first Game Seven in Mets history. So far in the '73 Series, our pitchers hadn't given up a single Oakland home run. Then in Game Seven Reggie Jackson and Bert Campaneris both hit two-run homers in the third inning off Matlack, and we never recovered. Our incredible, improbable "Ya gotta believe!" run ended in a 5-2 loss in Game Seven of the World Series.

* * *

Our season was over but the phrase "Ya gotta believe!" lived on. I kind of knew it would. Everywhere you went that summer there were signs with "Believe" in them and people using it for all sorts of projects. The whole city got it. The whole country, really. Eastern Airlines even started using the phrase before they went bankrupt. They had it on the sides of their planes, on their advertising.

They called and asked me if I wanted to sign anything, and I said, "No, it's fine just the way it is, you guys play with it, have fun with it." They mailed me a check for $5,000 anyway with a letter from the company's president. I wasted no time cashing the check, but overall it was probably a dumb business decision on my part. But at the time I thought, "Hey, I didn't say it because I was trying to make money. I said it because I was in desperate need of inspiration. So inspire me." That's how naive I was back then. But if I had picked up that money, for the rest of my career maybe everybody would have been thinking that every time I opened my mouth, I was trying to make money, and it would have been true, so I just left it alone. Ya gotta believe I regretted that one.

CHAPTER 11

Tim's First Call

Over the years I had always kept Betty's phone call and the possibility of having a son out there in the back of my mind. It's not that I thought of it often, but some nights, while I was on the road and lying in a hotel room, the possibility would cross my mind. I wondered if this kid—I think she said she'd named him Tim—was good at sports, and if he was I arrogantly assumed he must be my kid. Now, if he was a good student, I laughed to myself, then he couldn't be mine. Don't get me wrong—I would be giving myself too much credit if I said that I spent a lot of time pondering what this boy was like. But I did think of him over the years. A lot of times I started to pick up the phone and call, but I never did. I guess I was afraid that it could be true, and if it was, what would *I* do? In my own selfish way, it was easier to deny than confront.

Betty had sent me pictures somewhat regularly, and while I never saw a resemblance in the boy, I guess I did half-ass believe that he could be my son. Although I didn't think he looked like me, I never threw the photos away. I kept a couple of them, in fact, in my locker in Philadelphia.

I told Phyllis before we got married that one day there could be a knock at the door or a phone call saying that I was someone's father. I didn't go into great detail about Betty, but I warned Phyllis that the call could come. I remember the conversation well because I wasn't sure how she'd react. We were sitting on the couch, watching a soap opera, and on the show a young woman came and knocked on the door. The door opened, and the lady inside looked at the girl and said, "Can I help you?" The girl standing there said, "Hi, Mom. I'm the daughter you gave up years ago." I started shrinking at that point—the scene was hitting a little too close to home. In my head I was envisioning this very same scenario happening to me. I don't remember what happened on the show after that because I looked at Phyllis and said, "What would you do if something like that happened to us?"

"I don't know," she responded frankly.

So I said, "You know, there's a possibility that somebody could come knocking on my door and say that they were my boy, my son."

I don't know if it was because she was into the soap opera or what, but Phyllis didn't seem too bothered by my revelation. She said we had a big house and always had room for more if that happened. Phyllis had an understanding way about her, so I shouldn't have been surprised by her response. As a flight attendant, she'd lived around the wild world of the sixties and always seemed to understand how things were.

So with that base covered, I just waited for the other shoe to drop, so to speak. It hit me in the spring of 1977 when I took the first call in a decade from Tim's mother, Betty. By then Phyllis and I had been married for nine years and had two young children, Mark and Cari, who were only six and four at the time.

I thought I'd be ready if Betty ever called. I wasn't. All I thought about—in my own very selfish way—was that the timing was bad. How would this impact my kids at home? How would it impact my career? I've been accused by people close to me of sometimes thinking only of myself. This was definitely one of those moments.

But timing for something like this couldn't be planned, and whether I was ready or not, Betty was reaching out.

By this time, I had been traded to the Philadelphia Phillies. Betty called the Phillies front office and left a message for me to call her. The note said it was "Betty, the girl from Jacksonville in 1966," and left a phone number in Louisiana for me to call. It had been over a decade since her mother had threatened to take me to court. As usual, I asked someone else to do my dirty work and screen the call to see what Betty wanted. The girl from the Phillies office who called for me had no luck with Betty, who said the call was personal and very important. I waited a few days and called Betty back at her job.

After we said our hellos, I asked, "What's wrong, Betty?" I tried to keep the tone conversational. After all these years, and despite how I'd acted, I still felt some fondness for her.

"Tug, Timmy knows that you are his father, and he wants to meet you," she explained.

"First of all, quit referring to me as his dad. Just because you say that I am doesn't mean that I had anything to do with it. And how does he know that I am his father?"

She said, "Well, number one, Timmy found his birth certificate, and number two, I told him it was true."

"Why did you tell him that?" I asked. This was the first

time I heard that my name was on his birth certificate. I couldn't even address that part, I was so stunned.

"Because it is true," she responded. "Tug," she said with obvious anger in her voice, "this child is only eleven and it's a complete shock to him. He wants to see his father. I don't want anything from you. You made your choice back in 1966. I've never bothered you, but this is for my son—your son."

Your son. The words hit me like a ton of bricks.

Betty explained that Tim had always been a good kid but had started having problems at school since he found his birth certificate a month earlier. Evidently, Betty told the doctor who delivered Tim that we were married so he would put my name down as the biological father. I guess if a woman wasn't married back in those days, the birth certificate declared the child "illegitimate"—and she didn't want that for Tim. She said she wanted Tim to know who his father was when he was old enough to understand and wanted to make sure that legally he could use the name McGraw if he ever wanted to.

Betty told me about Tim finding his birth certificate in a shoe box in her room while looking for pictures for a school project. She said he was so upset that he called her at work and asked her to come home immediately to explain.

Tim had always thought that his stepfather, Horace Smith, whom Betty was divorcing, was his real dad. Betty married Horace when Tim was about a year old but made Horace promise that he would never adopt Tim and never tell him who his real father was. Over the years Betty had gone to great lengths to cover up the time gap between Tim's age and Horace and Betty's marriage. Each year on their wedding anniversary they would say that they had been married one year longer so that Tim would not catch on that he was born before they were married. Horace never told Tim the secret that his mother asked him to keep, but would often taunt Betty with the truth about Tim's birth. After years of Horace's drinking and being physically abusive to Betty and Tim, she and her now three kids left him, and she filed for divorce. She was working two jobs to support the children and there had been a point where they were so poor they all lived in a barn with hay on the floor. Their story would provide the basis for a great novel were it not for one thing—it is all true.

So once Tim had found my name listed on his birth certificate, he flipped. In one of life's great ironies, he had my baseball card on the wall of his bedroom alongside his other favorite player, Houston Astros center fielder Cesar Cedeno. At school, he started telling his classmates and teachers that his father was major league baseball player Tug McGraw. Naturally, they did not believe him, since all of his life he had been known as Timmy Smith. He began getting into fights with other students who accused him of lying.

For Tim, finding out that I was his father was cool. Even though Louisiana is nowhere near Pennsylvania or New York, he was a huge fan of the Phillies and the Mets. I later learned that Betty had always encouraged Tim's love of baseball and over the years even told Tim that when she had lived in Jacksonville, she had known some of the ballplayers he was watching on TV. She especially pointed me out every time I was on the tube, telling Tim I had lived in the apartment right below hers. She said she told Tim all this so that one day, when she explained I was his real father, he would have positive thoughts about me and not be so surprised since we had been friends. At the same time, she didn't pressure me in the hope that I would be receptive to Tim's call when the time came and would never resent him. I've got to hand it to Betty. She really thought this out.

After a long pause, I told Betty that I would have to talk this over with my wife and would call her back. I told Phyllis about the call and how Betty wanted me to meet Tim. I told her about Betty's marriage, and how her husband treated her and the kids, and about Tim getting into fights at school over him telling people that his dad was a major league baseball player. Open minded as always, Phyllis agreed that I should go meet up with them for Tim's sake.

"Okay, Betty. I'll do it for the kid, not for me," I told her when I called her a few days later. "But from now on refer to me as Tug to Timmy, not as his father."

We decided to meet at the closest city that had a National League team, which was Houston. The Phillies had assembled another good team in '77. The previous year we began what would be a great run culminating with the 1980 World Series. Since the days when I had dated Betty, I had really come into my own on the field. Now I was getting ready to meet my own off the field.

My reaction to all of this was to hurry up and get to the bottom of it. I honestly thought that this meeting would put to rest the saga of Betty and the son she claimed I fathered. I told Betty where I would be staying and to contact me when she got there. Betty borrowed a car from a friend so that she and Tim could drive down from Louisiana. I left on my own, with the team following me to Houston.

I checked into the Marriott near the Astrodome and waited for Betty to call and let me know they had arrived. As promised, I stayed in my room, waiting for her call. I found myself pacing, staring at the phone. I had tried to convince myself this wasn't really happening, but if it wasn't, then why was I pacing around like a caged lion at the zoo? When the phone rang in my hotel room, it really jarred me. I am not sure why but I guess I was more nervous than I thought.

I headed down to the lobby to meet Betty. It wasn't too hard to recognize her although she looked quite a bit different from how I remembered her at the Jacksonville apartment complex over a decade ago. She'd developed into a woman and was no longer a girl. Tim was sitting there next to her.

I went over and said hello, only this time I didn't delegate it. I said to myself, "This is mine to handle." We started talking, and Tim was really nice and well mannered. "Yes, sir" and "No, sir" was how he answered all my questions. He was very shy—which made me think that he could not be related to me. I have been called quite a few things over the years but quiet was never one of them. Looking back on it, I now realize that to an eleven-year-old boy, this meeting was more than him meeting someone who he was told was his father. To him, I must have seemed like a baseball card come to life. I was one of his heroes and someone that he had seen on TV for years. He probably never thought that he would one day meet a ballplayer whose baseball card was pinned to his wall. It must have been very overwhelming for him—kind of like it must be for one of his young fans getting to meet him today.

I had arranged for us go into the hotel bar and get some lunch before it opened so we could be alone and talk. Tim and I both ordered hamburgers and milkshakes. I would later learn that Tim liked only vanilla milkshakes back then but ordered chocolate because I did. During lunch we talked about life and sports. Tim really liked all kinds of sports and was evidently quite the avid athlete. He told me that Greg Luzinski was his favorite Phillie and that he loved baseball. I asked Tim about the trouble he had been having in school. He sheepishly nodded his head, acknowledging the fights he had gotten into. I told him that sometimes life doesn't always give us a fair shake but we live with what we've got and have to make the best of it.

"I know you're having problems at school," I told him. "And you're having trouble dealing with this situation.

You're carrying that chip on your shoulder and you need to knock it off and stand up. You've done nothing wrong. Anything that adults do sometimes falls back on children, but it's not their fault." That was pretty deep for me. He was such a nice, polite kid, and I did not want him to feel bad about what was going on with his mother and me. I thought about how when I was his age, I had had to deal with my mom drinking and later leaving us. I figured that if I could handle it, so could he. I was never handled with kid gloves and never really knew how to handle someone else that way— even a young child. I figured it was more important to be honest than kind.

I could tell he was looking for me to acknowledge that I was his father, but I just wasn't convinced. "Well, no disrespect to your mom, but I don't know for sure that I am your dad. What happened between me and your mom had nothing to do with you. So from now on, why don't you just tell everybody that we're friends? You can refer to me as your buddy."

"Yes, sir," he replied with obvious disappointment.

"So, do you want to go see a ball game?"

"Yeah!" Tim replied, and with that we headed over to the Astrodome.

At the ball field, I did just what I said I would and introduced Tim as my buddy. He met Mike Schmidt and the rest of the team, and you could tell that he was having a great time. He played catch with Greg Luzinski and then watched the game from above the dugout with his mom. Ironically, with Tim and Betty watching, I gave up my first home run of the season that game.

After the game, some of the guys gave me hell over Betty and Tim. Evidently some of them saw more of a resemblance between me and Tim than I did. Schmitty even went over to Betty to ask her about Tim. While I was playing catch with Tim, Mike asked Betty how old Tim was. She told Mike he was eleven years old. Then he asked how long she had known me. Betty replied with the same answer—eleven years. Schmitty just smiled and said, "I thought so." Leave it to your friends to handle situations like this with sensitivity.

Once I returned to our hotel, I called Betty in her room to see how Tim enjoyed the day and to make plans to say good-bye before they left. On the phone I told Betty once again that she needed to stop referring to me as Tim's dad and to just let this all pass. "It would be easier for Tim to move on and deal with this if you would stop saying that I am his father," I explained. Needless to say, she hung up on me after telling me that I was a pig for thinking only of myself and not Tim. She was right, I was thinking only of myself—but that was typical and I had been able to get away with it for years. I always thought that it was possible that I was Tim's dad, but I had just ignored it and hoped it would go away.

The next day, I met Tim and Betty in front of my hotel to say good-bye. I knew that Tim wanted to take away much more than a professional league baseball hat from our visit, but I just wasn't ready to give him that. I had my own family at home, and my kids were too young for me to drop this on them. Maybe, deep down inside, I knew that Tim was my boy. I thought, "I've gotta buy some time here so I can figure out what to do." And I kept telling myself I wasn't convinced that this boy was my child.

As you would expect from a boy of his age, Tim heard almost nothing I said. He wanted to be Tim McGraw, son of a major league baseball player. He wanted it so bad he went home and, though I didn't know it, changed his last name. To McGraw.

I didn't have any contact with Tim or Betty for a while after that, but a year later, when baseball season came around again, I received another call from Betty saying that Tim wanted to come see me play a second time. Even though a year had passed, I wasn't ready to spend more time with either of them—I was afraid that this might turn into an annual event and I didn't want to explore the matter further. As usual, I thought only of myself and of how pursuing this relationship would affect my career and my family. But I told Betty I would get them tickets to another ball game in Houston and would have the tickets waiting at the Will Call window under Betty's name.

So Betty and Tim, now twelve years old, came to Houston once again, but this time I barely acknowledged their visit. Betty brought Tim and a buddy down to the dugout for me to say hi—it was going to be a big deal for Tim to be able to show his friend I really was his dad. But when she asked if I wanted to see Tim later or have lunch, I told her I was too busy. That obviously upset Tim—they left during the third inning to go to Six Flags and didn't contact me again for many years.

I was such an ass that after the second visit, when I basically ignored him, he went home and immediately changed his name back to Smith and barely spoke of me.

Hearing that later in my life really got to me. Not that I blamed Tim for changing his name back. I blame myself for hurting him bad enough that he made that decision as a young boy and I never knew it.

In a lifetime of mistakes, this is the one I feel worst about making—and the one I'd most like to go back and correct.

CHAPTER 12

The Phillie Years

It was a Jack Daniel's trade, a whiskey deal. In 1974 the Mets dealt me to the Phillies as part of a six-player trade. It happened at the winter meetings in New Orleans and it wasn't unlike a lot of trades that happen during that event. The owners and general managers always get on the players for drinking but you should see what happens when these front office types get going. The owners and the GMs, they sit around and drink all night at their winter meetings, and at about three a.m., after draining a bottle of Jameson or Jack Daniel's or something, they make a deal.

I was at my off-season house in San Diego at the time, and I got two late-night phone calls, which is all a ballplayer needs to know. I got one first from the Mets and then one from the Phillies. I had been traded down the New Jersey Turnpike to Philadelphia. The Mets got Del Unser, a decent-hitting outfielder without a lot of power, a young catcher named John Stearns—the man the Mets really wanted as Jerry Grote was going to need replacing behind the plate soon—and reliever Mac Scarce. The Phillies got me, center fielder Don Hahn, and utility outfielder Dave Schneck. Everyone was saying the Mets were going through a transition; "juggling the lineup" they called it. I got juggled.

In retrospect, I shouldn't have been so surprised about the deal, but I sure was at the time. During the 1974 season I was experiencing some pain in my scapula in my shoulder, and it was affecting my pitching. I had a high ERA (5.14) even though I managed to save sixteen games and pitch well in spurts. But I also gave up four grand slams, and the press started calling me "Grand Slam McGraw." Toward the end of the year, I was getting concerned because I'd go out and pitch a couple of innings, the next day I couldn't throw, but then a couple of days later, I was fine. So I started taking Darvon, a painkiller. I also tried to get the Mets to find out what was wrong with my shoulder. They didn't take a strong interest in it. What they thought in the front office was that after ten, eleven years, we got all we can out of him and now we can get rid of him. In August I had gone in to see one of the Mets' doctors and he said that all he could do was prescribe painkillers. Then the ball club said they had planned to use me again as a starter. They said it was to check the shoulder, which they couldn't do if I was a relief pitcher. As a starter I could pitch and then they could monitor the shoulder and I'd be all right. I didn't understand it then. I understood it as soon as I got traded.

They just put me on display. By starting, it made me look like I was healthy, which was important because the word had started to spread around the league that I wasn't. So they put me on display as a starter after being a reliever all those years. The Phillies, who had finished last in 1973 but had moved up to third in 1974, eight games behind the Pirates, bit.

The 1974 season was a tough one for the Mets. After overcoming all the injuries and adversity we had in '73 and taking the A's to the seventh game of the World Series, we slipped to fifth place, twenty games under .500. Tom Seaver had a sciatic nerve condition in his hip and he went 11-11, though he pitched 236 painful innings. I went 6-11, Harry Parker went 4-12, and George Stone hurt his arm and fell from 12-3 to 2-7. The hitters didn't hit in the clutch like in '73, and attendance fell. I remember meeting with Joe McDonald, who had just been named general manager of the Mets in August. He called me up to his office and I told him, "If you're thinking about trading me, I won't go to the American League. I flat out refuse."

He said, "Why?"

I said, "I don't believe in the DH. I don't want to come to any ballpark on this planet without the idea in my head that I might get my ups today." You gotta get your ups in baseball—that's why you play the game. You can't score unless you have a bat in your hand.

He took it to heart, I guess, because he traded me to the Phillies, a division rival. That's rarely done. Usually you trade players out of your division and get them as far away as possible. He traded me ninety miles south, for crying out loud. That's why I'm saying it was a Jack Daniel's trade. What sober GM would do that?

Maybe one who thought he was unloading a ruined pitcher on a close rival. And considering what the Phillies didn't know when they got me, maybe their guys were a bit sauced, too.

The trade really hurt me at the time. I'd been with the Mets from the start, and I thought I'd always be a Met. The Mets were my baseball family. I'd had a taste of the spotlight in New York, and I loved it. I didn't want to leave. Although the Phillies had been a couple of games under .500 in '74, they had been twenty games under in '73 and had been pretty bad for years. I didn't know what a great move it would turn out to be, as the Mets headed into a nosedive that lasted from 1977 to 1983.

I reported to spring training for the Phillies in February 1975, and on the first day I went into the trainer's room and said, "What about my shoulder?" I was asking if they had a plan for my shoulder.

Don Seager, the trainer, said "What *about* your shoulder?"

I said, "The shoulder problem I had with the Mets."

Everyone got real quiet. I sat there for a few minutes, and the next thing you know, Paul Owens, the general manager, came in and then the manager, Danny Ozark, came in, and they said, "What's up with your shoulder?"

I said, "I thought you guys knew."

Paul said, "No, we don't know anything about it."

The team doctor, Dr. Philip Marone, was there, and he said, "This is off the wall. We didn't know anything about this."

I said, "Well, we gotta try to fix it, or cancel the deal or something, I don't know. You tell me."

Paul said, "We'll get your health file from the Mets."

I said, "You don't already have it?"

Dr. Marone said, "No, we don't have anything on your health from the Mets."

I said, "Well, I'll give you a good idea."

It was crazy. I told them everything I knew about the shoulder and everything we had tried in New York. Dr. Marone said, "Well, there's no sense in repeating what they did. Why don't we just send you up to Philly, and we'll send you over to Dr. John Templeton, and we'll see what he can find. He's a thoracic surgeon."

So I went up to Philly and checked into a hospital there, and the doctors looked at me with X-rays and all sorts of stuff. They couldn't find anything. I said, "I haven't pitched yet, and so I doubt you will find anything. It usually comes after I pitch."

Dr. Templeton said, "We'll have to go in there and operate so we can find out what's in there." Although the last thing a major league pitcher looks forward to is shoulder surgery, I figured what the heck, something was wrong. If they couldn't find it and fix it, my career would be pretty much over. Surgery was scheduled for the next morning. Before I had the surgery, I had to sign two documents. One was permission for them to operate, and the other was for permission for them to take out a lung or a rib or whatever they had to do if it was malignant.

Before I went into the operating room, they put a guard on my door because I was getting a lot of visitors and I needed my rest. And this is before I had played even one game for the Phillies! The next morning, though, just before the surgery, this one very cute nurse came in and said, "Is everything all right?"

I said, "Yeah, as far as I can tell."

Then she said in a certain way that made me realize she wasn't talking about just bringing another pillow, "Is there anything you need?"

Well, hey, I figured why not give it a shot. I was going in for surgery anyway. So I said, "Yeah, there is one thing I need. Would a blow job be out of the question?"

She said, "No." And away we went! Unfortunately, the doctors came to get me a little earlier than I thought they would. Right in the middle. Thank goodness they knocked on the door first. She jumped off of me immediately. Then they put me on a gurney and wheeled me out. I was lying on my belly, which at least concealed what had happened because it just wouldn't go down. It didn't go away until we got all the way to the operating room. Fortunately, that was a long ride. I arrived at the operating room and finally turned over in order to get onto the operating table, and it was gone. Whew!

They did the surgery on St. Patrick's Day, and when they operated on me they found this growth of fatty tissue about the size of a poached egg. It was a benign mass of gristle that had built up over the years. Removing it was a simple procedure. I was able to throw freely after that, so in hindsight, although John Stearns turned into an All-Star catcher for them, the Mets got the worst of the whiskey trade. If they had just done the procedure, I would have been fine. But they just thought I was done. It wasn't like there was even a long rehab. I had the operation in mid-March and I was back on the active list by May. I even made the All-Star team that year. St. Patrick's Day was lucky for me—the surgery added another ten years to my career.

For most of the late 1970s the Phillies were a good team but a frustrating one. In 1976 and 1977 we won 101 games apiece. We won the NL East from '76-'78. But we couldn't get over the hump and get to the World Series. In 1976 we ran into the defending World Champion Big Red Machine that swept us in the playoffs and swept the Yankees in the World Series.

In 1977 we took Game One from the Dodgers at Dodger Stadium. It was the kind of game that gave us and our fans heart attacks. We were up 5-1 when Ron Cey tied it with a grand slam. But we rallied for two in the top of the ninth, and I got the save when I shut the Dodgers down in the bottom of the inning. Then, in Game Two, Dusty Baker hit a grand slam for the Dodgers to give them the win. In Game Three, we were up 5-3 with two out in the top of the ninth when the Dodgers put together a rally to score three runs and win the game at the Vet. Thirty-eight-year-old Vic Davalillo beat out a drag bunt on a disputed call and thirty-nine-year-old Manny Mota hit a fly ball that Greg Luzinski couldn't handle. It went for a double. After a couple more Dodger singles, we were done. Instead of being up two games to one, we were in the hole. And then, in a constant, steady rain, Tommy John went the distance to beat Steve Carlton and win the pennant for the Dodgers.

In 1978, we again lost three games to one to the Dodgers. This time, I was on the mound in the tenth inning of Game Four. With the score tied 3-3, our usually unflappable center fielder Garry Maddox, a Gold Glover, dropped a line drive at the top of his shoes. He just lost it in the sun and never got a good look at it. I gave up a single to shortstop Bill Russell to drive in Ron Cey with the pennant-winning run. Man, that hurt.

Some people say we underachieved, we should have been a little better, but in fairness to the team, we ran into some very tough Western Division teams in the Reds and Dodgers. Philly can be a rough place to play for some players. The press is very tough, very inconsistent. Mike Schmidt had a great line. He said, "Philadelphia is the only city where you can experience the thrill of victory and the agony of reading about it the next day."

I happened to love the fans and love the press, but by this point it was getting difficult. The Phillies hadn't won a World Series since starting the team in 1883 (they finished last in their first season, by the way). The franchise had won exactly two pennants, in 1915 and 1950. In 1915 the team was led by thirty-one-game winner Grover Cleveland Alexander but were defeated in the World Series by the Boston Red Sox and their ace pitcher, Babe Ruth. In 1950, the Whiz Kids, led by twenty-game winner Robin Roberts, beat the Brooklyn Dodgers on the last day of the season and then were swept by the Yankees led by Joe DiMaggio and Yogi Berra. The Phils blew the 1964 pennant by folding down the stretch. Every time you turned around someone reminded you of it. Because of that, and because in the end we always lost, the press was afraid to write good things when we got on a roll.

One of the reasons I was brought in was to loosen things up. They had great players such as a power-hitting young third baseman named Mike Schmidt, who had his first big year in 1974, the incredible strikeout machine Steve "Lefty" Carlton, the powerful outfielder Greg "Bull" Luzinski, and the slick-fielding shortstop Larry Bowa, among others. But they needed a shot of adrenaline. I figured that was as much a part of the trade as my screwball. I didn't say much in the locker room but I went out and did things that you knew nobody else was doing. I would catch balls behind my back. I would go over and shag balls at first base, take grounders at second base—do things that pitchers normally don't do. I wasn't just a pitcher, I was an athlete, so I was all over the field.

At that time I started naming my pitches. I had a whole bunch of them. There was the Peggy Lee, named in honor of the singer from the 1940s and '50s who had a number-one hit called "Is That All There Is?" I used to take things like that and translate them into baseball terminology. So when I'd be ahead of a batter on a 3–0 count, I'd throw a little dunking batting practice fastball right down the middle of the plate. It wasn't a changeup and it wasn't like I was trying to blow the guy away. It was just a nice comfortable little fastball to hit. The hitters would see it and their eyes would light up and they'd want to jump on it, and the next thing you know, they'd pop it up or hit a grounder. I called it my Peggy Lee pitch because they'd swing and pop it up, and then they'd say "Is that all there is?"

Then there was the Bo Derek, which had a nice little tail on it. Gotta have a little movement on it. I threw mainly straight fastballs, four seams, and I hit the corners with it. I could pinpoint my fastball. I would outline the strike zone with my regular fastball, and then I'd change speeds and put a little movement on the Bo Derek, and that would get them to hit a grounder to shortstop. Then I'd throw a cut fastball, which I called Cutty Sark, because it would sail. I'd sail one in on their hands and they'd hit a ground ball out to second. The John Jameson was hard and straight, just like the Irish whiskey. It was the pitch I used when I reached back for a little something extra. Then there was the Frank Sinatra, the home run pitch. That was the "Fly Me to the Moon" pitch. That was usually a postdelivery name, instead of a predelivery name. I never meant to throw the Sinatra!

On December 5, 1978, the Phillies signed Pete Rose as a free agent to give us another spark and add a superstar. The feeling was Rose, Charlie Hustle, would will us to victory. Initially he came in and he tried to do everything. He knew we were almost there, and that our team needed something to get us over the hump. Just like everybody else, he thought that he was going to be the guy, so he overachieved. The problem was, everybody else watched him overachieve and we didn't achieve anything. After finishing first three years in a row, we ended up finishing fourth. It was brutal. We were decimated by injuries—Larry Christenson broke his collarbone on my charity bike ride in California, Greg Luzinski missed a lot of games because of a bum knee, Bake McBride also had bad knees, Dick Ruthven had elbow problems, and Warren Brusstar had a bad shoulder. It seemed like everybody was hurt at some point. The last month of the season, Danny Ozark was fired and Dallas Green, who had been a relief pitcher and spot-starter with the Phils, Senators, and Yanks in the 1960s and was now the team's farm director, was brought in to evaluate the team as the interim manager. During the off-season he told the front office that nobody could handle us better than he could, and he wanted the job. He got it. Perhaps it was the final piece of the puzzle.

When the 1980 season started, however, we were pitiful. We also had a drug scandal. Just like today, drugs were always talked about in sports. In baseball in the seventies and early eighties, the popular drug was amphetamines. Getting amphetamines was difficult unless you had established contacts. With the Phillies, the drug contact was the team doctor for our Double-A team in Reading, Pennsylvania. He would write out prescriptions for diet pills in the names of the wives, the wives would give them to their husbands, and the husbands would take them and then they'd go out and play baseball. Diet pills contain five milligrams of amphetamines, and doctors prescribed them to women all the time back then. Doctors still prescribe them today. Somehow word got out that the wives weren't using them. So there was an investigation, and the doctor ended up going on trial. The scandal threw the team off kilter for a while. It would take less time to mention who wasn't taking them then who was, although I didn't take them. I don't even think the bust stopped anything though. Everyone had enough to last them the rest of the year. But the publicity was terrible, and the newspapers were full of stories. I still remember the headline: "The Philadelphia Pillies."

It blew over when we started winning. Winning cures all. That came gradually during the year, though. It took us all the way to August to really get our act together. Dallas was a big reason for our improvement. Until then we had had such strong egos that nobody could put us in check. Nobody could get in your face, put his hand around your throat, and say, "Listen, you motherfucker, *this* is the way it's going to be around here as long as I'm manager." Dallas was big, six-foot-five, 250 pounds, and strong enough and confident enough that he could take you on. Although it wasn't his usual style of management, there were several instances during the season where he went around locker to locker, and if he felt like somebody needed a little face, he would give them some face. He would make it loud enough where he'd make your ears flap. He knew all the writers were outside with their ears to the door. You didn't want to fuck with Dallas. As a result, a lot of guys misread him. They thought he was doing everything for the media. In some ways, he was. He wanted the media to focus on him so the players could just go out and play. It's an old managerial trick, but one that doesn't always work.

I remember that when we showed up for spring training in 1980, the clubhouse was full of signs with big red letters reading, WE, NOT I. All the veterans rolled their eyes at this one. But Dallas knew that he had to do something to shake us up. We hadn't made it over the hump in our three playoff series, and we'd been pretty bad in '79. "We, not I" became our big slogan. Dallas, who once described the 1980 team as twenty-five different players who couldn't stand each other, did what he had to. A lot of guys didn't take well to Dallas, but hey, it worked. I've heard it said that it was our hatred of Dallas that made us win the World Series title. I don't think I'd go that far, but Dallas knew how to poke us in the right places to get results.

We had a team meeting on August 10 between games of a doubleheader where Dallas really got through to us. We were 56-52 at the time, and Pittsburgh was in the process of sweeping us in a four-game series. It was our worst stretch of the season, putting us in third place, six games out.

Our season was sort of on the line. Dallas just yelled at everybody. He just got in everybody's face, called everyone out, challenging our character. As a player I had been in lots of meetings, but most of them were bullshit. This one was real. It was like a slap in the face. It was so rough that reliever Ron Reed had to be restrained from going after Dallas right then and there. What Dallas was saying went right to the core. Sometimes it's not what's being said as much as it is who's saying it and when they're saying it. By this time of the year, Dallas had earned a lot of respect. We all knew he was real and wasn't just a blowhard. So after the meeting, we went out and won eight of nine, including five in a row from the pitiful Mets. But it still wasn't smooth sailing. A few weeks later, GM Paul Owens, known as the Pope, came into the locker room and addressed the team. Pope cursed us out but good, and singled out Bowa and Maddox. He was ready to fight them, that's how steamed he was about our play. He and Dallas knew we could still put things together and win it.

Well, they were right. We went 21-7 down the stretch, and we won by one run an amazing fourteen times. We swept a four-game series with the Cubs to at least assure ourselves of a tie with Montreal, who were sweeping three games from the Cardinals. We went into the final series of the year at Olympic Stadium tied with the Expos, but we were confident. We had Rose, who never thought he'd lose, and we had Schmidt, who was having a career year with 48 homers and 121 RBIs. Schmidt was the hero—he hit game-winning homers in the first two games to clinch the division. The second one came in the top of the eleventh inning. I shut the Expos down in the bottom of the eleventh, and we had taken the NL East flag.

Dallas was instrumental in helping us learn how to deal with the friction on the team. There were a lot of stars, so there was a lot of friction—a combination of ego, talent, and frustration from too many losses. I remember one tense time in Houston. One of our better players had proclaimed himself to be a born-again Christian. Everybody knew that was a crock of shit, because he always had the finest women, especially in Chicago at the Playboy Club. So, we were in Houston, and this guy had imported a tomato from Chicago. Fine, fine, fine. Before his religious declaration, nobody had ever criticized him for any of his beef. (Some of the guys used other food groups when referring to women.)

But in Houston, he was in the clubhouse playing cards, and another one of the guys was starting to needle him: "Born-again Christian, my ass." The first guy started getting agitated, and the second guy kept coming on a little stronger, "Hey, born-again Christian, who's the beef you brought down from Chicago?" Before long, the first guy finally got fed up and jumped to his feet, turned the card table over, grabbed the second player by the neck, and had him under his arm. The Houston clubhouse has these columns, and he was about ready to smash his teammate's head into one of them, which would have killed him, when some of the guys pulled them apart and broke it up. That's how volatile our clubhouse was. Nothing was sacred. Not your religion. Not even your tomatoes.

A lot of people consider our NLCS with Houston the greatest playoff series of all time. The Astros were terrific that season and beat out the Dodgers by one game to win their first NL West title. Houston won 93 games behind twenty-game winner and knuckleballer Joe Neikro, my old teammate Nolan Ryan, and the young phenom J. R. Richard, who had an ERA of 1.90. It was a best-of-five series, and there wasn't a single calm moment. We won the opener 3-1 behind Lefty, who had won twenty-four games in 1980 to lead the league. Down 1-0, Luzinski hit a two-run homer in the bottom of the sixth off Ken Forsch, who went the distance for the Astros. Strangely enough, that would turn out to be the only home run hit during the entire series. We scored another in the seventh, and I came on in the eighth to get the save. After that, each of the remaining four games went to extra innings. With the score tied at 3-all in the top of the tenth, Houston scored four runs and tied up the series with a 7-4 in Game Two.

The next three games would be at the Astrodome, which was a tough place for a visiting team to come into and win—at least for a visiting team used to playing on grass. We played on artificial turf at the Vet so it didn't really bother us. My buddy Larry Christenson pitched six shutout innings before giving way to Dickie Noles in the seventh. I came on in the eighth, finished it out, then pitched scoreless ball in the ninth and tenth. Joe Neikro pitched ten scoreless innings for the Astros—a terrific performance. In the top of the eleventh, Joe Morgan led off with a triple, and then I gave up the sacrifice fly to Denny Walling that lost the game, 1-0. We were on the brink of elimination again. For a team that had lost in the NLCS three times before, we were desperate. I think we would have been tarred and feathered and run out of town on a rail if we didn't bring back a pennant this time!

Houston was up by 2-0 when we scored three runs in the top of the eighth to take a 3-2 lead. Houston scratched back for a run against Warren Brusstar to tie the game, and we once again headed to extra innings. Pete Rose singled, and then Greg Luzinski doubled. With the score tied 3-3, Rose made the kind of play he'd been acquired for—bowling over Astros catcher Bruce Bochy at the plate to break the tie. Manny Trillo doubled in the last run of the game and we wound up winning 5-3. I closed it out in the tenth for my second save of the series.

Then came the dramatic Game Five. We were down 5-2 after seven and facing Nolan Ryan, who was merely 112-3 when he had a lead in the eighth. Well, we made it 112-4 because we scratched for five runs off of him, Joe Sambito, and Ken Forsch to take a 7–5 lead. I almost blew it by giving up two in the bottom of the eighth to tie the game again. But then in the tenth, Garry Maddox got a huge double that drove in Del Unser—who had rejoined the Phillies after we had been traded for each other—with the winning run to give Philadelphia its first pennant since 1950. Mets broadcaster Ralph Kiner had a great line about Garry that I'd like to repeat here: "Two-thirds of the earth is covered by water; the other third by Garry Maddox." To this day, Garry is a hero in Philly for that hit and I am not a goat. Thank you, Garry.

I got off a couple of good lines after we beat Houston. The tense series was filled with great plays and incredible swings, and I said, "It was like riding through an art gallery on a motorcycle." It was a good thing we won. If we had lost again, when the team plane landed in the City of Brotherly Love we would have faced a pretty un-Brotherly greeting— "A machine-gun pillbox set up at the airport." Manned by our fans, no doubt.

After losing to the New York Yankees in the playoffs in 1976, 1977, and 1978, the Kansas City Royals swept the Yanks in the 1980 ALCS to win the franchise's first pennant. We opened the Series in Philadelphia and won the first two games. And we did it in nine innings both times. The Royals had jumped out to an early 4-0 lead from a pair of two-run homers by Willie Mays Aikens—you think his parents wanted him to be a baseball player?—off of starter Bob Walk. We broke out for five runs in the bottom of the third to take the lead, powered by a three-run homer by Bake McBride. We added single runs in the fourth and fifth. Amos Otis got to me for a two-run homer in the top of the eighth, but I hung in there and got the save as we won 7-6.

Lefty got the start in Game Two and had a 2-1 lead until

giving up three in the seventh. Dan Quisenberry, the Royals' relief ace, was brought in to save it. He led the AL with thirty-three saves in 1980, along with a 12-7 record. He wasn't a big strikeout guy, but his unorthodox sidearm/underhand delivery was tough on hitters. But we jumped on him for four runs, including a pinch hit double by Del Unser and another double by Schmitty.

So we were up two games to none when the Series moved out to KC. Rufus—Dick Ruthven—pitched nine strong innings, but despite a homer by Schmitty, we couldn't overcome homers by George Brett—who flirted with batting .400 all summer before ending the year at an outstanding .390—and Amos Otis. The game was 3-all going into the tenth. So I came in and tossed a little gasoline on the fire. With Willie Wilson on base, Willie Aiken hit his first major league triple to win the game, pinning the loss on me, 4-3.

Home field advantage held in Game Four. Willie Aikens again hit two homers in the game, becoming the first player to have two multiple homer games in the same Series. LC—Larry Christenson—lasted only a third of an inning. Dallas and the coaching staff knew he was injured but threw him out there anyway. Dennis Leonard and Quisenberry shut us down to give KC the game, 5-3.

Game Five was another nail-biter. We were down 3-2 in the top of the ninth, with Schmitty on base. Del Unser came through in the pinch again, doubling Mike home to tie it up. Then Manny Trillo singled off of Quisenberry to send in the the go-ahead run. I pitched three scoreless innings, and after loading the bases in the bottom of the ninth, I struck out Jose Cardenal to get the win. No wonder Rolaids sponsored the award for the Fireman of the Year.

Now we were heading back to Philly, up 3-2 with two chances to win the Series. The last month of the season and in the playoffs I had pitched in something like 17 out of 26 or 27 games. I was worn down. By the time Game Six of the World Series came around, whenever I would throw certain pitches, especially the screwball, I felt like I was banging my elbow on the corner of a table. I had to be careful because I knew I had only a limited amount of pitches left, especially the screwball. And I knew we wouldn't be there if I didn't have the screwball.

In the eighth inning I came in to relieve Lefty, who had pitched great. We were winning 4-0, although he left me two men on. I gave up a run on a sacrifice but got out of the inning without another run scoring. As I went to the mound for the ninth, Dallas said "You all right?"

I said, "Yeah, I'll be all right." I didn't know I was going to have to throw another fifty pitches, or whatever it turned out to be. At the time I was all right. But, shit, the next thing you know I had the bases loaded and one out. I had struck out Amos Otis on a screwball—always important to get the leadoff hitter in every inning. Then I walked Willie Aikens on a 3-2 count. Onix Concepcion pinch ran for Aikens and went to second on a slicing base hit to right by Jon Wathan. And then the seventeen-year veteran Jose Cardenal lined a single to center. At that point I was close to calling Dallas and having him come and get me. I didn't want to give up a slammer, especially to Willie Wilson, a guy who had struck out eleven times in the Series at that point.

The thing that gave me hope was the pop-up by Frank White. With one out, White hit it over by our dugout. Our catcher, Bob Boone, chased after it even though it would normally be the first baseman's ball. But Boonie never heard Pete Rose yell for it. He was looking all around, thinking, "Where's Pete, where's Pete?" With no Pete, Boonie reached out to catch it, and it popped out of his glove. The ball started to go down into the dugout—it was going to be another devastating error in the cursed Phillies history—

until, all of a sudden, Pete was right there, Charlie Hustle on the spot. Pete stuck out his glove and cradled it before it could touch the ground. Man, if anybody played harder than Pete Rose, he had to be an outpatient. It was unbelievable! Anyway, we were one out away, and Boonie brought the ball over to me on the mound and said, "Tuggles, isn't this exciting?"

I said, "Boonie, you sure talk funny when you're nervous."

Everybody's different when it comes to nerves. When I get to the point where I'm at the limit of my physical and mental capabilities, I get acutely aware of everything that's going on around me. Some people are just the opposite. But I'm a sponge soaking it all in. When I get ready to take my sign and it's time to do my job, then all of a sudden it's zoom, I can focus. If I focus too soon, then I'm going to waste energy. So I notice everything. With two out in the ninth, the Philadelphia police started bringing these huge horses out. There were horses and dogs all over the stadium that night, but they didn't want to bring them out too soon because we've already had plenty of excuses for losing in the last ninety-seven years and the mayor didn't want to take the hit if we somehow managed to blow this thing. So he waited until the last possible minute that he could, and finally he gave the green light for the horses and dogs.

The canine corps had been around our bullpen during the game. It was getting real crowded in there. Even though I had a seat on the bullpen bench, I had left my glove over by one of the mounds. A German shepherd was lying down over there and had gotten comfortable by using my glove for a pillow. The phone rang in the seventh when Lefty started to get in trouble the first time, and Dallas said, "Get McGraw up." I went over to the mound and reached for my glove. The dog was now awake, and when I went to reach for my glove, he showed me his big German shepherd teeth. I said to one of the canine cops, "Can you help me get my glove? I kind of need it." He said, "No problem," and got the dog up. I got my glove and started tossing, although Lefty got out of the seventh without my help.

That was the beginning of the experience with the dogs and the horses. I noticed them again just before Willie Wilson came to bat in the ninth. I was standing on the mound watching a horse over by the warning track in foul territory. It was ready to handle the crowd of almost 66,000 when we won. All of a sudden this horse lifts its tail and drops a big mud pie. Right there. A strange sight to see before pitching the final out of the World Series, you know. I saw that happen, and I just thought "Hmm, if I don't get out of this inning, that's what I'm going to be in this city. I'm going to be horse shit."

Since it was final out time and the bases were still loaded, we needed a plan. Boonie asked, "How are we going to handle Wilson?" Even though Willie Wilson was having a tough time at the plate in the Series, he'd batted .326 during the season and led the majors in hits with 230. He was fast, too.

I said, "Well, I don't have any screwballs left, and he's looking for a screwball. The only thing I can think of is if we start him off with a screwball, and get it in his head, and then after that, he doesn't get any more." Boone thought that was a good idea, so he got behind the plate and he put down the signs for curveball, slider, fastball—he put down about four or five pitches—and then finally he wiggled his fingers, calling for the screwball. He kept wanting me to shake, shake, shake. By then Wilson must have been thinking, "I have no idea what he is going to throw me." So even though he probably knew he was going to get a screwball, we tried to plant a seed of doubt. I threw the screwball. Hurt like hell. Strike one. So it's time to do the same old song and dance. This time Boonie puts down screwball, screwball, screwball. Wiggling four fingers each time. I keep shaking my head.

Then he put down slider, and I threw a slider down and in. Wilson fouled it off his foot. For a pitcher, you can't hope for any better than that. You got a guy down 0-2 and he just fouled one off his feet. He's in pain.

I got the ball back, took some deep breaths, and got back on the rubber. Boonie did the screwball thing again, and I kept shaking him off, and then finally he put down fastball and I wanted a fastball up high, under his chin. I just want to shave his little Adam's apple. I wanted to get in his world a little bit. I felt like I could and I had a ball to waste. It turned out I was too confident because I tried to hurry the pitch, and the ball drifted out over the plate. It was a real meatball. He could have hit that out, but he didn't. It was a blessing he just took it for ball one.

I'm a little shaken up now. So I'm thinking to myself, "Look for a sign that this is going to work out." I've got Willie Wilson up there, bases loaded, ninth inning, World Series on the line. I need a strikeout.

At that point Boonie starts walking out to the mound. I hoped he had the answer to that last pitch—I was clueless. My eyes were big as pancakes, looking to Boonie for . . . something. Boonie, of course, had no clue either, and he was coming out to see if I knew what had happened. When he got to the mound, it was like, "Yeah? Well?" And all Boonie could say was "It was high." We just looked at each other, and I broke out laughing. Boonie was dumbfounded at my reaction, and he started laughing, too. Then, before the umpire could come out and ask us what was going on, Boonie turned around and headed back to the plate, laughing and shaking his head.

Although Bob had broken the tension, I was still desperately looking for a sign everywhere other than from my catcher. I'm looking for spiritual signs. Anything. I look over by Dallas in the dugout and again there are the dogs.

There is a German shepherd and a cop standing there, ready for crowd control. I think to myself, "It is a canine corps and I need a strikeout." How about that? "Canine—that's K-9. This is the ninth inning and I need a K—the baseball score sheet mark for strikeout." And there it was, there was my sign. It was beautiful. It was almost as if somebody shot me with adrenaline.

By this point Boonie, who'd played the entire Series on a bad ankle, has gotten back down there, and this time he puts the fastball sign down right away. Instead of shaking it, I said yeah, but this time I remembered to get my elbow up. I came right out over the top and had a little hop on that last John Jameson fastball. The rest is history. I have watched that final pitch and my celebration after it a thousand times, and I will tell you, I never get tired of seeing that pitch. And I won't, at least as long as Willie keeps swinging and missing. That was his twelfth strikeout of the Series, setting a record.

It was actually a pretty good fastball but they said it was the slowest pitch ever thrown in Philadelphia. It took ninety-seven years to get there. It was the end of an incredible journey. As I said at the time, "I get the feeling that W. C. Fields is out of his grave tonight celebrating with us. I gotta believe that even old Ben Franklin is turning over in his grave."

I had no idea that down in a little town in northeast Louisiana, two young boys, Tim and his close buddy Lance, were staying up each night during that 1980 World Series and privately rooting for me and the Phillies. Because everyone else in the house was asleep, they had to sit quietly in the dark, the volume on the TV turned down, to watch the action.

When I threw that final strike, Tim was loving it. He knew I was his dad—even if I hadn't acknowledged it—and I was sitting on top of the world. He was enjoying the moment with me.

Then, as the champagne was flowing in the Philadelphia clubhouse and the reporters were circling around, I was asked on television how I felt about the moment. I babbled on and on, then ended it by saying I couldn't have done it without my family. "I want to mention them," I said. "Thanks to my wife, Phyllis, my son Mark, and my daughter, Cari. You're the best!"

Fifteen hundred miles south, Tim got up quietly, walked over, and turned the TV off. He went to bed without saying a word to Lance. I had crushed him once again.

The pitch to Willie Wilson would have been the perfect storybook way to end my career, but at thirty-six I wasn't ready to retire from something I loved doing and that paid me so well. I wanted a four-year contract so I could pitch until I was forty at least. I thought I could do it. I didn't realize that the following season I was going to have elbow problems. Plus, the players went on strike in the middle of the '81 season, so it was a strange season. We were in first place at the time of the strike, and when the season ended up being split in half, we knew we were in the postseason. We ended up in a division series with Montreal—the team that came in first in the second half. Home field advantage held when the Expos won the first two at Olympic Stadium and we won the next two at the Vet. I pitched the last three innings of Game Four and got the win when George Vukovich hit a pinch walk-off homer to set up a decisive fifth game. We had our ace, Steve Carlton, on the mound going up against Montreal's ace, Steve Rogers, who'd bested Lefty in Game One. Rogers did it again, throwing a six-hit shutout and ending our efforts to defend our championship. Montreal ended up losing to, yes, the Dodgers—who had beaten Houston in the

AP/Wide World Photos

I'd rather be in Philadelphia. I haven't thrown a pitch for my new team yet, and I'm already being visited by pretty fans. Actually, it's Phillies secretary Barbara Conroy visiting me in the hospital after my shoulder surgery. I'm demonstrating on a baseball-shaped yo-yo that I can now turn my arm over to throw the screwball.

AP/Wide World Photos

Want a ride? I bicycled from Philly to Clearwater, Florida, for spring training in 1978 with my pal Larry Christenson (left). Also along for the crazy ride were Steve Carlton, Jerry Martin, and the Eagles' Roman Gabriel.

AP/Wide World Photos

Kiss me, I'm a Phillie! I loved celebrating St. Patrick's Day during spring training. The Phillies' handy zipper-front uniform allows me to reveal to manager Danny Ozark that I believe the Phils can go all the way in '79. So I was a year off....

AP/Wide World Photos

The Cheshire Tug. At the Astrodome before Game Three of the 1980 NLCS. I had a good feeling about things….

AP/Wide World Photos

Blast off. I've never jumped as high as I did when the Phillies won the 1980 pennant. I guess the defeats in '76, '77, and '78 made it that much more exciting. It was also the first Phillies pennant in thirty years.

Sports Illustrated

Houston, we have a problem. Manager Dallas Green gives me the mission—beat the Astros. Mike Schmidt and Bob Boone are there to lend support.

Sports Illustrated

Sweet! Phillies Hall of Fame broadcaster Harry Kalas (left) will have to wait his turn for a taste of the bubbly. First, I'm going to have a swig. Broadcaster Richie Ashburn has already sampled it.

AP/Wide World Photos

Norman Y. Lono, *Philadelphia Daily News*

Glove save! It's the top of the ninth, bases loaded—again— with one out. Frank White's high foul pop-up pops out of catcher Bob Boone's mitt. But Pete Rose hustles over to save the day, and now there are two outs.

Whew. Game Six of the 1980 World Series. Eighth inning. Royals batter Hal McRae is out at first to get me out of a bases-loaded jam. The fans weren't the only ones experiencing heart palpitations.

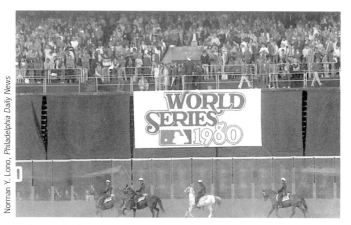

Norman Y. Lono, *Philadelphia Daily News*

Where's Seabiscuit? Mounted police and K-9 units begin to ring the field in the top of the ninth. I was both worried and inspired by them.

One for the ages. I've just struck out Willie Wilson to win the Series. The thrill was unbelievable. After all, I didn't play in the '69 Series, and I lost in '73. So to be on the mound was very special—the high point of my career.

AP/Wide World Photos

W. R. Everly III, Philadelphia Daily News

The pride of Broad Street. Waving to the fans during the victory parade with Pete Rose and Larry Bowa.

Sports Illustrated

We Win! The headline of the *Philadelphia Daily News* says it all.

AP/Wide World Photos

Joy in Philly, but none in Mudville. In November 1980 I performed "Casey at the Bat" with the Philly Pops, conducted by Peter Nero. Hammy? Nah.

Courtesy of Tug McGraw

Hey, this stuff really works. Sipping from the Fountain of Youth, no doubt the source of my nineteen seasons in the big leagues. The fountain was running dry by 1984.

Corbis

I'll miss you guys! I say good-bye to the big leagues after nineteen years in my retirement press conference on February 14, 1985. I retired on Valentine's Day because it symbolized my love affair with baseball. All right, I did ham up this one.

Courtesy of Tug McGraw

When the cheering stops. I went on television, of course. I spent seven years as a reporter for WPVI Channel 6 in Philadelphia, but never really felt comfortable in the job.

Courtesy of Tug McGraw

Life of the party. Here, I felt comfortable. Having a ball at Mardi Gras in 1990 with New Orleans resident and former teammate Ron Swoboda (far right). Ron and I hit it off as roommates on the '65 Mets. He taught me how to spit beer through my front teeth, and I taught him two new words for women's breasts—blorts and watatas.

Courtesy of Tug McGraw

I only saved games, not lives. But the Philadelphia Fire Department saw fit to award me for my support of the firefighters and the city.

Would you like fries with that? I always did love to cook, and I planned to open my own restaurant.

Courtesy of Tug McGraw

And now, heeeeere's Tug! Sometimes, when I spoke at an event, I felt the need to wear a funny hat…

Courtesy of Tug McGraw

Courtesy of Tug McGraw

…or jump in a vat of grapes…

…or pump my fist in the air one more time and shout, "Ya gotta believe!"

Courtesy of Tug McGraw

Courtesy of Tug McGraw

Fine produce. Sampling the "tomatoes" competing in the English Leather Calendar Girl Challenge at the Showboat in Atlantic City.

You had a grand opening, and everything went wrong? Next time, call me.

You did what? Next time, call me! I posed for an ad hyping the promotion company I'd set up with Diane.

Courtesy of Tug McGraw

I guess we really do look alike. Tim and me.

Courtesy of Tug McGraw

Courtesy of Tug McGraw

Enjoying the good life. Maybe a little too much. Having a drink with Bull, Phillies slugger Greg Luzinski, in 2000.

H. Lee Moffitt Cancer Center & Research Institute

X-rays of McGraw's head show nothing. Unfortunately, this was not the case. Dr. Steven Brem, M.D., of the Moffitt Center in Tampa, operated on my noggin for six hours to remove my brain tumor.

Duke University, Medical Center

I gotta believe. Dr. Henry Friedman, Mets fan and miracle worker at Duke University.

Associated Press

We believe. Phillies manager Larry Bowa in front of a sign during spring training, 2003. It was the beginning of an outpouring of affection from the fans.

On the road again. I signed so many autographs over the years, maybe it's time to start collecting them. Only a month after my brain surgery and Willie Nelson signed my tambourine.

Courtesy of Tug McGraw

Associated Press

You apply pressure to the seam here to throw the screwball.... I'm showing off my new bald look and my baseball-like scar at a press conference at the Vet on May 29, 2003.

Laurie L. Hawkins

I think I have more hair, Matt. NBC's Matt Lauer sits with me and my son Matthew in the dugout at the Vet. We taped a segment for the *Today* show that would air on July 3, 2003.

Courtesy of the New York Mets

Home, James. The current #45 on the Mets, lefty screwball reliever John Franco, drives me in from the Shea bullpen to throw out the first ball in a pregame ceremony celebrating the thirtieth anniversary of the 1973 "Ya Gotta Believe!" Mets.

Associated Press

Vet countdown… Matthew helps me change the sign on the outfield fence counting down the games remaining before Veterans Stadium is torn down. The Phillie Phanatic looks on.

Courtesy of Tug McGraw

Can I borrow a comb? Me and Hank during my fifty-ninth birthday party on August 30, 2003. My hair is starting to grow back. Hank has never had that particular problem. I love this photo because it makes me look taller than him!

Jennifer Brusstar

On the Road. I didn't have Jack Kerouac with me on my cross-country RV trip in November 2003, but I did have loyal friend John McManus.

Jennifer Brusstar

Two cool dudes.

West's division series. And this time it was the Dodgers who got over the hump and beat the Yankees in the World Series.

Even though I led the team in saves in '81, I really wasn't back up to speed until the end of '82, but by then the calls to "get McGraw up" were less frequent. I saved just five games in 1982 and none in thirty-four appearances in 1983, when Al Holland became the new relief ace in town, racking up twenty-five saves. I was still pretty good but not good enough. When we won the NL East that year, I was left off the active postseason roster. I just sat and watched us beat the Dodgers in four games for the pennant, and then sat and watched us win the World Series opener in Baltimore—the same team I didn't pitch against in my first World Series fourteen years earlier—before losing the next four straight. I made twenty-five more appearances in 1984, but that was it. At age thirty-nine, after nineteen big league seasons, I retired with a 96-92 record, 180 saves, and a 3.13 ERA.

Not to mention two World Series rings.

CHAPTER 13

Last Call

It had been more than five years since I last saw Betty and Tim, who was now seventeen and beginning his senior year of high school. Over the years, Tim had sent me letters care of the Phillies main office and even left a few messages, but I never responded. One time he wrote me a letter while he was sitting on the side of the road down in Louisiana. There he was, sixteen and sweating in the sun's heat because his car was broken down, and he wanted me to know how wrong it was that I was his millionaire biological father and that he had a worthless car and no way to get to school. I could definitely feel his rage.

I just was sure there was no chance this was my son—heck, he really didn't look like I remembered looking as a twelve-year-old—and I just sensed this boy was being set up for a big letdown.

As Tim grew up, Betty never contacted me demanding child support or recognition for Tim, but one day her mother's threat of "We'll see you in court" came calling.

In the fall of 1984, Tim was starting to think about college. Betty had remarried and divorced her second husband and had to work two jobs to make ends meet and take care of her family. She had always told Tim that she didn't want to ask me for money or cause any problems out of fear that it would affect my career and make me resent Tim. Evidently, she had still hoped that one day I would be somewhat of a father figure to Tim and that he and I would have a relationship. She always gave me more consideration and credit than I deserved. Tim was a respectful young man who listened to his mother—until February 14, 1985, when he saw in the newspaper that I had announced my retirement.

"Mom, didn't you tell me the reason you never asked Tug for child support is because you didn't want to bother his career?" Tim asked. "Well, he announced his retirement today, and college is coming and I don't want you to have work another job to send me to college. Why don't you ask him to send me?" Betty told Tim she would look into the idea even though she still didn't feel comfortable asking me for anything. Over the years I had never even called to ask how they were or to see if Tim needed anything, so she had no reason to think that I would help now. But at Tim's insistence, Betty wrote, asking me to finally step up and help send Tim to college.

I chose to ignore the request, hoping everything would go away—so Betty found another way to get my attention. I heard her loud and clear when I received notification papers from the State of Louisiana claiming I owed more than $350,000 in back child support. By now Tim was halfway through his senior year of high school and she was getting concerned that he wouldn't be able to go to college in the fall. Betty had gone to the Department of Family Services in Louisiana, showed them Tim's birth certificate with my name on it and a newspaper article detailing my $1.5 million contract for my last season, and come up with an amount for seventeen years of unpaid child support. Let me tell you, that sort of mail will certainly dull your buzz! So in typical Tug McGraw fashion, I called someone and told him to handle it. I had a Boston-based business manager at the time, and I had his law firm contact Betty.

They did and asked her to explain the logic behind her claim for back child support. She told them that if they worked for me and I told them to call her, then I must have told them what this was about. Betty was tough that way. She is a very sweet lady but when backed into a corner, she'll kick your ass.

"Is there proof that this is Tug's child?" the lawyer asked Betty.

"You could look at him," Betty responded.

"But is there documentation?" the lawyer pressed.

"No, but I know he's the father and Tug knows he's the father," she explained. Betty told the lawyer that she was working two jobs to take care of her family and that Tim was a straight-A student and deserved to go to college. She felt that she had raised Tim for seventeen years and now it was my turn.

My lawyer asked Betty if we could settle this out of court, and she told him that she never wanted to go to court—if she did, she would have filed papers years ago. She just wanted Tim to be able to go to college. After a while Betty and the lawyer decided to come up with some figures for Tim's schooling and began to negotiate back and forth on numbers and stipulations. Tim wanted to go to both undergrad and law school, so Betty asked for seven years of college tuition, spending money, and a car for Tim. Betty came up with a figure of $42,000 for the seven years. My lawyer nixed the car. Everyone agreed on the total for the settlement, and my lawyer drew up the papers for Tim and Betty to sign, but the lawyer added one extra clause.

Upon the signing of the papers and receiving the results of a paternity test to determine if I was indeed Tim's father, Tim could never contact me or my family again or use the name McGraw. I never really read the contract closely, and although it was in there, I never realized what the clause truly said or how hurtful it was until years later. And while it angered me that it happened, it adds to my amazement of Tim. It's hard to imagine why he still wanted to see me after having to read that.

Tim read the contract and agreed to the terms, but he had a clause of his own to add. Tim wanted to meet me face-to-face one more time before he would agree never to contact me again. I don't know why Tim asked for that final visit. It may have been to punch me in the nose, or it may have been to say good-bye, but either way I once again found myself heading to Houston to meet Betty and Tim. Even though I was retired now and didn't have a game in Houston, it seemed to be neutral territory for us all. So off I went with my agent, Phil McLaughlin. At the time Phil handled my speaking and other engagements and had negotiated my contract with WPVI, Philadelphia's ABC affiliate, which I was now working for. More important, I knew I could trust him.

I was standing in the hotel lobby with Phil when he spotted Tim and Betty. I had my back to the elevators, so I didn't see them coming.

"Tuggy," Phil said. "Here comes your son." Phil could tell just by watching Tim, who was now six feet tall, walk across the lobby. Phil said that my walk, that hop I do, was in Tim's step, making the resemblance impossible to miss. Once I turned around and saw Tim, I knew that he was my boy. Right then and there I told the lawyers to cancel the DNA tests because there was no doubt that Tim was my son. I was shocked at how much he had grown—I was still expecting a young boy to be standing there with Betty. Instead it was as if I was looking at a picture of myself twenty years earlier. The resemblance was striking. Tim and I shared mannerisms and similarities that could only be explained by genetics.

We all went to lunch—Tim, Betty, Phil, and me. Phil was not too happy with me being so open about Tim being my son. In his mind the deal was signed and sealed, and my open admission of Tim being my son was going to cost me more money and ruin their negotiated settlement. But I never worried about money. Hell, I'd sign anything someone put in front of me—no matter what it would cost.

During lunch I tried to find out more about Tim and what he was planning to do with college. I had heard through the lawyers that he had received a full scholarship, and being the one-track-minded jock I was, I just assumed that it was for sports.

"Tim, I understand that you have some scholarship offers?"

"Yes, sir."

"Baseball?"

"No, sir."

"Is it for basketball?"

"No, sir."

"Is it for academics?"

"No, sir. It's for music."

Now imagine my surprise and confusion at this point. I had never heard of a scholarship for music. What the hell did that mean? "Music?" I asked. "I didn't know you played anything."

"I don't. I sing."

"They give scholarships for singing? Wow, he's going to be a singing lawyer," I joked to my attorney, who looked like he could've choked me at this point for quashing the paternity test and risking our agreement. "You must have gotten that from your mother's side because I couldn't carry a tune in a bucket," I told him, even though I sang a role in *The Gondoliers* by Gilbert and Sullivan in high school. After lunch and a few hours of talking, I wanted to get to know Tim better. What a likable guy he was.

Looking for ways to spend more time with him, I suggested we play some tennis. Tim had never played tennis and in fact I had to buy him tennis shoes and shorts and a racket at the mall, since all he had on was jeans, a shirt, and cowboy boots. While on the court, Tim gave me a run for my money and certainly wasn't holding back when he pounded the ball back across the net. In the meantime, my lawyer stood on the side staring at me, wondering how I gave up the deal he had negotiated without a blood test. You gotta love lawyers—always looking out for you. I guess the lawyer realized that I no longer needed him, so he took off. Betty decided to go shopping so that Tim and I could go to dinner to talk by ourselves.

At dinner Tim and I decided that we would never look back and always move forward with our relationship. Again I asked him what he wanted out of all of this, and he said he "just wanted someone he could call Dad who knew they were my dad."

I said, "Well, I am the one, I am your dad." I must admit that if I were in his shoes I might not have been so understanding after all my years of blatant denial. No calls, no birthday or Christmas cards, no regard for him whatsoever. But he was willing to give our future a chance, and from that point on I was Tim's dad and he was my son.

It felt good to finally get it out in the open. Tim was such a wonderful kid that I wondered what I had done to deserve his persistence. If it hadn't been for his insistence on our "final" meeting, we wouldn't have been there that night beginning a relationship. Over the course of dinner, Tim and I talked about his college plans, his life back in Start, Louisiana, and sports. I learned something I had never heard before: Tim lettered in five sports in high school—football, basketball, baseball, track, and, of all things, rodeo. I didn't know you could letter in rodeo and still don't understand it.

After dinner we headed back to the hotel to tell Betty about our deal. I had downed a few drinks and was feeling pretty good.

"Betty," I told her with my arms around Tim, "Tim and I have come to an agreement."

"And what is that?" Betty asked.

"Tim's my son and I'm his dad."

"No kidding," Betty said in a sarcastic voice, as if she hadn't been telling me this for seventeen years and all of a sudden I heard her.

"I want this boy in my life. He's wonderful. He likes sports like me, he likes everything like me. Now I have to figure out how to handle this and tell my family, but I want him in my life," I told her. "And don't worry about college; I'll be here for him. You can just throw out those papers. That is lawyer talk. I'll take care of it."

Betty smiled, we all hugged, but she added: "If you don't mind I'll still hold on to these papers." I guess she wanted to make sure that I was really going to live up to my promise to Tim before she threw out the signed agreement. She was cautious, skeptical even, and given my history with her, I don't blame her.

After Tim and Betty left for Louisiana, I had to figure out how I was going to tell Phyllis that Tim was definitely my son and that I wanted him to be a part of our family. Now don't get me wrong—it's not like I was expecting to bring him into the Cleaver home. I hadn't exactly been there for my other two kids, so Phyllis was definitely wondering what I planned to change. I would also have to decide how to break this news to Mark and Cari. I never told them that they may have a half brother out there somewhere, and Hallmark didn't exactly make cards for this type of occasion. I wasn't sure how they would handle this. They could be really pissed, accept him, or even worse, resent him and our relationship.

Phyllis was fine with my acceptance of Tim. She even told me that had she seen a picture of him years ago, she would've known that Tim was mine and would have forced me to be a part of his life. She had always thought that some of the things I said to Tim were too harsh for a young boy. But she stayed out of it—I guess she figured that was my business.

A month or so later Betty sent me an invitation to Tim's high school graduation, but I didn't think it was a good idea for me to go. I was afraid that my being there would take some of the spotlight off Tim. At least that's what I told him. I know that Tim really wanted me there but I just didn't think it was best for me to go. Of course, looking back on it, I wish I had gone. Tim was the salutatorian of his graduating class and even gave a speech. He had his mom, his sisters, and Betty's parents there. Tim was a strong, secure young man and didn't need an "atta boy" from me—he hadn't received any so far and was doing just fine.

The summer came and went, and I hadn't really spoken with Tim. By now he had started his first semester at Northeast Louisiana University in Monroe, and I sent him tuition and spending money as promised. I later learned that Tim used the spending money on his mother and his sisters. He bought his mom a nice gift and took his sisters shopping. That was how Tim was—always generous and thinking of other people.

That winter I decided to look for a way to introduce Tim to Mark and Cari and to see if we could build this into a fun—if not a little weird—family. I told Phyllis that it was time to let the cat out of the bag and tell the kids. I was going to Florida to visit friends at spring training in a few weeks, so Phyllis and I decided that that would be a good time for Tim to meet our family.

I called Betty and asked if Tim and a friend would like to come down to Florida on his spring break and meet my family down at the Phillies training camp in Clearwater, Florida. I wanted Tim to bring a friend in case he didn't get along with Mark and Cari. I figured if Tim had a friend there, his buddy could serve as a buffer and absorb some of the friction. She said she thought it was about time and that Tim would want to bring his friend Lance Butler. Lance and Tim had been friends for years and had been baseball and basketball teammates.

I had been invited by the Phillies to come down and work with a few minor league pitchers, so I figured there would be no better place for me to build a relationship with Tim than on a baseball field. Lance was a pretty good pitcher—he would go on to play in college—and he loved it, too. Evidently the guys were very excited and even joked that they were going to show all of the players how well they could pitch and play ball. Lance later told me Tim was actually more excited about meeting the other Phillies than he was about spending the week with me!

As the trip got closer I wrestled with how I was going to tell the kids about Tim. I tried to tell them before we left but just couldn't get up the nerve to do it. I told myself that I would tell them in the car so that I had a captive audience. We had a one-thousand-mile drive, so I had plenty of time to do it—but I waited until we were twenty minutes away from Clearwater, right before the exit. Phyllis knew I was stalling and I knew that I was running out of time, so I pulled the car over on the side of the highway and acted like I was getting out to check the ties on the Hobie Cat that we were towing. Once I got back in the car Phyllis looked at me and rolled her hands like "Spit it out" so I did, right there on the side of the highway.

"Mark, Cari," I began. "You have an older brother." I just threw them a fastball. I sat there and let them absorb what I said and waited for one of them to respond.

"You mean, he is not my only older brother?" Cari asked, pointing at Mark, who was sitting next to her in the car.

"Yeah. That's what this means, Cari."

"That is great! He's always badgering me, so I am glad that I have another older brother." Cari and Mark always fought, so she was happy to know that she had another brother.

Mark's reaction was that he was glad that he would no longer have the responsibility of being the older brother. I think he thought it was great that there was another one out there who would now be the oldest. Boy, Tim didn't know what he was getting into being the oldest of my children and joining this family—but he would soon find out. After we all talked about it for twenty minutes or so, I told the kids they'd be meeting him that weekend and that I hoped that they'd all get to know one another. "I would hate to think that our expanded family couldn't get along," I told them.

"I'm sure we'll get along, Dad," Cari piped in.

"We'll get along. He looks like me," Mark added.

I had brought a picture of Tim, which Betty had sent me years earlier, to show the kids. In a strange turn of events, years earlier Cari had found the photo and asked about it, and I had blown the question off.

"Cari," I asked, "do you remember when you found this picture and asked who this boy was? Well, that was your brother and this is a picture of him now—he's seventeen."

"Dad, he looks just like you!"

So after that bombshell we continued our trip to Clearwater and arrived at our rented condos. There was one for me, Phyllis, Mark, and Cari; one for Tim and Lance, so they would have their own place; and one owned by our friends Sonny and Mitzi Hepps. We'd known them since my early days with the Phillies, and they would watch our kids when we came down to spring training. Sonny is a very successful businessman—he had a large beer distributorship at the time. He's a few years older than me, about my size, but professorial-looking. Mitzi, his wife, is thin and petite. She's a great party giver and does a lot of community work with a school for troubled boys.

I didn't know how the weekend would go so I wanted Tim to have a place to escape to in case things went south. Since Sonny and Mitzi wintered in Florida, they were there, as they were every spring, and I hoped that having them around would make introducing everybody easier and create a comfortable atmosphere.

We got unpacked, parked the boat, and got ready for Tim to arrive. The next day we all went to the airport to pick up Tim and Lance. The kids made a game out of trying to see if they could pick out Tim as he was coming off the plane. Tim sauntered off the plane like he was a traveling pro even though it was only the second time he had ever flown. I heard later that he gave Lance some shit since it was Lance's first flight.

The "pick your brother" game wasn't too difficult. Right away you could see the resemblance between Tim and me. Mark and Cari saw it, too. It was weird but great to see all my kids finally together in the same room and they all seemed to be enjoying one another.

The week was a blast. We all went sailing and the conversation flowed. Tim and Lance were in heaven walking down

Clearwater beach at night and through the baseball park during the day. At the ballpark, I gave Tim a pair of the team's spikes and outfitted him like a Phillie prospect. He was like a kid at Christmas. And I was like a proud papa, introducing Tim to the Phillies players as my son—and enjoying the double takes my longtime teammates gave me. At the beach, the kids went out for a sail on the Hobie Cat without us grown-ups there to interfere. What an adventure.

After that meeting, I kept in touch with Tim but still wasn't even what anyone would call a part-time father. I called him from time to time at his fraternity house in college and even stayed at his frat house when I visited. Not that fraternity life was much different than my life in baseball—in fact I felt very at home there.

We saw each other every once in a while and went on a few trips over the years. Tim came to visit me in Philadelphia two or three times, met Hank and my father, Big Mac, and even came to Dad's seventy-fifth birthday party in Napa Valley, California. Tim went skiing with our family in upstate New York, and everyone just loved being around him. I even gave him one of my Major League Baseball All-Star rings, so he'd have a little something from my past that might create a link. On another occasion Tim and Lance were working with a baseball instructional camp for high school and younger kids down in Louisiana. Tim invited me to come down and work with the players. I not only came, I brought my brother, Hank, along. We were in our forties, but we hung with those college kids the entire time!

One time during his sophomore year, Tim and four or five of his buddies came over to Mississippi to meet me and catch an Ole Miss baseball game. I was doing an ESPN College Baseball broadcast and figured it was a good opportunity to hang out with Tim. I got him and his buddies a couple of rooms and we partied a little bit—drank some beers. We continued the party all the way down to New Orleans for Mardi Gras. He seemed to enjoy himself but we still had an arm's-length relationship. I guess it's hard to build an instant father-son relationship after missing out on almost eighteen years of his life.

I finally did get Tim that car he wanted—even if it was a few years after he asked. It wasn't a "manly" car like he wanted, though. It was a little Honda CRX. Tim was grateful and appreciative—not that I would expect anything less. He was raised that way and appreciated everything he had.

Tim doesn't give up easily. You can tell that by his career—and by his desire to make this relationship work. He's aggressive and intelligent and very understanding about other people. You put that combination together and you get a guy that's willing to take a second shot at anything—even me!

After that visit, Tim changed his name one last time. He became and would forever be Tim McGraw.

CHAPTER 14

Tim Goes to Nashville

As the years passed my life started to change more and more. By 1987 Phyllis and I were estranged. I had been retired for a few years and was starting to really miss my ball-playing days. I had no idea how much I thrived on being in the spotlight and being a major league ballplayer, and it really rocked my world when it all went away. But some of the biggest changes were on the horizon.

While I was still working on building a relationship with Tim during his first years of college, my relationship with my other kids became horribly challenging. Phyllis and I were separated and Mark and Cari felt, as most teenagers do, like they were caught in the middle.

Tim and I would talk now and then and I visited him at school a couple of times but it didn't seem like we had bonded yet. But as time went by and I started to see what kind of a kid Tim was, my fondness and fatherly pride began to grow. There's just something about Tim that makes you want to be around him. He's just so normal, which you couldn't say about most of my friends and family. My challenge was figuring out what to say when we were together and it, at times, actually made me nervous. I sometimes feared asking too many questions about his upbringing, because that eventually had to lead to the conversation I didn't want to have—the one where he looked me in the eye and said, "You should have been there."

I was running and gunning, working jobs all over the place, and didn't really give Tim much time. He'd call my secretary, Ernie, every once in awhile when he needed cash. He dropped out of college during his second year and moved to Florida to live in an apartment near his mother, working odd jobs and singing wherever he could. Frustrated by the pull of trying to pursue his music while still putting food on the table, he moved back to Louisiana and reenrolled in college.

That didn't last long. One day, in the middle of Tim's third year at Northeast Louisiana University, he made the decision to give up on higher education and go try to earn his master's degree in hard knocks.

Tim had been singing throughout college with a glee club called the Electones and had begun to realize that singing and performing were what really made him happy. Needless to say, that type of extracurricular behavior brought him quite a bit of razzing from his fraternity brothers. I had never understood the whole singing thing myself, although I think Tim's done a pretty good job of making me understand it now. Anyway, one day he went to the pawnshop there in Monroe and bought himself a guitar. He didn't know how to play a single chord but over the course of a few months he taught himself the basics. After a little while he began getting gigs in local bars and restaurants around campus and got to the point where he was actually pretty good. He even played his guitar around the campfire at my dad's seventy-fifth birthday party in California. People gathered around to listen to Tim sing and play. While it was obvious he had some talent, I remember thinking, "Don't quit your day job." At the time I thought even Hank's folksinging was better than Tim's. Well, maybe there is a musical gene somewhere on the McGraw side of things.

Tim would spend hours watching country music television shows and playing his guitar, and then one day he decided that it was time to drop out of school and take his chances in Nashville.

He called his mom and told her what he wanted to do, and she told him to chase his dreams. Betty always believed that you have to try something before you let it go, and she could tell this was something Tim needed to do. After talking with Betty, he laid his plans on me during a weekend visit during Mardi Gras in New Orleans. I tried to do the fatherly thing and I advised him to stay in school. Tim had a great comeback: "Didn't you drop out of school to go play baseball?" He had me. But to cap it off, he reminded me he had attended one more semester in college than I had!

So Tim sold all his stuff, including the car I gave him, packed his bags, and headed for Nashville. I thought that boy was nuts. That crazy stunt—taking off with no plan like that—made him even more of a McGraw in my eyes. That's something I would've done.

When Tim got to Nashville, he started working odd jobs to be able to eat and sang in local dives for about twenty dollars a night. He was amazingly focused and wasn't about to give up. He loved Nashville but it was very different from Monroe, Louisiana. He was broke, he loved playing his guitar and singing, and he wanted to make it badly enough to stick out the hard times.

Tim had managed to get a demo tape made and started

shopping around for record deals but to no avail. He sent me a copy of the cassette although I didn't know what I was supposed to do with it.

He was just starting to get frustrated when he caught a break. At a ten-year reunion dinner for the 1980 Phillies a few months later, I was seated next to a man named Bruce Wendell who was a big supporter of the team. Bruce had grown up in Philadelphia and had befriended a number of Phillies over the years. You can imagine what that 1980 championship meant to him, a huge fan. He loved our team and what that championship did for the city. During dinner we started talking, and he mentioned that he worked for a recording company, Curb Records. I saw an opportunity here so I offered him a ride back to his hotel.

Once in the car, I popped in Tim's demo tape, which I'd listened to already, and told Bruce that Tim was my son and that his tape was worth a listen. Within days Tim had a meeting with Bruce's recording company. After his first meeting, the label signed him—due to Tim's persistence. At the meeting, the company's vice president told Tim to leave his tape with him and they would give him a call. Tim insisted that he listen right then, and halfway through the song the vice president told Tim that he had a deal. They loved his demo and felt they had a star in him.

I was very proud of him, although I still didn't get the "I want to be a country star" thing. I knew that all Tim needed was a foot in the door and I was glad I could help him achieve his goal in some small way.

I believe it was fate that put Bruce Wendell at my table that night—it was meant to be, for Tim. Finally, after years of disappointment and rejection, Tim was actually able to benefit from being my son. Funny, isn't it, that it would take me until Tim was in his twenties to find something good I could bring to his life. On the autograph I signed for Mike

Borchetta, the Curb Records vice president who met with Tim, I wrote: "Mike: Ya gotta believe in Timmy." And he did.

Once signed with Curb, Tim began putting together his eight-member band and headed out on the road. I couldn't do much for him because this was a business I knew nothing about. But I bought him a van and a U-Haul trailer so they could start making a name for themselves by driving all over the south and southwest. All they worried about was putting gas in the van and trying to get a hit song.

They would play anything with a stage. Most of their gigs were in places that had bullet holes in the walls or at fairs where they sang on stages overlooking cow manure. If Tim's singing career could be equated to the early days of my baseball career, right then he would've barely been in the minor leagues. But it didn't matter to Tim where they sang or how many people they sang to—he would give it his all for five people just as he would for five hundred. This was his dream and he was determined to make it. Mike Borchetta used to tell Tim that he was the perfect act because all the girls wanted to date him, the guys wanted to hang out with him, and the women wanted to mother him.

On several occasions, especially later in his career when he was in the northeast, I'd make trips to see him play. Forget the music, I loved watching the crowd and listening to its reaction.

It's funny to think about now that he's achieved so much, but there was actually a stage in the early nineties when Tim needed gigs so bad he even enlisted me to help him find places to play. On one of those occasions, my friend Sonny Hepps and I went out and got a bar called Cheryl's Sky Lounge in Newcastle, Delaware, to put Tim up onstage. The place was a real dump—I don't think it even exists anymore. Sonny and I had a friend, Chris Whaley, who worked for Sonny at a liquor distributorship, and she helped us get

Cheryl's to sign Tim for a gig. The most amazing part of this story is what this dump demanded in order to put Tim onstage. They required Chris and her distributorship to ante up cases of free beer—and I had to agree to show and sign autographs—so that Tim could play! Imagine that. Forcing friends of a future superstar to offer free beer to get him to sing. Outrageous. Tim was a hit—and I even joined him onstage to sing "Hell Is the Price Tag for Loving You." Some might argue Tim should have sung that song to me! Amazingly, for all Tim did for business that night, the folks at Cheryl's demanded the same bribe when he came back and played there a few months later.

On another occasion in the early 1990s, Tim was invited to play a major picnic event in central Pennsylvania that was an annual fund-raiser for firefighters. I grabbed some friends and drove 120 miles over to watch him play for an hour, turned around, and drove back. They had a bunch of pictures on the wall of the pavilion of stars who had come through and played that event, including big names like Tammy Wynette. Tim looked at the wall and told his hosts there would be a day they'd put his name up there. He and I may have been the only ones that believed that.

After developing a great reputation while touring, Tim went to work in the studio cutting his first album. He wanted to pick his own songs and even put one of his touring favorites, "Indian Outlaw," on the first record but Curb told him no. Being a freshman artist, you don't have much of a say on your debut album, and unfortunately the critics didn't have much to say on it either. Tim's first single, "Welcome to the Club," released in 1992, was a flop. His 1993 self-titled debut album did a little better, and a couple of the songs became minor hits on the country charts, but he didn't like the songs and felt he'd barely gained any recognition for the album.

Tim began to get worried, and you could sense his desperation beginning to build. One of the executives at Curb even told him that he couldn't sing and that it might be better for him to pack up and go back to Louisiana, but Tim wouldn't listen. With the same persistence that led Tim through his life as a teenager and brought him to Nashville, Tim asked the recording company for one more chance—but he wanted it his way. Tim doesn't give up easily. He told them that since it was his career on the line, he wanted to produce the album and pick out his own songs, and he did. *Not a Moment Too Soon* was released on March 15, 1994— pretty close to St. Patrick's Day—and sold more than six million copies. It was a multiplatinum album, Billboard's bestselling country album of 1994, and the fifth bestselling album of the year of all genres. Of course, it hit number one.

"Indian Outlaw" by John D. Loudermilk, a song that Tim had been playing on the road for almost four years, was the first song released as a single from his second album. In what seemed like an overnight success, it became a huge hit. Tim was on the radio and had made his mark. But before we could all celebrate, controversy surrounded his single and it started being pulled from radio station rotation. Chief Wilma Mankiller of the Cherokee Nation took offense with Tim's song and a media frenzy ensued. They thought the lyrics were derogatory and offensive to Native Americans. Tim made a public apology, explaining that he never intended to upset anyone. From that day on his career took off. The coverage from that first song was enough to make Tim's name known in Nashville and across the country. His second song, "Don't Take the Girl," also climbed up the charts and helped Tim's album sales skyrocket. In 1994, he received a bunch of awards from country music critics, and within months Tim became a well-known country music artist— just like he believed he would be.

This is when the basis for my celebrity began to change. After years of being baseball player Tug McGraw, I became country music star Tim McGraw's dad. I couldn't have been more proud. We even cut a commercial together in 2000 making light of the transition we were going through. The national spot was for Bud Light, Tim's longtime sponsor, and featured a cop pulling Tim's tour bus over for speeding. When the cop came to the door, Tim was sitting behind the wheel of the bus. "You're Tug McGraw's kid," the officer said after Tim handed over his driver's license. "Your dad had the best screwball I ever saw. So you're a bus driver, huh? Well, not everyone can have an arm like Tug." Tim was rolling his eyes. We shot the commercial out in the California desert near Twentynine Palms, and it was a full day of laughter and good times. I appreciated Tim including me in the spot—I know he was throwing me a bone. And while I enjoyed the humor, I knew the torch already had been passed. Those cops who knew me and not him were far and few between.

I was doing a few motivational speeches for groups of two hundred businesspeople, but Tim was selling out twenty-thousand-seat arenas. Five years after Tim left Monroe, Louisiana, to become a country music star, he had become a household name and one of the most sought after country singers on the circuit. He had come a long way from the gun-shot saloons he had played in for so many years—but his life was about to change once again.

In 1996, while Tim and his band, the Dancehall Doctors, were on tour, he met a young lady who knocked him off his feet. Faith Hill was a budding country singer like Tim and was performing with his tour. She immediately caught Tim's attention. During a concert, Tim and Faith sang a duet, and at the end of the song, onstage, Tim planted a juicy kiss on her. The crowd went wild and it just took off from there. Tim and Faith quickly became inseparable, and one night in his trailer before a show, he asked her to marry him. When he came back from his set, Faith had written *yes* on his mirror in lipstick, and they were married that October 6. They had a small family wedding in Rayville, Louisiana, and it was a sight to see: the oddball McGraw clan along with Tim's sisters and Betty on one side and then Faith's wonderful and very normal, down-to-earth family seated opposite us. Man, is Tim lucky!

Tim and Faith were all over television and magazine covers, and even performed together at award shows. Every time they sang together, they brought the crowds to their feet with their chemistry, and I couldn't have been happier for him.

Now Tim and Faith are the proud parents of three little girls. Tim is a great father and is determined to give his children everything he didn't have growing up, including a dedicated father. Tim is a better man than any of the men that have been and are still in his life. No matter what hardships Tim had to endure growing up, he became just what his mother said he would be—something special both as a man and as a professional.

I know now, and I probably knew then, that Tim deserved better from me during the first half of his life; at the very least, he deserved for his letters and calls to be acknowledged. But I was focused on hitters, not kids, back in those days and don't think I could have done anything differently. I spent half of my time on the ball field and the other half in a bar. At the time, I figured that if this kid was truly my son, he was better off where he was than with me. I'd have to say that while I tried for so many years to deny that I fathered Betty's child, deep inside I must have known that he was mine. That is the only explanation for my confession to Phyllis that I may have a son, my never throwing out his pictures that Betty sent me, and my reluctance to do a paternity test until the day I met him, all grown up, face-to-face.

I credit Tim's success and his being such a terrific person to his mom, Betty. She is a great mother and did an amazing job raising him. She always put her son and her family first, and she thought of their well-being before making any decisions. Everything she did was for her family's future benefit.

Tim is who he is today—a successful, generous man who is a wonderful father and loving husband—because of how he was raised, and that is a credit to who he is inside and who his mother raised him to be. But I had only begun to see what kind of a man Tim McGraw was. He would further amaze me years later when the tide once again changed.

CHAPTER 15

Life After the Game

For most folks, retirement brings relaxation, serenity, and downtime—but for me, it brought more chaos to an already chaotic life. During my nineteen years in the major leagues, I always planned for, and even expected, to one day be out of a job and searching for my next gig. But when the time actually came for my life to no longer be centered around a baseball diamond, I became lost in the reality of life after the game.

I knew my marriage and family had suffered because of my busy schedule and indiscretions over the years, but I never expected it to all come to a head when I finally got out and faced the world without baseball. I always assumed that if my personal life could handle my professional life while I was in the league, the years after retirement would be a piece of cake. Boy, was I wrong.

Phyllis hadn't been happy with me for quite some time, and while she had overlooked my one-night stands over the years, she often gave me the ultimatum that I either had to shape up or ship out when it came to spending time at home and with the kids. It wasn't that I didn't want to spend time with Mark and Cari, or that I didn't care. Something else just always came up. If I wasn't on the road with the team, I was working on other projects or appearances, or making myself available for the next gig. There is no doubt that I worked my ass off—and that didn't change once I retired from baseball. And I was also a partyaholic.

During my final season in 1984, Phyllis came to me one day and told me she was tired of covering up for all the important events I'd missed over the years. She was afraid that now that the kids were getting old enough to understand, they would blame her for making excuses for me. She asked me to give her one month after the season ended without any distractions or jobs so we could rent a Winnebago and travel cross-country like we'd done when we were first married— only this time without my mother! We never really got the honeymoon we'd planned more than twenty years ago and had had only a handful of vacations over the years, and she wanted us to finally take a vacation by ourselves. I nodded my head in agreement and promised her I wouldn't start any new projects or jobs for at least a month.

But the week that the season was to end, I came home and had lined up four post-baseball jobs. I agreed to work for a cardboard company, as a reporter for local news station WPVI Channel 6, and as a representative for First Pennsylvania bank, and I got a lot of speaking gigs, including work as a spokesman for 7UP and Gillette—and was to start all of them the following Monday.

That was the last straw for Phyllis. She had been a baseball widow for as long as she could handle it and wasn't willing to continue on into my retirement. She took the kids to the Jersey shore without me and that was the beginning of the long and drawn-out separation that led to our eventual divorce. I guess I was subconsciously trying to force the issue by taking all those jobs, since Phyllis and I both had a sense that divorce was on the horizon anyway.

By the time Phyllis returned from the shore, I had moved out and started my new jobs. Folks I was close to called these my "lost" years. While I was going through the divorce, which was finalized in 1987, I moved into an inner-city Philadelphia neighborhood. John McManus, who became a good friend of mine, was tending bar up the street.

He was a former college professor and I was a former baseball player. We were both kind of lost. It was just crash, burn, crawl off the floor, drop off the ceiling, pass out. It was an ugly cycle.

I never was too thrilled about the job with Philadelphia's Channel 6, even though I did end up staying with them for seven years. I was a community relations reporter and also covered sports. The community part was okay, but believe it or not, I actually struggled being a sports reporter. I hated going down to the clubhouse and having all the ballplayers look at me standing there in a suit with a microphone in my hand. We used to heckle reporters—calling them green flies—and now I was one of those annoying flies being swatted at by my former teammates. Man, that job was tough! You needed to be able to go for the jugular vein to do that type of work, asking the hard question of the athlete—or in my case, the former teammate—who had just screwed up. I'm always amazed when I see guys do that on TV: go from the field to the booth and immediately start blasting people. That was impossible for me because I was still a ballplayer at heart.

My favorite assignment while with Channel 6 had nothing to do with baseball. I called it the story of the "doll with the dolls." She was a doll repair lady who wrote me a letter, and I followed up and did a story on her. She was in her fifties and her house was covered in doll parts. I always wondered how someone gets started as a doll repair lady. Still do.

My second job was as a representative for First Pennsylvania Bank. I did all of their billboard, radio and television ads. This job proved to be life changing because it didn't just help me keep my mug out there for the people—it led me to meet, and fall madly in love with, the bank president's twenty-one-year-old daughter, Pamela Butler.

When I first met Pam she was working for an advertising agency, and I knew right away that she was someone I wanted a relationship with. I waited until she was twenty-two to start dating her—I was forty-one at the time. She actually asked me out on our first date and we went for a cruise on my boat on the Delaware. With my celebrity status, our obvious age difference, and the fact that I was still married, her father wasn't too keen on us having a future. Still, he tolerated our relationship for the three years it lasted.

I was recently separated from Phyllis when, a year after I retired, Pam and I decided to move in together. Over the next two years, she continued to pressure me to tell Phyllis about us, even though Phyllis and I were going through a divorce. I eventually told Phyllis—though it was one of the worst kept secrets in the city—and while she wasn't too happy with me dating someone so young, she accepted it. Not too long after, Pam decided she wanted to break it off. I still don't know why she ended our three-year relationship—I guess she didn't like me or love me anymore. Truthfully, what should I have expected? Isn't this what generally happens when some forty-one-year-old guy gets smitten with a twenty-two-year-old hottie? Yet I never was able to play with the odds. I always figured I could beat them.

To top matters off, I also lost the job at the bank. I gave it up before she left and never even got the $50,000 they owed me. Another one of my brilliant financial—and personal—

decisions. I wish I'd been smart enough to see a theme developing here. Bad personal life choices are expensive!

I really wish Pam and I had stuck it out. If I had to a pick a woman who I would absolutely say I loved, it would be her. I always felt she made me be a better man during our years together. As has been the case in most of my relationships, I'm not sure I was as good for her. She later married and divorced, and she called me when I became sick. I haven't seen her in five years—but I still continue to think of her regularly.

After Pam and I broke up in 1987, it came time to finalize my divorce from Phyllis. True to form, I once again delegated responsibility for my affairs to other people. I basically left it up to the lawyers to decide how to divide up our assets. Phyllis's requests weren't unreasonable, and quite frankly I never paid attention to money matters before, so this was no different. Phyllis said years later that I actually gave her more than she had asked for because I didn't take the time to really look over the divorce papers.

When it was all said and done, we shared custody of Mark and Cari and she did very well financially. We sold the big house in Media, Pennsylvania, and Phyllis built a house nearby so the kids could stay at the same school. I will always have a special place in my heart for Phyllis even though we ended our twenty-year marriage with some very hard feelings. She was my family and I will always think of her that way. She's a great gal, and while our marriage didn't last, my admiration and respect for her always will.

Phyllis immediately began to move on with her life after the divorce, but never remarried. I, on the other hand, did—but that marriage also was doomed from the start.

I struggled with my relationship with Mark and Cari. It was bad enough that I was seldom there with them when I was married to their mother. Now I was off trying to build a new life and was even more distant. Cari, who always found a way to hit me right between the eyes with the obvious, did so in the way she knew best . . . a poem.

"One Day"

Do you know what I'm feeling?
In one way I feel like healing.
But in another way,
I feel like nothing's changed since yesterday.
I miss you so much,
I always want your touch.
I want to hug you
And squeeze you so tight.
I feel like loving you
With all my might.
Sometimes I feel like you really love me,
Then sometimes I feel you just want to be.
I'm over the thoughts of dying,
But I still feel like crying,
All the time.
I want you to only be mine,
And spend all your time with me.
I know you're busy with your job.
And I feel like mom's so into Bob.
I know deep down she loves me,
But then I wonder "does she really?"
I guess I can't accept it,
Her loving me.
But then I do, but just a bit.
Please help me understand,
Even if we have to go hand & hand,
I'm willing to try.
No matter how much I have to try.

I'm out of things to say,
So now I'm going to bed & I'm gonna pray.
Oh, one more thing I want to say.
I love you more & more every day.
And maybe you'll also learn to *show* me
    & say.
I love you too!
Maybe, one day!

When she wrote that, I realized I needed to look for new and better ways to be around her. I worried that she was depressed, and I couldn't imagine what life must have been like for her. It was a real eye-opener. I started scheduling time for us—just the two of us.

I met Diane, the woman who would become my second wife, in 1991. When I first met Diane she was the director of the Philadelphia Sports Congress and I was still with Channel 6. The job often sent me to Diane to discuss events at the Spectrum, where the Flyers and 76ers played and where she put on events. My first impression of Diane was that she was a hot tomato. I would quickly learn that she was a damsel in distress with a host of issues. But back then my mind was wide open and the other side of my bed was getting cold.

Like during my relationship with Pam, I never looked for reasons not to move forward, so when some of Diane's issues started popping up, I just ignored the signs and kept going with the flow.

One day, I went down to her office to pick up tickets for the Ice Capades, which I was covering for Channel 6, and overheard her crying on the phone. She motioned for me to come in and sit down, which should have been my first clue that she would be a tad dramatic. When most people are upset at work, they ask you to wait outside, but she told me to come in and sit down while she continued her heated discussion for another ten or fifteen minutes. When she finally hung up, and before I even had a chance to utter a word, she began to tell me the story of her in-laws in Holland and her prick husband who was a bad businessman and now was living in the Caribbean. She met him in New York, got married, had two boys, and was raising them by herself while he sat on a beach. Her saga went on and on, and to be honest, I really wasn't all that interested in her story. I had just come by to pick up some tickets and ended up in this tomato's office listening to her pour out her whole life story to me. I didn't want to hear it, but I was acting interested just in case I wanted to get on that, which I did. So when she finished talking, I picked up my tickets and invited her across the street to the Brew Club. I figured a glass of wine would settle her down. We sat at the bar and had a few drinks and made a lunch date for later in the week.

Over the next few months, I got to know her kids, Ian and Christopher, and really took a liking to them. They were well behaved, athletic boys and I became the only father figure they had. Six months into our relationship she asked to move in with me in my row house in Fairmont Park near the Art Museum district of Philadelphia. It was a good place to live if you didn't mind stepping over the dead bodies on some of the stoops in the morning. Oh, I'm exaggerating. That only happened once or twice in the ten years that I lived there. Diane was being ousted from her apartment in New Jersey after a fight with her landlord and needed a place to stay with the boys. Since I had an available bedroom I offered it to her for the summer until she got back on her feet. That never happened; she stayed at my place. She was like my brother Hank—I would ask when she was getting her own place and she would tell me, "Don't worry, next week sometime." Next thing I know, she tells me she's not getting along with her boss at the Sports Congress and wants me to move to Orlando, Florida, with her and the boys.

I had just quit the job at Channel 6 after seven years and really had nothing job related keeping me in Philadelphia. During the last two years of my job as a reporter, you could tell that I had lost interest in the gig. My bosses were patient and kept waiting for me to regain my interest, but I never did and we agreed to go our separate ways. So at the time, I was just doing appearances and speeches and wasn't hooked to any geographical location. I thought it would be a good thing for me to change my life a little bit—so off we all went to Orlando.

We were in Orlando only two years before Diane started getting into fights with her new boss and decided to take a job in California. Once again, her propensity for picking fights was another sign of the troubles to come, but I shook it off. I stayed back in Orlando and waited until the boys got out of school and then brought them to San Moreno. Diane had an eye for good neighborhoods and set us up in a nice house, and I was the home daddy—Mr. Mom.

We were doing well in California, but in 1995, a good four years into our relationship, I got another surprise—at the age of fifty-one, I was going to be a father again. After Diane, who was in her early forties, told me she was pregnant, we decided to get married. We were married in a small ceremony in 1995 at the Rancho Caymus Inn in Rutherford, California. She always says that I married her because she got pregnant. She's right. I was close to breaking the thing off when she told me we had a child on the way. I wasn't going to make the same mistake I had made thirty years earlier with Tim.

I ended up getting thoroughly drunk on our wedding day,

November 25, and while the wedding was beautiful, it was awkward. Most of my family was there, including Hank, Mark, and Cari. Even Tim called in on a cell phone during our ceremony to wish us luck. Hank tried to make Diane feel welcome by giving her an old Irish coin to put in her shoe for her "something old," but she wasn't too impressed by his gesture. I was impressed that he at least tried, even though he knew that I really did not want to get married.

Five months later my son Matthew McKenna was born in Pasadena, California.

In 1997 we moved back to Philadelphia because Diane began to get into fights with yet another boss and we wanted to be closer to my friends and family in Philadelphia. Things were going pretty good for a few years but Diane's business ventures would prove to be explosive to me and my family. While my life with Matthew was beginning to take shape and gave me structure and meaning again, my relationship with Diane began to take an ugly turn. The financial stress of all these changes was taking its toll on our marriage.

Things got more complicated when, while both of us were out of work, Diane suggested we form a company to manage special events. I figured if we used my name and her understanding of the events business, it might make sense. It didn't.

Once again, I found myself in a chaotic situation—with no possible happy ending in sight.

CHAPTER 16

Disconnected Dots and Humor Bombs

I love being Irish. I think being Irish is one of the fun things to be in life. I'm proud of being Irish. We have a reputation to maintain. We have to be able to tell good stories. We have to be able to have a nip now and then. We have to act like nothing bothers us.

That's the way I've always lived my life, so being a left-handed Irish relief pitcher—three characteristics that tell most folks you're different—has been perfect. How can you not love the stereotypical Irish profile? Lucky charms and leprechauns. We know how to have fun and take life with the proverbial grain of salt. We don't plan too far ahead—unless it's to party. The good thing about being Irish is you think you can drink. After two drinks, you're gone and that's it. You just go back to your room and you go to sleep—depending on how long it takes you to get those two or three drinks down!

I wrapped myself in that leprechaun lifestyle—so much so I've long worn a little gold leprechaun around my neck—

and loved St. Patrick's Day more than Christmas. It had been that way in my family for as long as I could remember.

I've loved being Irish so much that I made it a point twice to load up the whole family—me, Phyllis, Mark and Cari, my dad, and Hank—and take them to the motherland, even though Phyllis's background was German. We felt awesome there, like we were among our own. What a beautiful place and what a great time.

I made being Irish the focus of real good times every year on St. Patrick's Day at spring training. My first spring with the Phillies, I stopped on the way to the ballpark and I bought a couple of packets of shamrock green Rit dye. I got to the ballpark and I asked the clubby—the clubhouse utilityman—to throw my uni in the washing machine and dump the dye in there. He didn't want to ruin a uniform. I convinced him that it would be okay. When it was time for me to come into the game, I wanted to make sure I left an impression. I knew I could pitch; I was looking for other ways to stand out. It's just playing with that Irish thing again.

Anyway, I got into the game, and out I came with a green uniform on. The umpire, Nick Colosi, lost his mind. When I was done with my warm-ups and was ready to start the inning, he called time-out, walked out to the mound, and said, "You can't pitch with that uniform on."

I asked, "Why not?"

He said, "Rule book. All uniforms have to be the same, even in spring training."

And I said, "You son of a bitch. If it was Columbus Day you wouldn't have a problem with this."

He said, "You may be right. But today's not Columbus Day. It's St. Patrick's Day." He told me to leave.

I said, "I'm going to have to call a long time-out."

See, it wasn't just my jersey and pants that I'd dyed green. It was everything. Socks, sanitaries, everything. I went and made a quick change and came back out. By that time, everyone knew what was going on, and when I made it to the mound, the crowd booed Colosi.

In the years that followed, I always made sure the Phillies scheduled me to pitch on St. Patrick's Day. I would take long underwear and I'd dye it green, and then I'd put it on under my uniform. When I was brought into the game, I'd drop my pants and give the crowd—and the umpire—a good look at my Irish pride. Everybody in the stands just loved it.

My attachment to the Irish thing was perfect until someone had the bright idea to call Hank and ask if they could research our family history. It was some college researcher, and he was trying to trace our family and some other family. Next thing you know, he brought us a bomb, ruining everything I've built my life around.

Hank called and laid it on me—*we're not Irish!* According to this researcher, we have about a thimbleful of Irish blood in us. I couldn't believe it until Hank showed me what the guy had found. How can you have a mother who is a McKenna and a father who is a McGraw and not be Irish? As it turns out, most of the family is from somewhere around what is today the Czech Republic but in the days when my ancestors came to the United States was part of the Austro-Hungarian empire! I now know I had family from Eastern Europe—possibly Slavs from Russia—and that my mother's family was from the Bohemia region, so I'm not sure if that makes us Czech or Slovak.

There is *some* Irish in me—at least enough that I can say that all those years of loving the Irish weren't wasted!

The upside to becoming a veteran in major league baseball is that spring training becomes less a proving ground and more a time to have fun. I certainly had more than my share of memorable moments down in the Florida sunshine as my career progressed.

We used to have what they called the Piña Colada Open golf tournament every year among players and coaches. We'd pick an off day and get tee times on one of the great golf courses in the area for everyone to play. The guys would all take jugs of piña coladas with them. We would raise hell on the golf course and have an unforgettable time hitting the ball around.

We were so crazy that we never were invited back to the same course a second time. Once, late in a round where we were totally smashed, several members of a real upscale golf club had complained to the club pro about our behavior. The pro pointed out the two women who had called us in and he told us that they thought we "needed to be more polite and gentlemanly." Well, two holes later, those women were on a hole adjacent to the one we were playing. You can guess what happened: As they got ready to tee off, we all dropped our pants and mooned them!

A dozen thirty-year-old men dropping trou. Pretty sophisticated, huh? No wonder they didn't invite us back.

But the key moment of each year's Piña Colada Open came on the eighteenth green. When we got there, we always had it set up so that my group was the foursome just ahead of the manager, who at the time was Danny Ozark. So after we all holed out to end the round, my foursome would pee in the cup, and then Ozark's group would always let him putt out first into the cup.

Childish, I know. But what a damn good time!

We also had a big pig roast at the end of each spring for all the players and their families. We'd get a pig and keep it at a house on the beach one of the veterans had rented, then take it by boat the next morning to an island in the middle of Clearwater Bay where we'd let it cook all afternoon. Late the next day, we'd line up seven or eight boats at the dock to take all the guys who wanted to go across the bay for the roast. If islands could have cut us off like golf courses did, we might have run out of places to hold that party.

One year, when my son Mark was little, it was our job to keep the pig the night before the barbecue—just to make sure Larry Christenson didn't sleep with it! Although I tried to get the pig into the bed, it kept jumping off. My line the next morning was, "It wasn't the first time I tried to get a pig in bed with me." I even served it beer, but all that made it do was take a crap in the bedroom. The pig ended up sleeping on the floor. The next day, the pig was shot with a .22 rifle right through its forehead, and then was boiled in scalding water to get bristles off. We cooked it over an aboveground campfire, rotating it every thirty minutes or so. LC poked both eyes out with a fork and ate them.

As the years progressed and more guys started making money, they started buying boats of their own. When you're in a beautiful spot like Clearwater and have access to all that blue water, you have to get out in the afternoon.

Finally, I had to join that club. A couple of years before my retirement, I went out and bought a boat just in time for that spring's pig roast. Sonny Hepps and I went over to the causeway to launch the boat. We backed it down the boat ramp, and I couldn't have been more excited.

As we launched it off the trailer, we stood there with looks of horror as the boat started to fill up with water and sink. We forgot to put the plugs in the damn thing! We had never owned a boat before and didn't know about plugs. We stood there with silly expressions, watching the boat sink. Fortunately, it was in only a couple of feet or so of water, but we had to hire a guy to come pull it out, drain it, and put the plugs in! It took all day and nearly made me late to the pig roast.

* * *

Over the course of my lifetime I've generally been known for two things—my screwball and my sense of humor. The former helped get me attention. The latter helped me keep it. It didn't matter where we played; sportswriters hovered around hoping I'd drop one of my humor bombs.

Growing up, I learned that by dropping these funny lines on people, I could get them off my back. In grammar school people were always trying to ruffle other guys' feathers, even bullying some of the smaller guys, and some of them did it a lot. I found the way to keep them off me was to verbally just drop funny bombs on them. It seemed to work.

It helped me combat being small, too. The fact that I was small gave the jerks extra reason to pick on me. When they got tired of picking on me verbally and they were ready to beat the crap out of me, I would drop a funny bomb. How could you beat up a guy who was just trying to be funny? Once in a while, I'd get popped, but not as often as I might have. And then, when I'd made it to the majors, look who I played for: Casey Stengel and Yogi Berra, two of the most quotable, funniest guys in baseball—at least as far as the writers were concerned.

I used to read quite a bit and I'd pull stuff out of some of those books. One of my favorite humor bombs was drawn from a book about sales. It was after I walked in the winning run on Opening Day in Cincinnati in 1981. Since we won the whole thing in 1980, the League scheduled us to open with Cincinnati. In those days, because the Cincinnati Red Stockings were the first professional baseball team and became one of the original teams in the National League, Cincinnati would open at home the day before the rest of the league. It's one of those nice traditions that baseball has so casually thrown out the window. And the starter for the Reds was my old pal, Tom Seaver. Anyway, I walked in Tony Perez on a 3-2 pitch that was real close to lose the game.

Scotty Palmer—a sports reporter with Channel 6 in Philly—came up to me after the game. There was a whole bunch of reporters around me because the last time they saw me pitch in a real game was the World Series. Scotty jumped in there and said, "Tug, how does it feel today? You walked in the winning run. The last time we saw you pitch you struck out Willie Wilson, and you won the World Series. You just walked in the winning run on Opening Day. How does that make you feel?"

Drawing from the book I'd just been reading, I said, "Scotty, it's like this. Science has proven that the sun is going to last another fifty billion years. When the sun burns out, the Earth is going to freeze over and take on the appearance of a frozen snowball. And when that day comes, who's going to give a shit? I'm thinking fifty billion years down the road." So everybody laughed—that was a humor bomb. I saw all the bullshit coming, and I dropped the humor bomb on them. Most of the reporters just turned around and walked away, shaking their heads.

I remember reading those lines and thinking to myself, "I'm going to use this someday." Then I just had to hope the line would be there when I needed it and not lost in one of the brain cells I killed smoking pot.

Speaking of pot led me to another memorable humor bomb. This one came to me in 1974, when a reporter in San Francisco was working on a story about what surface I liked to play on. Within a five-year period, the Giants had gone back and forth from grass to Astroturf to grass. So this reporter was asking players around the country what they thought. The question seemed simple: "Which do you prefer—grass or Astroturf?"

My answer was just as simple: "I don't know, I never smoked Astroturf!"

That one made *Sports Illustrated*'s quote of the week, the first of several times I was chosen for that honor.

I don't remember making an effort to be quotable. I never knew if one of the things I said was going to be funny enough to travel, but a lot of times they did. It's amazing how many fans read and remember that stuff. I had people coming up to me all over the country, especially after the Astroturf quote. I got mail from people who made little torpedoes out of Astroturf, wrapped them in rolling papers, and sent them to me with a note reading, "Let me know how it is, bro." Those kinds of notes came in from all over the country.

But my wacky quotes didn't start when I got traded to the Phillies. When I was with the Mets, a writer from one of the financial magazines wanted to do a story on how players were preparing for their careers after the game. I had by then established myself as one of the top relievers in the game. I wasn't really interested in talking with him because I don't know anything about money. He came up to me and said, "So, have you invested your money wisely over the years?"

I thought about it and said, "I probably invested my money more wisely than any of those guys," pointing to Seaver, who was the highest paid player on the team, and Kranepool, who was a Wall Street stockbroker in the off-season.

The guy looked at me like I was nuts, and I was. He said, "What do you mean?"

I said, "Ninety percent of my money that I've earned in baseball, I've invested in women, cars, parties, booze. The other ten percent I probably wasted."

Once in a great while the question was really about baseball. One reporter asked me how to pitch to the great Hank

Aaron. My answer: "The same as to anybody else, except don't let the ball go!"

I've had some other doozies over the years, quotes that ended up taking on a life of their own. Once, when I was struggling with the mental part of the game, I told a reporter: "I have no trouble with the twelve inches between my elbow and my palm. It's the seven inches between my ears that's bent."

Another time, as I was explaining how precarious a career like mine was, I said, "One day Cy Young, the next day sayonara."

And I even occasionally took to offering advice on how to grow up and become a big leaguer: "Kids should practice autographing baseballs. This is a skill that's often overlooked in Little League."

I can't explain how some of these come up, but I've never had a shortage of humor bombs. And they always kept the reporters coming back.

I have had three role models in my life. Babe Ruth was my first role model. He did things in baseball that nobody else was doing. He changed the game and made it an offensive game. I read and heard enough about the Babe that I just saw the guy as unafraid to try anything. The Babe pitched, he hit home runs . . . what else did he have to do? He changed the whole face of the game of baseball. When you're looking for a role model, look for the guy who will try anything.

That led to my second role model: Ben Franklin. Long before I played in Philadelphia, in junior high and high school in fact, I started paying attention to Ben Franklin. He did things that nobody else would do—he looked around and saw what needed to be done and got it done. He stood out. If the people needed a way to send and receive letters and documents, he started a post office. If people wanted to see wild and exotic animals, he started a zoo. If people's houses were at risk of burning down, he started an insurance company. If you needed to start a new country, he helped write the rules. He was just working it. Always working it. He lived to be eighty, died of the gout. What else do you need from a guy?

Then my third role model was the King. Elvis came along and danced and sang his way to fame. He made the tomatoes melt just by looking at them. He made more money than he could spend, although somehow he managed to spend it all. Hell, he's still making money today and he's been dead for over twenty-five years! In November 2003, Tim rented a motor home for me and Hank, John McManus, and my friend Mike Mahoney to drive across the country from my home in Pennsylvania to end up with the family out in Napa. Of course, we had to stop at Graceland to pay homage—and they got us for $25 a head to see the King's kitchen!

Just to put my love of Elvis in perspective, on August 16, 1977—the day Elvis died—the Phils were taking a charter flight to Chicago after a night game against the Expos. I spent the afternoon shopping in an underground mall in Montreal and came up with black jeans, a black shirt, a black leather jacket, black boots, and a jar of pomade. When I showed up at the ballpark, I *was* Elvis. I gave my personal tribute to the King every August 16 for the rest of my career.

I know I'm not the first to call him a role model. I probably wasn't the first to do this either: Every once in awhile, when the spirit moved me, I left tickets for Elvis at the ballpark. I'm not one of those who is convinced he's still alive. But I figured I'd leave him good seats just in case!

CHAPTER 17

The Fans

I have often said I loved baseball enough that I would have played it for free. I loved the game so much that I developed my own annual ritual: At the beginning of each spring training, before the pitchers would arrive, I would always go over to a bar in Clearwater called O'Keefe's, have a beer, then head over to Jack Russell Stadium—where the Phillies held spring training in those days—get down on my knees, kiss the ground, and say, "Thank you, God, for letting me do something I love so much."

I think fans understood my love. And they gave it back to me. So while ownership paid me to play—paid me well for a while—it was the fans who really got my motor running. There's no question I drew my motivation from performing in front of the crowd. It was obvious I loved them, I loved the game, and I loved the stage.

A lot of players talk about how they zone everything out except what is happening on the field. My Phillie teammate and friend Warren Brusstar had gunfighter eyes. When he pitched, he didn't see or hear anyone or anything. He locked in on the catcher and that was it. I couldn't do that. I was never that laser-focused. I had to bring it all—including the fans—in for me to be successful. If I was standing on the mound getting ready to make a big pitch, I needed to look into the crowd to see my dad or my brother or my family or friends before I could look back at the batter. I got my strength from those people sitting in the stands. Then I'd say to myself, "I guess it's time to do my job now," and I'd throw the ball. The second the play was dead, my eyes were back in the stands. Some coaches said I had Attention Deficit Disorder on the mound.

I think the way I acted on the mound allowed me to connect with the guy using a healthy chunk of his weekly salary to bring his family and sit in seats in the outfield. After a nervous moment, I would tap my chest. I wanted the fans to know my heart was racing just like theirs was. After a big out, I loved to jump off the mound and pump my fist. I'd blow kisses to my kids in the stands, and they'd blow kisses back. I'd reach out for the imaginary kisses and catch them.

To fans, that made me popular. To opponents, it made me annoying. And to some teammates, it made for a good eye roll. It didn't matter if it was the World Series or a mid-June game against a last-place team, I had the same emotions. When I had the bases loaded and was facing a great hitter, I was looking to the crowd, to the fans, to my family for help. It wasn't an act—I needed to do this in order to be successful out there.

And the fans were always willing to embrace me. It probably helped that I spent the last half of my career on a team full of guys who were amazingly cool, and I wasn't afraid to admit that I was just having a damn good time.

Another friend and former Phillie teammate, Larry Christenson, loves to tell stories of me—some of which are even true! When he was asked once about how much I loved playing baseball, he shared a somewhat embarrassing story. When we pitched together, LC, who towers over me at six-four, had the locker right next to mine. Once I was so excited during a game that I soiled my shorts on the mound. Larry noticed that as we were changing and has managed to include that in stories for years. Of course LC, a pretty good starting pitcher for several years—his best year was 1977, when he went 19-6—also likes to remind me that he would have been in the Hall of Fame if I hadn't come in and blown so many of his games.

I loved giving LC a hard time about the fact he could never pitch a complete game. Whenever he walked in the locker room on a day he was starting, I'd be sure to ask at the top of my lungs, "LC, you pitching tonight?" When he'd say "Yes, I am, Tug," I'd yell back, with my eyes wide and bright, "So am I!" It seemed like every game he pitched, I did, too!

I did wish I could hit like LC, though. He hit eleven career homers—three in 1977 alone.

Fans really do make the game great. But I have worried over the last several years that fans don't have the connection to baseball that they had years ago. Maybe it's the labor unrest. Maybe it's the skyrocketing salaries and the skyrocketing ticket and concession prices. Maybe it's spoiled superstars who refuse to sign autographs or show any on-field emotion. I don't know. All I know is there are too many near-empty ballparks and there is no easy solution in sight.

That's one of the reasons I began, in the months before I knew I was sick, my own personal fight to return the game to the fans. I called the effort "Ya Gotta Believe in Baseball," and I began working hard on a Web site to get fan input.

I was invited to be the keynote speaker at the Forty-fifth Annual Baseball Dinner in Nashua, New Hampshire, home of the minor league Nashua Pride in January 2003. I decided that since the presidential candidates kick off their national campaigns in this state, I would also launch my new Ya Gotta Believe in Baseball campaign in New Hampshire. People laughed when I told them I was launching my campaign there, even if it wasn't to get to the White House. Can you imagine me as President of the United States? I can't either.

Laurie Hawkins and I had been planning the fan-interactive campaign for several months, and it was now ready to go. I was going to talk about the campaign throughout the country when I made appearances. I also wanted to use the media, and I would ask the fans to join me in the effort, so it seemed like this was the best time to tell everyone about it and get it started. I'd had an e-mail box set up so that fans could send information, and I was getting ready to launch my Web site.

The purpose of the Ya Gotta Believe in Baseball campaign was to make baseball more fan-friendly and to restore it to its status as America's favorite sport. The campaign was different than what other people were talking about because it actively involved the fans. I wanted to go to the baseball fans of America, ask them what they thought, and then give power to their voices with a report from me to Baseball Commissioner Bud Selig. I figured that I'd be able to take that information to MLB and get someone to pay attention because of my years as a well-known player.

I told people that I was going for the biggest save of my life—the game of baseball. I wanted to honor the history of baseball and focus on its future; that was the campaign's central theme. We invited fans to use the Internet to send me their special memories of baseball as it related to them and their life. That was the history part. And most important, I wanted them to tell me what they'd recommend to make baseball better. The fun part for me was that I was throwing out some of my ideas and then asking them to respond. I got some smart answers and started to collect them for the Web site. It was great to learn that there were still so many baseball fans who cared so deeply about the game.

The audience at the dinner loved the idea, and the local media gave it some coverage, so it was a pretty good beginning. I'd also had a press release about the campaign sent to other areas, and that got picked up in a number of places. We quickly began to get some e-mails on it, and I started feeling more confident that there was interest and we'd get fan involvement.

I was getting ready to go down to the Phillies spring training as things got rolling. I wasn't very close to baseball at the time, and I was looking at it from a distance. That distance gave me, I felt, the right perspective to examine some issues that I thought were important to try to fix while baseball still had enough passionate fans to make a difference.

On the field, the individual talent is as great as ever, but I felt the game had become homogenized with the merging of the two leagues through interleague play. And I felt the press coverage so heavily centered on the economics made the game unhealthy and the future precarious.

One issue that many fans and I saw as destructive to baseball is the designated hitter. That was number one. I didn't like it when it first showed up thirty years ago and I don't like it now. The fact that the American League and the National League take a different approach to making their pitcher a full member of the team tells you something is wrong. I loved to hit when I was in a game—I think most pitchers do. I know LC, with his eleven career homers, did. Knowing that you'll come up to bat kept me engaged in the game the whole time. To allow the rules to take the bat out of an athlete's hand dilutes the game. And that's to say nothing of allowing guys to hit only when they don't go out in the field. If you can't put the whole package together—hitting and fielding—maybe it's time to retire or become a pinch hitter.

I despise the American League and the DH so much I have always refused to sign baseballs from the AL—that is, in the days before the leagues merged when they used different balls. If somebody asked me to sign an American League ball, I'd tell them, "No, I won't sign that ball because it would be like signing up for the Communist Party." And if anyone asked why, I'd say, "Because I hate the DH." I'd tell them that I'd sign an autograph on a piece of paper, or any other ball, but not on an American League ball.

The second issue that so many fans told me they wanted to see changed was the judging of umpires. For years, umpires ruled with no accountability. Players and managers had no recourse except arguing until the ump sent you packing. I never had any particular beef with the umpires—I felt that I got treated pretty well by them, especially after I'd been around for a while. So this isn't meant to be Tug's revenge on the umps.

Baseball has taken a huge step in this area in the last couple of seasons with the advent of QuesTec. The ability to have technology gauge whether the umpire was seeing the truly legal strike zone is huge. It was used in a few ballparks in the 2003 season, and some pitchers really hated it. But I believe that if it was used across the board and umpires were judged on their ability to make correct calls, the game could get better with a more consistent strike zone.

I absolutely believe that you ought to be able to have stats on the umpires like you have stats on the players. Suddenly, there would be a level playing field for everyone in the game. Players are paid based upon their statistics. Coaches are hired and fired based upon their players' numbers. Imagine if umpires were paid on something other than longevity and seniority. QuesTec gives you measurable stats. It tells how well home plate umps call fastballs, curveballs, checked swings, and so on. It gives umpires an accuracy rating. That should be a big benefit to the umpires. If they truly believe they are as good as they say they are, then they can back it up with their stats. If they finish in the top ten and then the number one umpire in the league goes up on the stage at the banquet and receives his Bill Klem Award for the most valuable or best umpire right next to the Cy Young and the Triple Crown guy, he can hold his chin up and he can be proud. It will also give the other umpires something to aspire to. Conversely, if you're on the bottom of the list, maybe you get sent down to the minors. "See you later, buddy. Work on a few things."

But the umpires hate it because it makes them accountable. And some pitchers who have made a very good living by getting strikes called half a foot off the plate hate it, too.

I worry sometimes that baseball management has lost its touch. I just think that people try to mess with the game too much. You can overtweak it to the point where it becomes ineffective. I can't stand interleague play. I hate it with a vengeance because nobody knows what to do with the DH. When Boston's in Philadelphia, they use no DH. When Philadelphia's in Boston, you've got to use the DH. It just messes everything up, it throws all the stats out. Divisional play—cool. Interleague play—not.

I think there has to be a better way to handle things if MLB is hell bent on interleague play. I think that if they had done a little research, they could have taken, say, the New York Mets and L.A. Dodgers and had a weekday series in Kansas City, or any other two National League teams in an American League city. You could take any combination of National League or American League teams, and you could plug them into an American League city during the week, a businessperson's schedule. No doubleheaders; it would just be Tuesday, Wednesday, Thursday, with Wednesday being a businessperson's special day game, and everybody gets a chance to see teams from the other league. You get two for the price of one. Instead of having to watch Kansas City play the Mets and then the Royals play the Phillies, you get the Mets and the Phillies three days in a row playing in Kansas City. If you live in an American League city and you never get to see the National League teams play, then that might be an incentive for you to come out, depending how they market it.

Maybe this idea is a bit radical, but it could work. Some of the ideas certainly caught fire with fans who wrote to the Web site. Unfortunately, by the time the Web site was launched, I had been diagnosed with a brain tumor, so we never got a chance to give it the attention it deserved. When I get my health back, I absolutely intend to go back and put pressure on management to think about the fans first. Right now it's difficult because I've got a brain to look after.

Baseball is falling off the map of the American young person today. I have a solution for that. In these new ballparks that are being built, the teams need to add, in my opinion, X-game parks inside the gates, not gourmet food and hot tubs. So if parents take a kid to a ballgame, he or she can come out there with a skateboard or Rollerblades and do their thing in the X-game park. The thing that will stop teams from doing it, or has already stopped them from doing it if anyone besides me has thought of it, is probably attorneys and liability insurance. It's an arguable point. But if you can find a way to put an X-game facility inside the turnstiles, Mom and Dad can go and watch the game, and little Johnny can go out into the skateboard park. Or the family can go to the game two hours early and let Johnny wear himself out at the skateboard park and then come watch the baseball game when he needs to chill out.

The teams can add a buck to the ticket for the kids for use of the park—or charge extra at the entrance to the area. Teams can't have it there for free, because they've got to make money on everything. I'll bet teams could find sponsors for the X-games park and use that as a resource center.

The kid goes out there for two or three innings and wears himself out, and now he's hungry and thirsty. Mom and Dad have a seat next to them reserved for him, and next thing you know, he's there with them. He watches two or three or four innings and bada-bing, he gradually becomes a baseball fan. It's stealth marketing the game to kids. When he gets older, he buys a ticket to a ballgame and takes his kids out there. MLB doesn't have to let the X-games steal from its fan base. Just cultivate it. Use it. Make it work for the game. That's my fix on that.

You'd think that with all my ideas, they'd just slide me in as commissioner one day, huh? Somebody with some ideas and some guts has got to step in there. Baseball is in a nosedive. Teams are building the stadiums smaller to make them look more full on TV and to create the sense that going to a game is a hot ticket, even though it's priced out of the range of most people. But TV ratings don't lie. Everything has a life span, and baseball's probably no different. I'd hate to see it die, but I think unless the honchos do some creative things, it will eventually die. We're moving into a high-tech world, and baseball is not a high-tech sport. It's probably about as low tech as it gets. A piece of wood, a ball, and the pace of a game mirroring life in the nineteenth century—not the twenty-first.

I'm looking forward to getting better—and watching baseball do the same.

* * *

I'm lucky in that my love affair with baseball fans has been a two-way street. Within hours of the media reports that I was in the hospital in Tampa, thousands of calls, letters, and e-mails flooded my way. Laurie Hawkins, who was monitoring the Web site from the hospital in Tampa, counted thousands of e-mails. She printed every one out for me and filled notebooks with them—twenty huge binders at last count.

Some of those fans wrote to remind me of a conversation we might have had twenty years ago while at a gas station. Some remembered me from autograph signings or golf outings or banquets. And they wrote to tell me how my years with the Mets or the Phillies had made them smile or brought them closer to family or motivated them to face a challenge. Despite what Laurie and others had been telling me since we had first started getting e-mails, I had no idea that so many people cared about me like they did.

The funny thing was how many of these encounters I remembered. I tried to remember and it's good to get those reminders, but as hard as you try, you can't remember all of them, especially after you've had your coconut operated on. I'd say I remember about seventy-five percent of them.

Some wrote to share a laugh with me over one of my funny lines dropped on the media years ago. Others wrote about some play that still gives them goose bumps—obviously most of the folks from Philadelphia mentioned the strikeout of Willie Wilson!

One of the things that was most valuable about those letters was that it helped me get a sense of the effect I've have on people during the course of my life. I always thought I was a little edgy. But apparently people have been able to forgive me for that. I always tried to be humorous, and maybe I was naturally a little flaky, but I didn't really know what impact that has had on fans or teammates or relatives. I didn't know where I stood sometimes. And then when I got sick, they told me. I've got to say it was kind of like attending my own funeral with everyone offering a eulogy.

When I first was told that I had cancer, I didn't realize that it was going to have any impact on the outside world. I'm overwhelmed by the response that I've gotten from people. I think it's pretty phenomenal. Actually, it's extremely phenomenal, not pretty phenomenal. If I get through this whole cancer issue, it will have a lot to do with that outpouring from the fans. Mentally, they will have taken me beyond the cancer. You hear about people doing that all the time—getting rid of the stress in their lives, getting some positive reinforcement, and suddenly beating extraordinary odds.

Most athletes, especially those playing today, have no idea about the impact they have on people. None at all. They have no idea what that conversation at the gas station might mean. I always thought I understood until these letters and e-mails started pouring in. Who would have guessed that a thirty-year-old conversation in the grocery store line could be remembered!?

Some of the more meaningful notes were from people who wrote to share personal stories about their battle with cancer. They were writing to offer hope, to offer encouragement, and to offer prayers. The cumulative effect of receiving all these cards—they came in all forms, from just a pleasant little joke to a big joke, a regular joke or a religious card—was like a snowball heading downhill and getting bigger and bigger and bigger. And the more of them you receive, the more you start believing in the power of spirit.

There's no underestimating the strength I drew from those letters. I asked the permission of a few of those writers to share their letters with the readers of this book, and they are graciously allowing me to include them here.

• • •

Subject: Praying for You
Tug—

I want you to know that I'm praying for you tonight. I know that you will pull through this illness.

I'm 30 years old now, but when I was a kid, my friends and I were avid baseball card and autograph collectors. While many players were cordial, sending autographs upon request, many did not. But nobody ever reached the level of Tug McGraw.

Whether the letters you sent us were standard form letters or not, the important thing was that you truly made me believe that not all famous sports or movie stars looked down upon the "little people." I truly believe that the time you took to give that personal touch to each and every fan made many of us better people—I know it had a significant influence on my life.

I know you will make it through this. You gotta believe, Tug. You will make it through.

God bless you and your family.
With all of my love and respect,

Jay B. Wilson

• • •

I was glad to see in the papers that you're feeling a lot better. I just turned 44, and grew up on Long Island, but have lived in Baltimore since August 1983. I was in North Jersey on business last September and went to the Mets-Expos game that Sunday, 9/22/02. It was my first time back at Shea in 19 years, and brought back many memories. By a stroke of luck, you just happened to be there that day to sign autographs and have photos taken. It was quite a thrill. You and your pitching have given me many moments of joy over the years. I remember reading your comic strip, "Scroogie," in the mid-70s, and really enjoyed it. I wish the strip had lasted longer, but it was fun while it lasted. I even remember the prima donna character you had in the strip, Royce Rawls.

I was unusual back then, since I liked both the Mets and the Phillies. I wasn't the only fan who started tapping his thigh with his mitt when he played, just as you did. I'll always remember your strikeout of Willie Wilson to win the 1980 Series for the Phils. I'll also remember the appearance you made on CN8 last year, on Lou Tilley's Sports Connection, when you suddenly broke out singing opera from *The Pirates of Penzance.*

Tug, you can't imagine how much joy you have given to so many people over the years, both on the field, and with your careful, friendly Mr. Everyman attitude off the field. You have been a treasure for major league baseball, and I wish you the best of health as you continue your battle. It was an honor to meet you last September, though briefly, and I and many others are thinking about you and pulling for you. Ya Gotta Believe!!

Sincerely,

Michael Greenhill

• • •

As a young southpaw baseball fan and little leaguer growing up in the Pocono Mountains of Pennsylvania in the

'60s, I followed the Phillies and the Mets closely, reading the box scores in the morning paper and collecting baseball cards. Being left-handed, I had special interest in guys like Jerry Koosman, Chris Short, Sandy Koufax, Steve Carlton, etc., but when I took the mound for my little league team and the ump yelled play ball, I was Tug McGraw. I wore my hat like the Tugger, wore my socks the same, had the windup down and as many of the mannerisms as I could remember, including slapping my glove against my right thigh as I was heading to the dugout.

I'll be 47 years old on Friday, but I remember those days as if they were yesterday. I was very saddened by the news of your illness. I just wanted to thank you personally for some of the happiest memories of my life. You'll be in my prayers daily.

Good luck and God bless you,

Lance M. Brasavage

• • •

Hi, Mr. McGraw. As a lifetime Mets fan you will always remain a joy and a wonderful memory of my youth. As a 9 year old I lived for nothing more than a Tom Seaver game and a Tug McGraw bounce out of the helmet-size bullpen cart. The memory of your tossing your glove to the batboy, wiping your perspiration, and going to the mound is unforgettable. You even managed to dig a hole with your spikes to the sounds of a wonderful Irish jig. It was so great. But two things have always made you special to me. I had written a fan letter to you (my first). You sent me an autographed picture with a note. It was so terrific, and it meant a lot. Secondly, we share the same birthday. I have followed your career and was fortunate to see you as your '69 teammates had their anniversary (30 years) reunion. I went with my dad and we took my son to his first game. Again you jumped to the foul line with your usual flair—gosh, it was great! I was shocked to have heard about your illness. I'm so glad to have heard (and seen) your progress. You will remain in my prayers. Thanks for giving me a few minutes to thank you.

Sincerely,

Peter Tacconi

• • •

Hi Tug,

I am and have been a fan of yours for almost 30 years. I bought Phillies season tix primarily to see you play up close on a regular basis. While you are now gone from the team, I kept the tix—I was there for the win and I wait for another win, because I BELIEVE!

Having faced a brain tumor and craniotomy one month to the day (Feb. 18 for me) before you, I appreciate some of what you are going through—the overwhelming fatigue and the fear. I am also a nurse and so I know waaaaaaay too much!

I am doing well and pray that you continue to beat the hand that has been dealt you. As you know, laughter and attitude have a great deal to do with it! I tried, especially in the beginning, to keep those who make me laugh the most around me.

I have sent you a couple of snail mail notes to offer support, as a fan and as a brain tumor survivor. The survivors are where I got most of my support and best information! (A survivor warned me that I would need more care when I first got home—more than any doctor or nurse or practical experience had told me.) Oh, and my daughter got married 10 weeks after my surgery. It became a question whether I would be able to attend, how long I would be able to attend or what condition I would be in to attend the wedding. I did, and did it well . . . as you seem to be doing 10 weeks after surgery!!!!

Be well and LIVE LONG!
Peace and Love,

    Judi Zdziera

This is from Springsteen's "Rosalita"—my mantra during this whole time: "Someday we will look back on this and it will all seem funny."

• • •

I was 10 years old on October 21, 1980, when you provided me with one of the greatest moments of my life.

I came back to the Vet in 1990 when you held up the "We Win" newspaper.

I came back to the Vet in 2000 when you held up the same famous "We Win" newspaper once again.

I had tears in my eyes last week when I saw you on TV telling us about what you have been through the past few months. You looked great, and I'm honestly rooting for you now more than I did on that October night in 1980.

I want to take my 2-year-old son to Philadelphia for a 30th anniversary in 2010. He will be 10 by then, and I expect you to be there holding up the same "We Win" newspaper. I can't wait to tell him about 1980, and the legend of the Tugger and the rest of those cardiac kids.

We love you, Tug! Ya Gotta Believe!!!

Sincerely,

Steve Goff

• • •

Tug,

I started following the Mets in 1965 as a 9-year-old and I do remember hearing about your career getting started at the same time. I have been a Mets fan ever since and will never forget either 1969 or that crazy period in September-October 1973 when you guys showed that heart can defeat logic when you have enough of it.

I have followed your recent battles with interest for several reasons. Your example helped show me since the 1970s that it was possible to have fun and be successful at the same time. I was the bookworm in school with no girlfriends and always studying. I didn't know or was afraid to find out that there was another way. Such narrow-minded thinking almost led me to suicide in the mid 70s but thankfully I was pulled away from that. But I never forgot you.

More recently my father suffered his second heart attack last month and now he was living alone, my mom having passed away 3 years ago. For two days he lay on the floor of his co-op in Flushing, but with the help of a local friend (I now live in Rochester, NY), he was saved and hospitalized, where he still is. I gotta believe he is going to make it. Slightly before that, I read of your recent battles and thought to myself there is a guy who will beat this because to me it's all about attitude. I believe you can make or break an illness depending on how you deal with it. If you have to wear a cap that says "Ya Gotta Believe" on it to cover a manhole cover–like scar on your head, you do it and you laugh at life and wonder what the future will bring.

My whole point of this is that I started growing up very logical and straitlaced, but thankfully found other influences that showed me not only is there another way but also that this other way leads to a fuller and more satisfying life. Not that I totally dismiss logic, mind you—I have plenty of that left too. I hope you have many years left and I want you to know you have always been a positive role model in my life right up to and including the pictures in my newspaper yesterday.

So here's to living-on-edge—you'll notice no one ever dies-on-edge. ☺

Gotta believing,

Howard Rubin

• • •

Tug,

Not sure if you will remember me by name, but we have met on several occasions over the past twenty plus years. One of my nicest encounters with you was back in the early 1980s. I owned a company, Aqua Terra Fitness Systems. We were doing aerobic dance marathons to benefit the American Heart Association for a few years in a row. This one particular year, you were helping us with publicity.

We were scheduled to do a photo shoot with you, the

American Heart Association reps, and my aerobic instructors to promote an upcoming fund-raising event. My young son was home from school that day, so I invited him to come along. Being a pitcher on his little league baseball team, my son, Brian, was totally excited at the prospect of meeting one of his heroes, Tug McGraw!

We all arrived at some bank (I forget the name). The photographer was late. While we were all waiting, you took my son aside away from the rest of us, and I noticed the two of you just sitting and talking. I walked over to catch the conversation you were having with my 7-year-old son. I remember Brian telling you his recollection of the 1980 World Series: "It was the bottom of the ninth . . ." Brian was so excited and he described every detail to you. It was really cute for me, as his mom, to watch this interaction, with you showing so much interest in my son.

You asked Brian if he wanted to be a pitcher in the major league. With big wide eyes, Brian said yes and listened intently to your advice. You proceeded to tell him that there were three important things that he needed to remember. Brian leaned forward eagerly, waiting to hear your words of wisdom. You reminded him again that there were THREE important things that he needed to remember. You very quietly leaned forward, too, and told him "Liver, lima beans, and peas." Brian said, "Yeah." You repeated, "Liver, lima beans, and peas." Brian again said, "Yeah" (waiting to hear what's so special about that). With that, you told Brian, "Never, never eat those things, they taste AWFUL!" I proceeded to chastise you for telling my son not to eat peas, which were the ONLY green vegetable, at the time, that Brian would eat.

We all laughed. It was just a lighthearted moment. Brian was admiring your World Series ring. You offered to let him try it on. In fact, you told Brian that if it fit him, he could keep it! Brian tried it on every finger and his thumb, hoping it would fit. Innocently, he handed it back to you and said, "It's too big."

Tug, this whole interaction with my son took just a short amount of time. But, it was very special to my son (and me). Over the years, my kids and I have met many sports personalities and celebrities. Many have been full of themselves and some, well, just plain rude. You took the time to just be nice. It was just a little thing, but it's the little things that we all remember. I'm sure this "little thing" is one of many, many little things you have done for many, many people. It doesn't surprise me that so many people care about your well-being. Your positive personality has touched many people that you don't even know.

I wish you the best for a speedy recovery. You Gotta Believe that power of prayer and positive thinking are an incredible force in healing. With all your friends, family, and fans, you have an abundance of prayer and positive attitude that I believe can make all the difference.

Thanks again for just being the great personality that you are. Best wishes for health and happiness and brighter tomorrows.

Sincerely,

Nancy P. Ottaviano

• • •

Tug,

Hope you are feeling fine and all is well with you and your family! I just wanted to take this time to say "thank you" to you!

Way back around the spring of 1981, I was sitting our hook & ladder fire truck down on Chestnut Street in Center City Philly and I spotted you strolling up the street, and being the life long Phillies fan that I am, I went nuts. I was in charge of the company that day, so I was riding shotgun in the front seat. Of course all the guys said I was crazy and that it was not you, and even if it was, that you would not come over to the truck. Even though I was a professional firefighter in charge of five men and a quarter million pieces of fire equipment, I yelled out like a little kid to one of my heroes, "Yo, Frank." I yelled and time froze for a second as you actually spun around and waved back to me. Nobody even knew why I yelled "Frank," but I did know your name and to my great surprise, you changed directions and came back to our fire truck and you gave me an autograph for my son without any hesitation! I believe that you mentioned that your father was a fireman too. Well, Tugger, that is why I am thanking you now. You helped create a very bright spot in my life that day. I have told that story to a million people. Tug McGraw, just off from winning the 1980 World Series, took the time to chat like an old friend with a Philly firefighter who got to meet his hero that day!

Thanks again Frank "Tug" McGraw!

Frank E. Katona, (Retired) P.F.D., and family

• • •

Over the course of nineteen big league seasons, fans gave me many great moments. But none compares with the feeling I had while watching the Phillies 2003 opening game. I had already been hospitalized and was going to miss the ceremony celebrating the last year of games at Veterans Stadium. I had been practicing with the team's owner, Bill Giles, to catch a baseball Mr. Giles dropped from a helicopter. The trick was I would catch it behind my back!

But as I lay in the hospital after surgery and watched opening day on TV, I heard Hall of Fame announcer Harry Kalas ask the big crowd to send me a message.

"Ladies and gentlemen, as you're aware, Tug McGraw could not be here today because he is in Florida recovering from surgery. We ask all of you to please stand and wave your Phillies rally towels to let the Tugger know we are thinking about him . . . and praying for him. Tug, as you taught all of us, Ya Gotta Believe!"

Harry then told the crowd that two of my sons were there to throw out the first pitch of the last season in a stadium where my greatest baseball moment had been played.

"Ladies and gentlemen, for years Tug McGraw walked in from that right field bullpen. Delivering the ceremonial first pitch today are Tug's sons Mark and Matthew."

I watched the boys jog from the bullpen to the pitcher's mound—both slapping their baseball gloves against their right thigh as I once did—while forty thousand fans waved white towels and chanted at the top of their lungs.

I cried for an hour. For all that's happened, all the mistakes I had made in life, fans still cared. And they were telling me they believed I'd beat this. That's a hell of a revelation when you're lying there in a hospital bed looking for reasons to fight.

CHAPTER 18

Life's Unraveling

I had been through one divorce years earlier and I knew the telltale signs. My relationship with Diane had deteriorated to the point where it was obvious neither of us was happy, but we were both attempting to hold it together in that age-old tradition of trying not to traumatize our son.

The beginning of the end came in 2000, when Diane and I came up with the idea of creating a for-profit arrangement to celebrate the twentieth anniversary of the 1980 World Championship. She was sure we were going to make a bundle from it. Against the advice of everyone I knew, we moved forward with the celebration.

The plan was to re-create not only the win but the hysteria afterward. Of course, that never really works. Our first mistake was holding the event on a Friday night in August, when almost everyone is on vacation at the Jersey shore. Our second mistake was holding it in Center City, the downtown part of Philly—not where the fan base was, which is the neighborhoods. The third and biggest mistake was that we made the tickets expensive—too expensive for the average fan to attend and bring his family. Back in 1980, the celebration had been free! The high price was a real turn-off, and the media was openly critical of the event. There was a real short parade, and then a musical variety show at the upscale Academy of Music that covered all the musical genres—jazz, rock 'n' roll, oldies, contemporary, dance, everything. The show lasted about an hour and a half. And at the end of the show, Schmitty and I and Lefty and a couple of guys sang "God Bless America." After the concert, everybody headed to a top-notch Italian restaurant nearby and was served a real nice dinner.

But only a handful of people showed up to the damn thing. At the end of the night, this bright idea had left us $100,000 in debt and had strained my relationship with a number of players who were embarrassed by how badly the whole thing had been handled.

To cover that loss, Diane made the move that sent me over the edge—she called Tim and asked for money. No, she didn't ask. She demanded money.

Diane and I already had had it up to here with each other. While financial difficulties will create stress in any marriage, a shortage of $100,000 creates a lot of stress. She tried to blame everything on Tim because she kept wanting money from him—all because he had it. I told her to leave him alone.

Tim came into town for a concert at the Spectrum, and I went down to see him and I told her to stay home. She had called him without me knowing it and asked to have lunch with him. Tim said okay. I don't know what was said at their lunch because I was down with his band at the Spectrum. After lunch, she came down there and accused me of blowing her off. I had told her not to come down in the first place. She brought Matthew with her to use as a shield. She knew I'd cooperate if I saw Matthew. It got so ugly that Tim had to tell his security people to keep her away from me because he knew I was really upset.

The whole day was embarrassing for me—but worse for Tim. She had put him in a real tough spot. To his credit, Tim stood his ground and said no. When we ran out of options to find money to pay for the event, I turned to the Phillies. Dave Montgomery, one of the owners, along with principal Phillies owner Bill Giles, personally helped us out. And my good buddy LC, God bless him, chipped in with $50,000 of his own money. Without their help, I would have been paying for the event to this day.

By the summer of 2001 it had gotten to the place where even Matthew wasn't reason enough for Diane and me to stay together. I had to leave.

These became, in the words of my friends, my dark days. In public, I put on the smile and told the jokes. But in private I began flirting with depression. I had moved out of the house and was living with friends. I was drinking like a fish and spending most nights in bars. Every time I went to visit Matthew, Diane and I ended up fighting. Although these are things and emotions many people go through in this kind of situation, I wasn't prepared for them.

At the insistence of John McManus, I went and visited a therapist, Peggy Fredereco. She didn't hesitate in diagnosing me as bipolar—the same disorder my mother, Mabel, had been diagnosed with all those years ago. Peggy prescribed drugs that she said would help me, but I disagreed with her diagnosis and never got the prescription filled. The one thing that talking to Peggy did, though, was help calm my anxieties. I was struggling at that time with finances, divorce, job issues . . . you name it.

Although I didn't want to believe it, maybe Peggy was right. Truth be told, I've probably suffered from some depression-related disorder all my life. But I grew up in a time period where medically you had to be nuts to be treated for bipolarity or manic depression—extreme highs and lows and all that good stuff. My actions were always excused as just extra energy or no energy, as the highs and lows of a competitor. That's the way everyone perceived it. "He's all wound up today." I was usually that way.

Looking back, I realized I had been that way for years. I remembered that one day in my sophomore year of high school, Sister Jordan called on me to go up to the blackboard and solve a simple geometry problem. I got up there and I froze. I couldn't do it. I knew the answer—it was one of the few times I was prepared in that class—but I went up there and froze. While I was trying to do this geometry problem, I started to laugh. Then the next thing you know, I wasn't laughing anymore. I had lost control of my laugh and then flipped over to a cry.

Sister Jordan asked me if I wanted to sit down and try to get hold of myself. She said I could try to finish the problem later. I sat down and I cried. I think after that, at the end of the class, she gave me another shot at it, and I started crying before I even stood up. Then she came over and had a talk with me after class. She was very hard edged on the outside—she never smiled. But deep within her soul beat the pulse of a warm, loving woman. So that part of her came over to me and settled me down.

My mother had been in the mental hospital by that time, so I was sensitive to the whole question of mental stability. I saw how her instability had hurt my father and damaged our family. But that was when I started to tiptoe around the subject of my own mental health. I had all kinds of little things in high school that used to take me up and bring me down. The geometry problem is just an example of one of them.

Had I understood what was happening, perhaps I could

have recognized an early warning sign of my potential for depression. But I didn't think of it in those kinds of words—depression and anxieties. I just thought I was a high-strung kid.

The same kinds of telltale signs were there throughout my career, too. I remember one time in San Francisco, you could say I was hit by an anxiety attack. It was in 1970 or '71 and Gil Hodges was the Mets manager. We were playing the Giants and my dad had come to watch me pitch. There I was, out on the mound pitching, and the Giants had a man on second. He's the tying run. Teddy Martinez, our young substitute shortstop from the Dominican Republic, was in the game.

Everyone on the team is supposed to know all the signs— it's not even an issue. Well, I was trying to put on a play at second. I wanted to pick this guy off. Teddy didn't know the signs. We only learned them in English, and he spoke Spanish, and he motioned to me that he didn't get it. I kept trying to get Martinez to understand, and finally Hodges called time-out. This was the bottom of the ninth. He came walking out to the mound, and he said, "Mr. McGraw, I suggest you focus on the hitter. If you screw this game up by trying to pick a guy off second, you'll be so far out of here, you won't even know what hit you."

I said, "Yes, sir."

I went back to focusing on the hitter, and everything worked out. We won the game. But afterward, back in the clubhouse, I wasn't doing very well. I was sitting at my locker just kind of gasping and barely holding on. But something about my exchange with Hodges sent me into a mental spiral. Joe Pignatano came by to try to settle me down, but things only got worse. A few minutes later Rube Walker, who had been Roy Campanella's backup on the Brooklyn Dodgers in the fifties, came by out of the shower, and he talked to me and he went over and got me a couple of beers. At that point I didn't know if I was laughing or crying, just like in geometry class in high school. Then Hodges came over and he tried to talk to me.

Think about it. All this over trying to pick a guy off second. Hodges sent the clubby to get my dad. Hodges was hoping somebody could bring me back to level. It took Dad several hours, a few drinks, and dinner to get me back. I should have known then that I needed help.

There were several other episodes over my career where I lost it emotionally. It seemed everyone was always willing to make excuses for me—and I made them, too. But now it was the summer of 2001 and I didn't have anyone making excuses anymore.

I filed for divorce, and, nearly broke, I asked Sam and Denise Miluzzo if they'd let me move in to their spare bedroom for a while. They let me, but I was definitely a third wheel in their life. They have long been good friends, but it sure strains relationships when you move in on folks.

While the Miluzzos were great to me, my situation with Diane was getting worse. On several occasions, she told me she was accepting jobs in other states and would be taking Matthew with her. That sent me into the stratosphere each time. The divorce proceedings got uglier and uglier and dragged on and on. I had great lawyers, but there seemed no way to make this happen in a timely fashion.

My connection to the Phillies at this time was very loose. I was a friend to the team and I did work on the team's behalf when they asked me. I would come in and make appearances for some of their corporate sponsors and attend just about any function they wanted to send me to.

In 2002, Larry Bowa invited me to come to spring training to work with a few players. I was looking to grab any dime I could. Diane wasn't working—she worked project to project and had nothing going on at the moment. I was doing the occasional speech and was trying to support both households. Diane didn't want me to go to Florida, but I reasoned that I could sit in Philly and make no money, kind of scavenging for things and waiting for the phone to ring, or I could go down to Florida, make some money, enjoy the sunshine, and be around old friends. What would you do? Go to Florida.

It was the first time I'd been intimately involved in the game in years, and I loved the experience. Just sharing the field again with Mike Schmidt, who also was brought in to teach the younger players, gave me a sense of purpose again. I had always said I couldn't be a coach or manager—I never thought I was cut out for it, as it demanded a kind of consistency I didn't feel I could provide. And being at the ballpark every day, especially with the responsibilities of leadership, didn't interest me. However, this experience of working with players showed me how much I missed—and needed—the game.

Larry, who was in his second year of managing the Phillies after an All-Star career, said he brought Schmitty and me in to give the current players a sense of Phillie history, pride, and work ethic. Every one of the players knew the greatness of Mike Schmidt, a Hall of Famer. Not as many knew who I was. I think Bowa was more honest when he said he invited me because all the guys on the team wanted to hear stories about my daughter-in-law, Faith Hill! And he knew that if I was there I'd bring a little life to the party. Smart man, that Larry Bowa!

I wanted to prove I was worth Larry's gamble. I thought if I just showed the players how to hustle, and brought a smile and some enthusiasm to the ballpark every day, then maybe once in a while somebody would come up and ask me a question about pitching, and I'd be there for them. I hustled my butt off, running from one field to the next between drills and setting an example. I made friends with everybody, had a great time.

Hard to believe, but I was actually nervous about working with the team—so nervous I went on a diet and lost twenty pounds before heading to Florida. I didn't want to be one of those old-timer coaches with my belly drooping over my belt. No one listens to those guys.

After I came back from spring training, it didn't take me long to wear out my welcome with Sam and Denise. In the summer of 2002 I moved in with Larry Christenson, who was divorced. LC had been a phenom with the Phillies in the late 1970s but was forced into early retirement after an elbow injury. He was smart enough to go out and get a great post-baseball job as an institutional investor. He is now a senior vice president with Phoenix Investment Partners. He earns a good living and has a wonderful home in Valley Forge.

I was still making stops on the speaking circuit and baseball card shows, but every time I pocketed a check for $1,000, Diane asked for $2,000. Like I did when I was divorcing Phyllis, I gave Diane everything I had in hopes it would make the process easier.

By the fall, LC asked me to move out. He had family coming to stay with him and he needed the room I was using. Sooner or later, he had to come up with some reason to get me out!

I had to get a place for myself. With no regular income and not enough cash on hand, I couldn't buy a house. I was lucky enough that another one of the owners at the Phillies stepped in to bail me out. Frances Middleton owned a series of low-priced hotels in the Philadelphia area called Macintosh Inns. So I went from LC's palace to an economy motel. The best thing you can say about the motel arrangement is I had privacy. From that point on I started getting more involved in my divorce. I have a lifelong history of delegating things, and it was time I got involved in this situation.

It didn't take long for me to understand how awkward this was. The first time Matthew came to visit, it became obvious I was failing. A motel room is no place for a kid to develop a relationship with his dad. I knew I had to get out of there, but I really had no options.

Here I was, a fifty-eight-year-old former world champion baseball player—at one stage the highest paid relief pitcher in the game of baseball—and I was homeless, penniless, and living in a budget motel with my former colleagues feeling sorry for me. Although I know I hadn't hit rock bottom, I didn't want to see what the bottom looked like. This was as close as I wanted to come.

When I talked to Tim, he asked about the Macintosh and my living arrangements. I didn't tell him much. I didn't want to bother him. It wasn't his problem. It was my responsibility to take care of myself. I kept telling Tim the hotel was a temporary thing, not to worry about it. He didn't know it was low-end so he never questioned it. It would have been embarrassing to admit how far I had sunk.

In January, I was out running errands in a snowstorm and had a car accident that totaled my Jeep Cherokee. It also knocked me slightly silly. I was in the left turn lane when a guy rear-ended me. I got a pretty good bump on the head that left me with a splitting headache, an injury that a few weeks later would be the excuse most people used for my extraordinary flightiness. Little did we know the real reason was tumors growing inside my head.

As the winter turned into spring, Bowa and the Phillies came to the rescue again. After spring training in 2002, when the team had me in for the first and last ten days of spring training, I had come up with a proposal that I thought would make me worth employing. I got a little frisky. I thought, I can do this better; I can bring something better to the table. I'll bring them a product. They'll have some results.

My idea was to have me come down and hang out at the major league facility every morning and work with the boys on the big league roster. Then, in the afternoon, after all the minor league guys had gotten their work done, I would go hang out with them. Just sit and talk and even toss a little. The team could just assign me three left-handers, guys who hadn't progressed like the Phillies were hoping they would. If they were A ball guys and nobody had been able to get them to AA or AAA, I would take a shot focusing on them. I'd do that by showing them how to move the ball around and maybe even throw some screwballs. I promised the team that I wouldn't hurt their arms. Everybody is afraid to teach the screwball—they think it's going to hurt your arm. But I think that after twenty-one years of throwing it, I could teach it without injury. After all, I wasn't like the old-time screwball pitchers like Carl Hubbell or Freddie Fitzsimmons who threw the ball in such a way that their arms were permanently crooked and twisted around, walking about with the palm of their pitching hand facing out all the time!

I told the Phillies I would work to develop these pitchers into the complete package. I would look and see if the youngsters had the guts, the arm, and the repertoire along with the passion for playing ball. Larry bought into my idea, even offering me an awesome $30,000 for the spring. He assigned me three youngsters, and I was excited about their prospects. For the first time in a while, I was excited about mine!

While I'd like to think Larry invited me to spring training because he knew I'd be able to help those three pitchers, the truth is I think he hired me because he felt sorry for me. Pity is a hard thing for me to accept, but, man, I needed help. It's a pretty shameful thing to admit, but I needed the money so bad I'd have done whatever he asked.

We got to Clearwater, and Larry assigned me to work with Beau Richardson, Mark Outlaw, and Chris Rupert. I was just starting to find it, just starting to click with them. My idea seemed, at least in my mind, to be working, and the Phillies seemed happy.

I was back in baseball, earning money and feeling good about myself. What a change.

CHAPTER 19

It's Back. . . .

The headlines in New York and Philadelphia screamed good news. Not long after six hours of cutting on my coconut, doctors from Moffitt told the world that I was as close to cancer free as a patient in my condition could get.

After leaving the hospital, I moved into a home in a nice North Tampa neighborhood, just minutes from Moffitt. Tim had stepped up again and paid for the place, paid for an amazing cook to make me nutritious meals that would keep me healthy, paid for everything. By the first of April, all the family members who had come in for my "funeral" had to get back to their lives. Everyone left except Hank, who stayed to look out for me, drive me to the many doctor appointments, and make sure I took the mounds of pills that were required. I wasn't sure for a while there what was going to get me first—the cancer or the pills, double ginger tea, and oatmeal I had to eat! The doctors told Hank to make sure I ate well and avoided anything that would cause stress.

Mark went back to work in Oregon and Cari to California. Tim was still on his concert tour. He provided me an enormous emotional lift when he called one night in early April from the stage while performing in Philadelphia. He held out the cell phone and let the crowd cheer my recovery. "Ya gotta believe!" he said, the crowd roaring in the background. What a rush!

In June, when it was time to leave Florida and move back to Philadelphia to be near Matthew, I went home to a wonderful three-bedroom place in suburban Berwyn that Tim had rented. It was completely furnished. When I walked in, I couldn't believe how awesome it and he were.

During all of this time, fans were sending e-mails, cards, and letters and calling my office and friends to ask how I was doing. We had not given the media much information about my prognosis or my condition, and the people around me weren't saying a lot either. It was better that way because I wanted to make sure that my family, especially Matthew, got correct information and got it from me. But we needed to let people know what was happening, so on May 29, 2003, I held a press conference at Veterans Stadium in Philadelphia. I picked that day because the Phillies were playing the Mets and we knew that all the media from those two cities would be there. We wanted to make sure that each team's fans would get the same information at the same time.

I was nervous about facing the media that day because this would be the first time I had made a public appearance since getting sick. I've never really been afraid to talk to the media about my baseball career or my life, but this time was different. I had a press release for everyone, but when the time came I didn't use it because I wanted to just answer their questions. I walked up to the podium and just said, "Well, does anyone have any questions?" I didn't know until after it was over that one of the local TV stations was carrying me live or I might have not made a few off-color remarks!

For instance, before the press conference I had visited the Phillies locker room with Matthew and talked with my buddies there. Seeing Phillies third base coach John Vukovich—a former utility infielder and teammate of mine, who'd had a benign brain tumor at the back of his skull removed in 2001—was really great and I was pretty emotional. The young players came over to me with their wishes and I felt good. At the press conference I described it as a lovefest. Everyone came over and had something nice to say. There were some hugs, and a few kisses. I thought that was kind of unusual and funny—not the kind of stuff that typically goes on in a macho baseball clubhouse. So I cracked a joke. "There are a couple of switch-hitters in there, I guess."

After the press conference, it was time to go to see the Mets. I took Matthew with me so he could collect some autographs. I got the same kind of greeting there, and my old buddy Tom Seaver, who was now broadcasting some Mets games on TV, spent time talking to me as did many others.

All of the media was there and I got a lot of coverage. There were many photos of me with no hair and my baseball cap with "Ya Gotta Believe" on it. Once again we were flooded with e-mails from friends and fans because almost every TV station and newspaper gave my e-mail address. Because I got so much coverage, I was now hearing from many people whom I had grown up with or lived near and hadn't spoken to in years. What a way to connect again.

It also meant that now people writing to me were asking me how to get a baseball cap like the one I was wearing. I heard from a son whose father—a lifelong Phillies fan—had been diagnosed with pancreatic cancer, and the son wanted hats for him and all of members of his family. I had so many requests that Laurie and I decided to have the hats made and people could get them through my Web site.

Back in 1984, when I retired from the Phillies, I held a press conference. The night before I had given an interview to Bill Conlin of the *Philadelphia Daily News,* and he wrote that I said to him, "What I'm doing tomorrow is pretty obvious," referring to my facing the media and announcing my retirement the next day. "It is my last gesture as a player, to have one more little rap session. I figure this will be the last press conference I'll call where everybody will come."

What a way to be proven wrong.

If all of that attention didn't tell me the fans were thinking and pulling for me, two other events certainly did.

The Phillies were spending their last season at Veterans Stadium before starting play in Citizens Bank Park, so special activities had been planned for the fans. One of them was the game countdown, with a number hanging in right field to indicate how many games were left at the Vet. At each home game, a former player or other dignitary was invited to ride out with the Phillie Phanatic in his cart to remove the old number and replace it with the next lowest. I was invited to change the number on July 3, 2003, the night before the Fourth of July holiday.

I'd missed the opening day at the Vet because I was still in Florida. So this would be my first public appearance with fans since my illness and surgery. The stadium was packed with fans because it was fireworks night. I heard the announcer say my name as our cart entered the stadium, and then I heard nothing but an overwhelming roar from the fans. I looked all around to see them on their feet, clapping and cheering and yelling my name. All of the Phillies team members came to the top of the dugout, and I could see them as I rode by. The roar continued as Matthew and I changed the number and returned to the entrance. What a way to come back to the Vet.

My return to Shea Stadium was later in July, with the celebration of the thirtieth anniversary of the "Ya Gotta Believe" season. The team got ahold of the old Mets bullpen cart that had been used to bring me and other relief pitchers from the bullpen. I rode in from the right field bullpen with Mets pitcher John Franco, who wears my old number 45. The fans gave me another standing ovation as I made my way to the mound, where I threw a pitch to my old catcher Jerry Grote. It was a great day that I got to celebrate with the fans, and with Tim and Faith and their girls, and with Mark.

At one of the press conferences, a reporter asked me, "What was running through your mind when they told you you had three weeks to live?"

"Cancer," I deadpanned. Everyone in the room laughed. They may have carved out a part of my brain, but they didn't get the section that allowed me to be funny.

"If you can laugh at it, you can live with it," I said. I kept repeating that to myself over and over.

I always used to crack the joke, "I don't know what disease I'm going to get, but I know I've paid my dues no matter what." Over the course of my career there wasn't a charity I didn't allow to roast me to raise money. I've been working all these charities out there—diabetes, heart disease, ALS, cancer. You name it, I've worked it. I just knew one of them was going to reach up and bite me in the ass. And I knew I'd have earned brownie points.

But I never would have bet on cancer. I raised money for cancer but knew almost nothing about the disease. I just knew it was out there. I had no idea of how many people it touches. I always visited hospitals, I always met cancer patients, but I was never confronted by it other than when my father passed. Even then, he was approaching eighty years old, and I thought less about cancer as the cause because he lived such a full life.

There is one thing I know about cancer: I know there are tons of people out there who have it and beat it or are still fighting it. It's a pretty amazing club. How can you put that into any kind of context?

It was interesting watching how people approached me during my treatment. During my career, I had visited lots of cancer centers and cancer patients, and I just tried to inspire the people who had it. It really never occurred to me that I would be a cancer victim.

The thing I keep thinking about is how we were able to put a man on the moon, but no one can prevent or cure cancer. Does that make sense? I don't know that we'll ever find a cure for it. What significant disease have they found a cure for in the last two hundred years? Modern science did find ways to prevent polio, malaria, the measles, mumps, and chicken pox, and smallpox has been eradicated. But cures? I don't think we've made as much progress as we'd like to think we have.

I know when I'm thinking like that, I'm not thinking positively. Sometimes I can't help myself. I've joked that really all that's left now is for me to become the poster child for some neurological cancer charity. But I guess they'll have to wait to see if I'm the right pick. See, if I die from the cancer, they'd have to put a red line through all those posters!

After leaving Florida and heading on my victory tour of Veterans and Shea Stadiums, it sure seemed like things were looking up. "Ya Gotta Believe" was working and my recovery was the feel-good story of the summer.

At the time of the press conferences, almost no one—myself included—knew that none of that was true. The tumors were back and more aggressive than ever.

Then, in late June, I was visiting Tim, Faith, and their kids when once again I lost control of my bladder. There I stood, just as I did during spring training when this all started, wetting my pants.

The doctors at Moffitt had given us a list of things to look for, and if there was new growth causing pressure on my bifrontal tumor, they said I'd relieve myself uncontrollably. A couple of days after it happened at Tim's, I was back in Philly and had gone to visit Matthew. Standing in Diane's driveway, it happened again. I heard Jennifer whisper under her breath, "Shit, it's back." I knew exactly what she was talking about. She e-mailed Moffitt and they said, "Get him down here, it's probably the tumor coming back."

Talk about feeling your world spinning out of control. I went from thinking I was home free to suddenly not knowing what day would be my last. On July 16, the doctors at Moffitt did another MRI and saw the worst: Not only had the tumors returned, but they were growing faster than ever. Moffitt wanted to arrange surgery within a week.

We had a couple of days to hang out before the surgery, so I thought I would jump on a plane and see Tim perform in Vegas. I went thinking this would be my last chance to see him perform.

I was exhausted but I wanted to come to him. Prior to the concert he and Faith hosted an intimate cocktail party for just me and his band members. The biggest surprise was when Hank showed up in a Versace suit. Tim had taken him on a shopping spree. Hank had been groomed—nose hairs and all. He looked great. We flew back to Tampa the next day to face a different kind of music.

Having dealt with the media frenzy during the first visit, we decided to try to keep this surgery quiet. All the attention that the first surgery had attracted had put pressure on everyone involved. Trying to be honest with the media created more problems than we could handle. It was a lesson learned that even though you wanted to go public, the problems that you can't control—speculation—make it almost impossible for those around you.

On July 22, we checked into Moffitt again for a second operation and to try the first of several more radical treatments. What my doctors had determined was that the tumor on the right side had responded positively to the first operation and chemotherapy. The tumor on the left side, though, had grown back and was as big as it was the day it had been removed in March.

This time Dr. Brem wanted to scrape the left-side tumor out and insert chemo wafers to sit on the cancerous area to try to burn it out. The wafers were invented by Dr. Brem's brother, who is a doctor in Baltimore. Dr. Brem has two or three brothers in the same field. They are all brilliant. Tim had really found some good people. Dr. Brem's brother invented these little wafer things that are full of the drugs used in chemotherapy, and they dissolve. They didn't put them in there the first time. They wanted to see what would happen. I know I'm oversimplifying this, but that's how I understood it.

It was tough talking to my kids, especially Tim, about this second surgery. Like me, they had all been so hopeful after the first surgery. Tim, in a conversation with Jennifer, got emotional about the need to think positively. "You need to take this one day at a time and we'll all get through this," he said when I got on the phone. It gave me strength to know how committed Tim was.

And strength is what I needed because I was no longer a surgical patient. I was now an experiment, part of research.

After the second surgery, the doctors told my family they had never before seen such reproduction of the cancer cells. Privately, the Moffitt folks worried that this thing was going to head south if the wafers and chemo couldn't overcome these aggressive cells. This was new to them. I was off the charts.

I say privately because everyone was good and positive to

my face. The kids, Hank, Jennifer, the doctors—they all tried to paint this second round in as positive a light to me as possible. But they apparently made a pact: whoever I cornered for the truth had to lay it out. No sugarcoating.

The game then began—which one of them was going to have to tell me. They all agreed that if I asked the question, they would tell me that based on statistics, the opportunity to one day be completely cancer free seemed slim. The other thing the staff at Moffitt told them was that the cancer was higher than a Level IV tumor—it was actually a Level VI.

Over the next few weeks, I sensed the conspiracy. My family is big into conspiracies, so we're always looking for them anyway. Hank is convinced one person killed all the Kennedys—JFK, RFK, and even John Jr.

Because of the surgery, the doctors felt that it would be safer for me to drive home rather than fly. Tim called his driver, Casper, and hired a tour bus to pick up me, Hank, Jennifer, and her son Jack, and take us back to Philadelphia. I made it my goal during that long drive to hit every Waffle House along the way!

I knew there was no way I was getting all the information. I'm a guy who loves to know everything—or at least know what I can know. So I started asking more and more questions. Finally, Jennifer drew the short straw. Standing in the kitchen of the home in Philadelphia that Tim rented for me, Jennifer gave me the skinny.

We had been talking about the second procedure done at Moffitt. During the conversation, I realized I had no clue about the different grades of brain tumors. I finally asked Jennifer point-blank what the probable outcome of this type of tumor was. Jennifer told me she was going to try to not get emotional. Then she spelled it out.

"Tug, it's time to get all your ducks in a row with your family and estate," she said. Whew! That was a kick in the ass. It took a few minutes to settle in. We talked about setting up a family trust and how I wanted to be buried. I think Jennifer expected me to say that I wanted the pope and the Vatican involved. To her surprise, I asked that it all be done at Father Victor's small countryside church in Chester County.

I've got to admit, my attitude changed from that moment on. I knew I needed to get stuff done, needed to get ready for the inevitable.

Apparently, I learned later, everyone was convinced that the day I learned how dire the situation was I would go into a funk, a depression, and that it would be all downhill from there. They figured the only way I could stay positive was if I was in the dark.

For a few hours they were right. I was afraid to take a nap that day. I had no idea if I would wake up.

Do you know how hard it is to be positive when people keep telling you how quickly you're going to die? I've made a career out of looking down the barrel and believing I had what it took to beat the odds—well, on a baseball diamond, anyway. Suddenly, I had no idea what odds even meant.

All I knew was that here I was, a man with the pride of a champion, and I couldn't walk more than thirty yards without developing the wobbles. My legs would quiver, and I knew I was one step from falling flat on my face.

Worse, the chemo had cost me control of some bodily functions. I had a loss of taste and a loss of smell. There's nothing more humiliating than having people standing near you telling you you've soiled yourself—and you had no idea.

My body started betraying me daily and it was moments like those that made believing so difficult. But the thing I was most bothered by losing was my pride. There was a day that I could walk from the dugout to the outfield—on my hands! Now I had trouble walking from the bedroom to the bathroom.

The weaker my legs got, the more nervous I got. The thought of using a walker or a wheelchair almost made me want to cry. I kept telling myself I wasn't even sixty and there was no way I was going to lose my ability to walk. The wobbles became more and more frequent. When it started, I mostly got the wobbles when I got out of the car. By the late fall, it was all the time. Every time my knees buckled, my mind asked if it was because the tumor was back.

I know people can't predict when they'll leave this earth. But the guessing becomes a bigger part of your day when you have cancer. You don't know if you have another couple of months, or a couple of years. What if it was just a couple of days? Some mornings I would wake up and wonder if today's the day. Other days I felt like, Hey, I'll probably make it. In August, I was convinced I wouldn't make it to my fifty-ninth birthday on August 30. I figured everyone else knew it, too— and they just weren't telling me. That explained why so many people showed up for a birthday party thrown for me by family and friends. See, combine my belief in conspiracies with a lack of information, and what was left of my mind went wild!

Jennifer tried to keep me positive. I kept asking her, "Do you think this is my send-off party?" She'd come back with, "Tug, stop that! Remember PT, positive thinking!" PT became her daily admonition when I started losing faith.

The one story that kept my spirits up was of the fight my father gave cancer at the end of his life. I had good days and bad days. On the bad days, I held on to that story.

Big Mac still died of cancer. But he did it on his terms. As my condition got worse, that became my promise to myself. I was going to fight this fight on my terms.

After they had operated on me twice and cut big chunks out of my brain, it was clear surgery wasn't going to solve my problem. This cancer was tougher than any batter I'd ever faced, and that left me with limited options.

In September, we went back to Moffitt for another MRI to see on-screen what the results of the second surgery had been. Flying down, I felt like it would be a great day. I had none of the telltale signs of relapse.

I should have known something was wrong, though, when no one would tell me exactly what had shown up on the MRI. They all wanted me to wait for Dr. Brem, and they asked Jennifer to get all the kids on a conference call. Then Brem was delayed in surgery, so they sent in his partner, Dr. Susan Snodgrass, to deliver the message.

She dropped the bomb. My condition had worsened. In fact, there was a new tumor forming at the back of my skull. I pressed Dr. Snodgrass on what she thought this meant. She said that barring a miracle, I was looking at a maximum of six more months to live. Now I was already six months up on the last doctor, so I wasn't sure what to make of it all. I came in full of hope. I left with my hopes crushed.

Even in my wildest dreams, I hadn't expected to have a new tumor. I had not expected to be told I had six months to live. Although I understood it was possible, I had just been feeling so good.

Dr. Brem came in after Dr. Snodgrass went out, and he talked and talked and talked. Truthfully, I can't remember a word he said. Then he gave me a hug—it was one of those hang-in-there hugs. It was an "I'm sorry" hug. That's when I got worried. When I first got there in March, everything was much more positive, Brem was much more enthusiastic. He was full of hope, too. Now, it was just a hug.

Dr. Brem and I had known each other for only six months, but there already was something special between us. Moffitt held a wonderful fund-raiser, the Magnolia Ball, earlier in the summer, and Dr. Brem had asked me to deliver a short speech and to help with the silent auction. So Denise Miluzzo got on the bandwagon and started calling our network of friends. I belong to the Mets Alumni Association and the Phillies Alumni. Tim has friends in the music business, and the next thing you know we had at least $10,000 to $12,000 in auction items: guitars, gloves, anything and everything.

It was kind of funny that I used some of that time to sort through mounds of trophies and pictures collected over a lifetime. When some of the family and I were going through the stuff that had been in storage, Tim found a silver bowl with the Jacksonville Suns logo on it. That was the team I was playing for when I'd been lucky enough to meet his mother years earlier. Tim asked if he could have the bowl. I had it polished and sent to him.

I went to Tampa loaded with good stuff for the hospital. Dr. Brem has a nine-year-old son and he wants him to grow up and be a good athlete. So at the dinner he asked me if I would sign a few things for his little guy. We were all dressed in tuxes, and we both had "You Gotta Believe" hats on. At the dinner, we gave each other hugs. I gave him a jersey encased in plastic.

I put all my trust in him, and it turns out that it was well placed. We developed a nice relationship during the post-op treatments.

But the problem with this type of medicine is that no two patients are exactly alike. What works for one might not work for another. So for all the affection I had for Dr. Brem and all the faith I had in the folks there at Moffitt, I grew to understand that everything we were doing was kind of like playing a big guessing game. There was no hard and fast answer, no right or wrong decision. Everything, basically, was educated guesswork.

When it became obvious that all the treatment, surgeries, wafers, and the like at Moffitt had not been able to stem the tide of these cells growing in my brain, I knew I had to move on if I wanted to try to beat this thing.

So I went looking for someone new to help me beat these odds.

Moffitt had one more treatment to offer me but I told the doctors there that I wanted to go home and talk to my kids about it and that I would get back to them. That flight from Florida home to Philadelphia was among the longest in my life.

The next morning Jennifer saw how down I was and told me there had to be another path. We jumped on the computer and started exploring other options. We e-mailed Susan Snodgrass and told her that I was going to wait on her last option. She e-mailed back and told us to look up David M. Bailey's Web site. David, who bills himself as a performing songwriter, is a young man who's had success treating a deadly brain tumor. His Web site offered hope and the name of Dr. Henry Friedman.

Jennifer said, "Tug, can you believe this doctor puts his pager number on the Web site? You want me to call?" I thought, Fat chance this guy will call back.

Fifteen minutes later the phone rang. It was Dr. Henry Friedman. He told us that he had been waiting for our call and that he had been following my case through the media, both as a doctor and an old Mets fan. Dr. Friedman told me that in regard to this disease, it was as if I had lost the first game of the World Series badly, but the good news was I had three games left.

The doc said that people who are real sick are pioneers, and we have darts in our backs. He didn't know how else to put it. He said, "We can all absorb so many darts, and then we die. And some of us can take a lot of darts, and then the next thing we know we get over the hump, then we're on our way and we're doing okay. So if you want to be a pioneer, you've got to be willing to go out there and be ahead of the pack and take the darts. People are going to be throwing them at you."

That included the medical community among the dart throwers.

"The truth is," he continued, "that you will probably die from this disease, but what Duke and my staff can offer is a longer, healthier quality of life and, most important, hope."

I was so happy when he got off the phone that I was actually singing. I couldn't wait to call my kids to tell them that I was seeking another opinion. Tim said it best: "If the treatment is not worse than the disease, go for it."

Dr. Friedman told me to gather all my medical records and head on down to Duke. Four days later Jennifer and I were on our way. Standing at the doors of Duke Medical Center on a Saturday morning was not your typical doctor. He wore blue jeans and sneakers and greeted us with a big hug. He talked fast and with great enthusiasm. He told us to call him Henry—that's something he insists all his patients do.

There was no time to spare. He took us to his office and introduced us to his colleague Dr. Allan Friedman, no relation. One thing that stood out to me was that in his office, there were no degrees hanging on walls. That wasn't him. Instead, the place was filled with computers, boxes, and papers. This was a workingman's place, an office that gave you the feeling you were about to engineer and construct a highrise. Henry walked me through my options—things that might work and things that might not.

He explained to me how aggressive my cancer was, showing me that the cells creating my tumor were basically doubling every day. "It's like offering you a job and telling you I'll pay you one dollar a day," he said, bringing it down to my level. "But every day, I'd double what I gave you the day before. One dollar doesn't sound like much. Neither does two, four, eight, or sixteen. But by the end of the month, I'd be paying you a million dollars a day. Now that's a bunch. That's what we're facing. You've got an aggressive tumor that is growing so fast it's like winning the lottery in reverse."

I was going to start my first clinical trial. That's doctor lingo for making me a guinea pig. Henry sent me to rest for two days before he would start treatment.

When it was time for all this to begin, Henry met us and took us over to the Brain Tumor Center. When we walked in it looked like a scene out of *M*A*S*H*. There were dozens of people sitting and lying around getting chemo treatment. I remember walking through and thinking, "My God, there are so many people here. They are so young." Mothers and fathers were holding the hands of their grown children as they were getting treated. The place, however, was not sad. It was the first time I saw other people with big surgical scars on their heads that looked like mine. And it wasn't so scary anymore.

We stayed for five days. Every night I was able to return to the hotel for the remainder of the treatment. Jennifer and I had dinner that night with June, an old girlfriend of hers and fellow flight attendant. June too was a cancer survivor. She showed me a photo of her when she was at her worst. I was shocked. I could not believe this was the same woman who was sitting in front of me. June definitely gave me hope!

I left Duke with that ray of hope. Henry wanted me to return in a month to see if the treatment was working.

In Philadelphia there's a place that can do the MRIs before my appointments at Duke. It saves time, and Henry can read the results faster to see if the treatment is working.

So a month after getting pumped up by Henry, I headed for my first MRI. Unfortunately, the MRI revealed that the treatment was not working. The disease continued to progress.

Henry had option B available. As long as there were options I felt safe. The problem was that Henry's option B would be costly. The drug he started giving me was FDA approved but not for his type of treatment. Jennifer called Daine, Tim's assistant, and told him that a one-month supply would be $5,800. Tim said, "Gotta do it." Thank God there are a Tim McGraw and a Faith Hill in my life. My treatment would have ended right there had he not had the resources. I couldn't help but think how many people and children are turned down because of finances. That was another of life's reality checks.

During this entire experience, I swear I've had the chance to meet real live here-on-earth angels. Start with Dr. Brem. Then Tim. The next angel wore blue jeans and cowboy boots. His name was Henry. And of course there was Jennifer and Laurie. There was also my good friend Mike Mahoney. Mahoney, a college professor with long blond hair, moved east from his home in Napa so he could be a part of my support team. Moe, as we called him, shared my love of vanilla ice cream and was at my house whenever I needed him. All of them have been looking out for me. Amazing.

I'd mentioned before that Tim rented a motor home for a few of us to drive across the country to Napa for a holiday family gathering. I left Berwyn a few days before Thanksgiving with Hank, John McManus, and Moe in the fully stocked RV and headed west. Hank and Moe split all the driving. What a trip. I think there was some belief that we wanted to do this as a kind of last hurrah, one final fling before I bit it. I really wasn't thinking like that. I just thought it would be a great road trip.

We swung through Nashville to have breakfast near Tim's house, then jumped on Interstate 40 and did the old Route 66 the rest of the way. We were a couple of miles outside Memphis when it hit me—we had missed Graceland. I couldn't pass through the Land of Elvis without visiting the home of the King! I had never, in all my years, made a trip to the Mecca of rock 'n' roll.

We turned the motor home around and wound our way through to Graceland. I was suffering from the wobbles pretty badly, but I now had a walking cane that Larry Christenson had given me. So we signed up to do a little private tour of the mansion.

While headed up the stairs, I had a medical moment brought on by months of chemo. I lost control of my bowels and crapped all over myself. In Graceland! The staff there rushed me out—I guess because I smelled so bad.

The rest of the trip, all I heard from the guys in the motor home was how I had soiled myself in the home of the King and how proud the rest of the McGraws were of me. Hank, in a moment of complete irreverence, even suggested the folks at Graceland were going to put a plaque on the wall that headed up the stairs: "Tim McGraw's dad shit here."

On December 8, 2003, I headed back to Duke for what I believed would be my last visit with Henry Friedman. Something told me I was losing this battle and that once Henry saw my MRI he'd tell me we'd run out of options.

We rolled into the hospital early in the morning for an appointment with the MRI machine. I hadn't slept well the night before, worried this wasn't going to be good news. I was so tired, in fact, that I fell fast asleep while in the machine. After the MRI and after having blood drawn, I went with Jennifer up to Henry's office to wait for the results.

We both sat there in this nervous quietness, not really sure what to say. The door was cracked and we heard a doctor across the hall sharing results with another patient. The patient, who was on his way to Europe for the holidays, took bad news. "Thank God they're not talking about your MRI," Jennifer said.

About that time, we heard laughter and hollering down the hall. Henry came around the corner and burst through the door.

"Good news!" Henry said. "Christmas has come early. It's freaking awesome! The therapy is working. *Your tumors are shrinking!*"

I sat there speechless, soaking in the words: *My tumors are shrinking!*

I couldn't believe it. Henry made so much noise that others joined in the celebration. One of the nurses asked me why I believed the tide had turned. "Henry and Jennifer," I said. "Without Henry to mix the cocktail and Jennifer to keep me motivated, I wouldn't be hearing these words. I wouldn't be standing here."

As excited as Henry was for me, his elation was multiplied by thoughts of what my experience could mean to others suffering from brain tumors. There were fewer than a handful of patients in the world who were trying this mixture of medicines. Henry had told me a "protocol" mixing these two drugs—one normally used for lung cancer patients, the other for transplant patients—was going to be tried clinically in about four months. I didn't have that long to wait. So the positive result I was having might speed up delivery of this treatment to hundreds, possibly thousands, of people.

"This is the medical equivalent of pitching a shutout," Henry said, his smile spread from ear to ear. "If we keep these tumors shrinking, it will be like pitching a no-hitter." He was talking my language. I knew this would be tough. But like that day in 1965 in Forbes Field, I thought that if someone was going to pitch a no-hitter, why shouldn't it be me?

As the good news found its way to my network of friends and family, a powerful phone message came my way. Ed Wade, general manager of the Phillies, wanted to make sure I understood his offer: "Get well, Tug, because we want you back at spring training when pitchers and catchers report in February 2004!"

The lump in my throat was as big as a baseball.

• CHAPTER 20 •

Life's Full Circle

W hat are the odds that a man could have cancer cells running through his brain and still call himself lucky? What is the chance a doctor can give you three weeks to live, yet you can sit back nearly a year later and say luck couldn't be more on your side? That's me. To paraphrase Lou Gehrig in his farewell speech at Yankee Stadium, I may be the luckiest man in the world.

I've always said that I had to prove myself on the field because it was luck that made me a baseball star, but it has been luck that has led me through my personal life as well. What are the odds that a young boy of meager beginnings from Northern California would grow up to spend nineteen years in major league baseball, win two World Series and play in a third, and bring baseball's biggest prize to two franchises in major cities for the very first time? And what are the chances that this flighty young boy would later father a child who, after years of being denied his father's love, would one day become one of America's biggest recording stars and give his father a second chance at life?

It seems like I've always had to load the bases before throwing that final dramatic strike and pulling out the save, and if you look at the record of my life, that is when all the good stuff has happened to me.

Born at the tail end of a devastating world war in 1944 and growing up poor in the prosperous fifties, I had an older brother who knocked down all the trees to clear a path for me, no matter how difficult it may have been. True to form, I stacked the deck against myself early on, but my big brother, Hank, came in to save me and put me on the road to becoming one of the few men who at the time could call themselves major league baseball players. If it wasn't for his insistence, I never would have been signed to the Mets, been sent to a series of minor league farm teams where I would eventually play on a team that would give the Mets their first minor league championship win, gotten noticed by the powers that be and offered a spot in the bigs after just one year, and started my ride on the elevator of pro ball—making a few stops at the top. Some have speculated that it was my talent as a pitcher and my zest for life that put me there on the mound for the 1973 and 1980 World Series. But I know that it was luck and the faith of a brother.

Lucky? You're damn right I'm lucky.

Over the years, folks have tried to connect fate to a chance meeting that produced a young man strong enough to persevere and believe in a father who didn't deserve the unconditional love and forgiveness that only a son could give. I believe that everything happens for a purpose and that each chapter in our life leads us to where we are today, but I can only credit luck and the strength of a good woman—his mother, Betty—for the man my oldest son, Tim, has become.

He was lucky to have been raised by a young lady who would teach him integrity, faith, and hope and instill in him the value of being better than all the other men in his life.

There is no doubt in my mind that Tim was better off not having me in his life until he was seventeen, no matter how hard it must have been to be denied a father's love for so many years. Luck and a mother's love made him the man he is today. Nothing I gave him made him the man who stepped up and said that my prognosis of three weeks to live was unacceptable and then helped me to live longer than I was supposed to, giving me a new lease on life.

Most people just assume that I am a rich man after all the money I've made in my lifetime. Bad assumption. Without Tim, I would be in a poor man's hospital fighting to make ends meet with my pension. My medical insurance covers some of my medical bills, but Tim has taken care of everything else: my expensive and sometimes experimental treatments, my house in Philadelphia, my meds, my travel and needed care. Tim even bought Hank a truck so he could drive cross-country to be with me after I became ill. There is no limit to his generosity and there is no limit to my appreciation. He may not have been lucky to be my son. There's no question I am lucky to be his father.

I have also been lucky enough to have been married to two women who have given me a family and made me a father of three more children. My twenty-year marriage with Phyllis brought my son Mark and daughter, Cari, into the world, and while I wasn't the model father for them while they were growing up, I have tried to tell them how proud I am of them and how much I respect their individuality. Then there was my second marriage to Diane, which gave me my youngest son, Matthew, who is my biggest symbol of good fortune. Matthew is my second chance, my chance to move forward, and one of the best things I have ever done. In his short life, he has shown me that I can be a good father and make a positive contribution to someone's life. Matthew is going to be the one child that I haven't let down—my chance to finally get fatherhood right. I am lucky to have Matthew and be given a second chance at fatherhood.

Luck, I know, is exhibited every day in this world in one form or another, even if some people never see it. Everyone has a different explanation for life's events. Some say it is fate, destiny, or even a blessing that guides us. Maybe it was fate that history repeated itself with the scout who signed Hank also agreeing to take me. Maybe it was my destiny to be a successful major league ballplayer who became known for his spontaneous displays of emotion on the field. And maybe it was a blessing that I was diagnosed with cancer and had my eldest son come to my rescue, giving me the opportunity to see my life more clearly and spend a few more months on this earth with my friends and family. But I say that I am who I am today, and I am alive, because I am one hell of a lucky guy.

In 1973, I said "Ya Gotta Believe" that the Mets could win the pennant. Now, thirty years later, I gotta believe that my luck hasn't run out yet. But if it has, and this is the end of my winning streak, then I am taking this luck to Vegas, baby—for one last shot at a win!

Ya gotta believe.

Epilogue: Final Inning

Following the good news and high fives of December 8, Tug and Jennifer returned to Philadelphia and prepared for a Christmas filled with good cheer. But the good days didn't last long. Inexplicably, the very medical cocktail that seemed to be beating back the cancer in Tug's head suddenly was powerless against the aggressive tumor.

For weeks, Tug had made it clear that he wanted to spend as much of Christmas Day as possible with Matthew. But Tug was very tired and barely conversant when December 25 arrived—only responding to questions but not initiating conversation.

Early on the morning of December 27, Laurie heard Tug wandering around upstairs. When she went up she found him half-dressed, his skin cold and clammy, and he didn't know where he was. Laurie immediately called Dr. Henry Friedman at Duke. Henry thought Tug was probably lightheaded from standing up too quickly. Henry told Laurie to give Tug a glass of orange juice with extra sugar in it, which she did. Tug asked for a glass of water, as well. About thirty minutes later, he took the first half of the thirty-two pills he took each day. The mixture didn't sit well and Tug threw up his medication.

Laurie called Henry again. He instructed her to get Tug to the emergency room. She called Larry Christenson to help take him to the hospital, as she couldn't do it herself. Tug's blood tests came back negative, so they took him home. By this time, Laurie had called Jennifer and told her what was going on. Jennifer took the first plane out to Philadelphia, arriving late Saturday night with her young son, Jack.

When Laurie reported to Henry that Tug's blood tests were okay, Henry asked her to keep Tug under close observation. Henry now thought Tug's condition might be related to the tumor and that it may have started growing again. He ordered an MRI for Monday, December 29, exactly three weeks after the cheers had gone up at the cancer center in Durham. Jennifer accompanied Tug for yet another MRI. When she looked at the film, she couldn't believe what she saw—the cancer was everywhere. Tug knew she could read the MRIs, but he never asked. Jennifer had her stewardess face on. Tug knew.

When Tug was out of earshot, Jennifer immediately called Tim. She was trembling as she told him about the MRI. She hated being the messenger of such dire news. "Jenn, I'm coming," Tim told her. "I'm on my way."

Tim and Daine flew into Philly on Tuesday for a conference call with Henry to hear his diagnosis of the MRI. The film had been overnighted to Henry, and it now proved Henry's theory right. The tumor had spread in the front of Tug's head and now was stretched across both frontal lobes.

Now it was time to make another big decision. Henry said it was obvious the cancer had beaten the treatment and that to continue would be futile. He had always said to Tug and his team that when the end came, it would come rapidly. As a group, Tug, Tim, Hank, Henry, and Jennifer agreed to drop use of the chemo medicines that only a month earlier had seemed so promising. It was a decision made with a very final outcome in everyone's mind. Henry assured the family that because Tug's treatment at Duke was now finished, he would be at home with his family to the end.

Henry hung up, and the silence was deafening. No one knew what to say. Finally, Tim got up, walked across the living room, and asked Tug if he wanted him to open the curtains for a little sunlight and a view of the backyard. Tug said no, but started thinking about the view at the cabin Tim had on a hilltop on his property outside of Nashville. Tug couldn't stay in Philadelphia; he knew how crazy it would get with the media once the story of his condition got out. He also didn't like the idea of having people see him fade. He considered going to Napa but it was just too far. After thinking it over, Tug said, "I'd like to go to the cabin."

On New Year's Eve, Tim loaded his father, Daine, Jennifer, and her son, Jack, on his plane at ten a.m. and headed west. After they landed in Nashville, Tim went to pick up Faith and the girls while Daine took Tug, Jennifer, and Jack and started out for the cabin. While Jennifer was on the phone with this book's editor, trying to wrap up a few remaining editorial changes, Tug suffered a major seizure with convulsions while riding in the front seat of the car. Jennifer, sitting directly behind him, put him in a bear hug. That and the tight seatbelt probably saved him from hurting himself. Daine pulled up to a policeman and they were escorted to the nearest hospital. Daine called Tim to tell him they had had to take Tug to the emergency room. Tim said he'd meet them at the hospital.

Meanwhile, Jennifer called Henry, and he advised her not to let the doctors try anything heroic. They would want to try to save him; Henry knew that they couldn't. Tim arrived and met with the doctors in the ER. They advised him to contact the rest of Tug's family. Daine began making all the arrangements to have them fly out immediately. The idea was to get Tug stabilized so that he could spend as little time as possible in the hospital and maximum time at the cabin.

After that episode, Tug evened out a bit. Matthew came out to the cabin on January 2, where he got to ride one of Tim's all-terrain vehicles and hang out with his dad, watching football games on the couch. Tug played with Matthew and entertained the immediate family with a pajama fashion show throughout the day, changing into a new set every couple of hours.

On the afternoon of Saturday, January 3, after Matthew had left, Tug requested the presence of a priest to deliver last rites, initiating the chain of events that would become the last "humor bomb" of Tug's life. A nearby church was called at around two-thirty in the afternoon, and a priest was dispatched. He hadn't arrived by three, or by four, and so the call went out again and the family was assured a second priest was on the way. The second priest arrived and offered Tug communion. He smiled weakly when the priest placed his hand over Tug's. Tug seemed comforted by the priest's presence.

Then, about four hours after the first call went out, the first priest—a man in his seventies—showed up, skittish and scared. It turned out he had gone to the wrong address, to the house of a middle-aged couple. The priest had knocked on the door repeatedly, and when he received no answer, he entered the house via the sun porch to wait, as is the custom in the neighborhood. From the kitchen, the wife heard the door open and slam shut, but her husband thought it was just the TV. When the husband, a large, strong man, walked into the front room and saw a man in black standing there, he tackled the intruder from behind, knocked him down, and sent his papers flying. As the two men scuffled, the wife got a pistol and pointed it at the man in black. Finally, they turned him over and discovered his true identity. Needless to say, apologies were made.

After the episode with the priests, a few old teammates—Bob Boone, Dickie Noles, Greg Luzinski—and Dave Montgomery, one of the Phillies owners, called to say one last good-bye. Visitors, including Cari and her daughter, Hank, Laurie, and Tug's cousins, among others, streamed in and out all day long. Tug rallied a bit and was even alert and smiling. He enjoyed watching the Tennessee Titans—Tim's favorite team—defeat the Baltimore Ravens on TV.

That night, when they were getting ready to put Tug to bed, Tim and Jennifer stood him up in his snowflake pajamas, and he suddenly began to shake and wobble. Tim and Jennifer started to panic, knowing that he was having another seizure. After about half a minute, Tug stopped, looked at them both, and began to laugh. His boyish humor was intact to the end.

Faith called in late at night to get an update from Tim. After talking to her for a bit, Tim put Tug on the phone. Tug, who had spoken very little in the last twenty-four hours, suddenly started speaking in full sentences to her. Jennifer turned to Tim with a look of total disbelief on her face. They just shook their heads, their mouths agape. Jennifer started to laugh, and she said to Tim, "Tug always was a sucker for pretty women."

Tim and Jennifer slept in shifts that night, to make sure someone was awake in case Tug needed anything. While Jennifer slept in one of the other rooms, Tim curled up on a chair and ottoman, holding Tug's hand as Tug slept in a hospital bed made homey-feeling with handmade quilts.

Sunday, January 4, was a quiet day. Tug was less responsive now, and Cari was praying that her brother Mark would get there on time. Mark had spent New Year's Eve skiing at Mammoth Mountain in California when news reached him of his father's failing health. Heavy snows had prompted the cancellation of some flights, but Tim had promptly made arrangements for Mark to fly to Nashville. The family knew he had left California, but they weren't sure when he would actually arrive.

Tim had gone to Daine's house down the road to grab a shower and a change of clothes, leaving Jennifer alone with Tug. It was unusually windy that morning; a storm was coming. Jennifer asked Tug if he wanted her to open the windows, and Tug nodded yes. She rolled the bed over to the window and took the sheets off so Tug could feel the breeze. His feet were practically hanging out of the low window. When the breeze came through, Jennifer said to him, "Look! We're windsurfing!" Tug gave an emotional laugh and held up his hand for a high five.

Tug hung in there for the arrival of his son Mark and his friend John McManus that evening. When he arrived, Mark was stunned to see how much his father's health had deteriorated. He found his father slipping in and out of an almost comatose state. At first, Tug didn't appear to know Mark was with him. He never opened his eyes or took notice that his younger son was there. Tim suggested that perhaps a baseball would help, and his assistant found one and gave it to Mark.

Mark walked over to his father and placed the familiar reminder into his father's hand. It was then that Tug opened his eyes to see his son standing over him. Mark leaned over and kissed his father. As he began to stand back up, Tug pulled him back down . . . and kissed him back. Then Tug drifted off to sleep.

"That was a very special moment for me and my dad," said Mark. "I am so thankful that I made it [to him] in time."

Once again, Tim slept on the chair at his father's side. On the other side, on another chair, was Mark.

Jennifer, Tim, and Mark kept a constant vigil throughout the night. Cari, Hank, and Tug's cousins came and went throughout the day. Being on deathwatch is a horrible feeling. Trying to anticipate when he was in pain and controlling it lay heavily on everyone's minds. At about four forty Monday afternoon, Central time, Tug began to have trouble breathing. Cari, Mark, Tim, and Jennifer were sitting around his bed. That morning, Faith had asked Jennifer where Tug's rosary beads were, and now Jennifer blurted out, "Oh, my God! The rosary!" Then she said to Cari, "Put that cross in his hand." Cari placed the beads with the small cross on it in Tug's right hand, and Tim placed a baseball in his left hand. Tug opened his eyes, and at four forty-five he took his last breath. At that exact moment, Hank walked in. Tug died peacefully and in comfort, surrounded by loved ones.

He was mourned and eulogized in not only the Philadelphia and New York newspapers the next morning, but on TV, on radio, and in newspapers all over the country. Tug McGraw had made believers of all of us.

Moving Forward

by Jeff McMahon, keyboardist for The Dancehall Doctors,
friend to Tug McGraw, and advocate for the
Tug McGraw Foundation

Tug and I first met in 1993 at a Phillies baseball game. I had just started playing keyboards in Tim's band, the Dancehall Doctors. It was hot, and I had my long hair tied back out of my face with a blue bandanna. Tug came up behind me—remember, we had never met before—pulled me by the hair, and said, "Hey, big boy . . . I love what you've done with your hair!"

Okay. So this is Tim's dad. I wanted to make a good impression. I snapped around and found myself face-to-face with the star pitcher. He immediately let go of my hair. I grabbed him by his collar with both hands, pulled him up into my face, and told him as professionally as I could, "Hey . . . you know, 'tug' is one of my *favorite* words."

We both just broke up hysterically, and he gave me a hug. I guess we hit it off. I saw Tug pretty regularly after that. Over the next ten years, he'd show up somewhere during a tour, hang with Tim and the band all day, and then catch the evening show.

After Tug was diagnosed with brain cancer in March of

2003, he made the decision to continue moving forward with his life, with his family, and with his career. He didn't like dealing with what "might have been." He chose to focus on where he was going and what was to come. He made plans and kept on moving. You've got to admire that. Even as he fought his own fight against time, Tug aspired to help those sharing his struggle find hope for the future. Together with Laurie and Jennifer, he began to make plans for a charitable foundation of his own.

The Tug McGraw Foundation was formed in January of 2004. Initial support came through Tug's friends and former teammates as various fund-raisers and charity events were assembled to honor his legacy. Both private and corporate donations increased as news of the foundation's mission began to spread.

In June of 2004, the Tug McGraw Center for Neuro-Oncology Quality of Life Research was established as a component of the Brain Tumor Center at Duke University. The center was formally dedicated on June 12 with Tug's son Tim, his brother Hank, and Dr. Henry Friedman in attendance. The Tug McGraw Center strives to improve the quality of life of both children and adults with brain cancer through exacting research and promoting support for both the patients and their families. In October of 2004, the Tug McGraw Foundation partnered with corporate sponsor UbiquiTel, a PCS affiliate of Sprint, to kick off the Diamond 45/Ubiquitel Regional Scholarship Program. The first twenty scholarships will be awarded to qualified applicants in the winter of 2005.

One thing Tug never got to share with us before he left was the remarkable impact of the song "Live Like You Were Dying." Tim first heard the song back in November of 2003. Tug was already pretty sick by then. The band was rehearsing in an empty warehouse, getting ready to record our follow-up album to *Tim McGraw and the Dancehall Doctors*. We were trying out new material, new arrangements, just getting started. One day Tim cruised into rehearsal with this song for us to hear—right then. "This is the first single on the album, period," he told us. The actual recording session was still a few months away; we had a lot of work to do. But there was no question in his mind.

Tim talked about the song in interviews. Reporters wanted to know about Tug and how their relationship was reflected in the song. He would always say that it wasn't all about Tug: it was bigger than that. It wasn't about death; it was more about an affirmation of life, about moving forward.

"Live Like You Were Dying" was the first single off the album, and it was huge. It hadn't been on the radio even a week when we performed the song on May 26, 2004, at the Academy of Country Music Awards in Las Vegas. By the end of the song, everyone in the audience was on their feet—they got the message. The applause seemed to last forever. And there was Tim, center stage, tapping his thigh with an imaginary glove, as if to say "Here ya go, Tugger."

The song took on a life of its own, shooting up the charts in record time and breaking a thirty-year record for consecutive weeks at number one. *Live Like You Were Dying* became the title of the album, and the album set a personal sales record for Tim, selling more copies in its first week than any album in his career. As for the fans Tug so cherished throughout his life, they're still here. They're at our concerts every night, banners in hand, waiting for the lights to come up and the music to swell. Phillies jerseys with number 45 and signs shouting "We Love You, Tug," "Ya Gotta Believe," and "Tug Rocks" are seen waving through the crowds in remembrance of his life and the spirit with which he lived it.

Hmmm. Just caught the calendar as I wind this up. It's

October 21. Today's the anniversary of Tug's big 1980 World Series win—twenty-four years ago today. Tug was right. Ya gotta believe. Tug, we miss you—and we're moving forward. You would be proud. The foundation is doing some great things, and you are remembered. Thanks.

Batter up.

About the Authors

Tug McGraw was born in Martinez, California, in 1944 and was raised in the Napa Valley. A two-time All Star, he pitched for the New York Mets from 1965 to 1974 and for the Philadelphia Phillies from 1975 to 1984. Tug retired after the 1984 season and was most recently a spring training coach for the Phillies. The father of Tim, Mark, Cari, and Matthew, Tug McGraw passed away on January 5, 2004.

Don Yaeger is a well-known *Sports Illustrated* writer who has collaborated on such books as *Never Die Easy: The Autobiography of Walter Payton*; *Under The Tarnished Dome; How Notre Dame Betrayed Its Ideals for Football Glory*; *Shark Attack: Jerry Tarkanian and His Battle with the NCAA and UNLV*; and *A Shark Never Sleeps: Wheeling and Dealing with the NFL's Most Ruthless Agents*.